Unit 4

A Lake Superior Lawyer

Chester A. Congdon

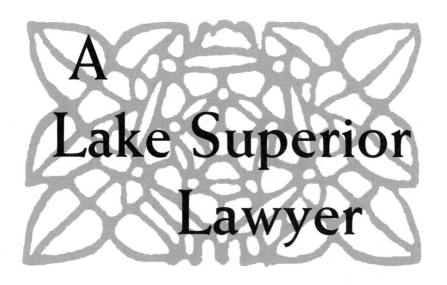

A Lake Superior Lawyer

A biography of Chester Adgate Congdon

Roy O. Hoover

Superior Partners ✦ Duluth, Minnesota

Superior Partners
c/o The Kutenai Press
P.O. Box 14107
St. Paul, MN 55114
(612) 645-1819

Dedication

To Majorie Ann Hoover, whose capabilities as a researcher, proofreader and critic were always valuable, and to whom this book is dedicated.

Contents

Acknowledgments   XI

Maps   XV

Introduction   XIV

1. The World of Chester Adgate Congdon   3

2. Congdon Ancestry   8

3. Syracuse University   13

4. After Graduation: An Uncertain Time   19

5. St. Paul   23

6. The Venture on Grays Harbor   30

7. Raymond   43

8. The Mesabi: Rivalry for Ore   48

9. Family   55

10. Agricultural Development in Yakima   62

11. The Western Mesabi   76

12. The Legislature of 1909: The Tonnage Tax   85

13. The Legislature of 1911: Redistricting the State   97

14. Bisbee   104

15. Expansion at Ajo   113

16. Pacific Panorama   118

17. National Affairs   132

Notes   145

Bibliography   167

Index   173

Publisher's Note

When Professor Roy Hoover of the University of Minnesota, Duluth completed his research paper on the life of Chester Congdon, the managing partners of Superior Partners (the investment arm of the Congdon family) decided that the paper presented an excellent opportunity to publish a biography of their ancestor. Prior to the publication of *A Lake Superior Lawyer* there was no published work documenting the life of Chester Congdon, a prominent business man and philanthropist in northern Minnesota.

The manuscript, which was intended as a scholarly paper, needed editing if it were to address itself to a broader audience. It was turned over to Sarah Dudley Plimpton, who placed it in the hands of Charlie Rogers, an experienced editor. Charlie Rogers made several trips to Duluth, and subsequently Professor Hoover rewrote sections of the book. The edited manuscript was then turned over to Emily Strayer of Kutenai Press, who undertook the tasks of designing and overseeing production of the book.

Several other people have been instrumental in getting the project completed. Mary Van Evera originally encouraged Professor Hoover in his project and frequently consulted with him. Vera Dunbar was especially helpful in locating photographs that are included in the book. Many other family members also made helpful suggestions and lent their support.

The result is both an informative and readable book, and we hope the readers will find our efforts worthwhile.

Superior Partners, Ltd.
James C. Dudley, Managing Partner

Acknowledgments

During the years of research and writing this biography, I relied on the services and assistance of a great many people and organizations. Without their help this book would not have been possible. Each person generously shared his or her knowledge and skills with me.

I owe special thanks to several persons whose names appear at the beginning of the list of acknowledgments. For their involvement and interest in my work, I extend to them a most grateful thanks.

Foremost among those persons who contributed to my work are Mary and William P. Van Evera, Duluth, Minnesota; they shared family documents and made it possible for me to use the files of The Congdon Office Corporation in Duluth, the materials at the Congdon Orchards, Inc. and Westhome in Yakima, Washington; Charles Rogers, Brooklyn, New York, who applied a gentle but sharp editorial pen to the manuscript; Beth Kwapick, Secretary of the Department of History, University of Minnesota, Duluth, for her years of support and especially for helping me sort out the mysteries of word processing; Kenneth E. Maine, Manager, The Congdon Office Corporation, Duluth, who provided information as well as work space and facilities; Judith Gillespie, Dean, College of Liberal Arts, University of Minnesota, Duluth, for her assistance and encouragement; Sam Krislov, Professor, Department of Political Science, University of Minnesota, who read and offered comments on a preliminary draft of the narrative; George R. "Rip" Rapp, Dean, College of Liberal Arts, University of Minnesota, Duluth, for his assistance and encouragement; Michael Lane, Director, Glensheen, who read the narrative on Glensheen, and the Glensheen staff, particularly Carol Chamberlain; Emily Strayer, Kutenai Press, St. Paul, Minnesota, whose skills converted the narrative into "printer's ink;" Vera Dunbar, Duluth, for her assistance with the photographs; James Dudley, New York City, whose interest in the project made publication possible; Thomas Congdon, Denver, for his interest and encouragement; Sarah Dudley Plimpton, New York City, managing editor of the printing process; Salisbury and Jean Adams, Wilson, Wyoming, for their kind hospitality at Westhome; Charles Boone, Manager, and staff, Congdon Orchards, Inc., Yakima, Washington, for their information and assistance; Roger Fischer, Head, Department of History, University of Minnesota, Duluth, for his encouragement and assistance; Ruby Shields and Ruth Ann Bauer and staff, Minnesota Historical Society, St. Paul, Minnesota, who gave a great deal of time and skill to my work; Staff, University of Minnesota, Duluth, Library; The Graduate School, University of Minnesota, for funding part of my research; Nancy Pryor and staff, Northwest/Washington Room, Washington State Library, Olympia, Washington, for help in locating materials; David R. Hoover, Boise, Idaho, who assisted in map preparation; Yakima Valley Canal Company, Yakima, Washington; Philip A. Schwartzberg, Meridian Mapping, Minneapolis, Minnesota, who created the maps.

The individuals listed below took an interest in my work and contributed a great deal to the project. I am grateful to each person.

Delores Beaudette, Chippewa County Historical Society, Chippewa Falls, Wisconsin; Rose Byrne, Arizona Historical Society, Tucson, Arizona; Donald Clay, Public Affairs Office, United States Steel Corporation, Pittsburgh, Pennsylvania; Nancy Gale Compau, Northwest Room Historian, Spokane Public Library, Spokane, Washington; Tom Copeland, St. Paul, Minnesota; Judy Copland, Evanston Historical Society, Evanston, Illinois; Amy S. Doherty, University Archives and Records Management, Syracuse University, Syracuse, New York; Lori Davisson, Arizona Historical Society, Tucson, Arizona; Timothy L. Decker, Chemung County Historical Society, Elmira, New York; Edward F. Donley, Pittsburgh, Pennsylvania; Gail A. Ferris, Alumni Records Office, Yale University, New Haven, Connecticut; Cynthia A. Garrick and Pamela Pratt, both of Yakima Valley Regional Library, Yakima, Washington; John Gonzales, Librarian, California Section, California State Library, Sacramento, California; Michael N. Greeley, Department of Mines and Mineral Resources, Tucson, Arizona; Mary Jane Haight-Eckert, Buffalo, New York; Charlotte Hazen and Mary Kate Heron, both of the Arnot Gallery, Elmira, New York; Jerome T. and Mrs. Heermans, Olympia, Washington; Mary Catharine Johnsen, Carnegie-Mellon University, Pittsburgh, Pennsylvania; Carrie Johnson, Arlington, Virginia; Diane E. Kaplan, Manuscripts and Archives, Yale University, New Haven, Connecticut; Mary Kay, The G. G. Hartley Trust, Duluth, Minnesota; Wisner Kinne, Ovid, New York; Frank Kurtik, Archives of Industrial Society, Hillman Library, University of Pittsburgh,

Pittsburgh, Pennsylvania; William C. Lagos, St. Mary Parish Land Company, Denver, Colorado; William L. Lang, Montana Historical Society, Helena, Montana; Dick R. Larsen, Wenatchee, Washington; Howard Levitt, Alameda Free Library, Alameda, California; Ronald II. Limbaugh, The Hold-Atherton Pacific Center for Western Studies, University of the Pacific, Stockton, California; Dallas R. Lindgren, Minnesota Historical Society, St. Paul, Minnesota; Susan Lovald, Duluth, Minnesota; Patricia Maus, Northeast Minnesota Historical Center, University of Minnesota, Duluth, Duluth, Minnesota; Pat Mestek, Hibbing Historical Society, Hibbing, Minnesota; Bruce Mitchell, Wenatchee, Washington; Elizabeth Mitchell, Belleville Public Library, Belleville, Ontario; Wayne Morrison, Ovid, New York; Ed Nelson, Iron Range Research Center, Chisholm, Minnesota; Janet Ness and Karyl Winn, Manuscripts and University Archives, University of Washington Libraries, Seattle, Washington; John Oliver III, Pittsburgh, Pennsylvania; John Oliver, Jr., Sewickley, Pennsylvania; William R. Oliver, Ligonier, Pennsylvania; Vicki O'Neill, Carolyn Ocheltree, and L. Dale Patterson, all of the General Commission on Archives and History, The United Methodist Church, Madison, New Jersey; Nancy J. Perrin, Corning Area Public Library, Corning, New York; Alan F. Perry, National Archives-Kansas City Branch, National Archives and Records Administration, Kansas City, Missouri; Kevin Oliver Rea, Pittsburgh, Pennsylvania; Diane M. Rebar, The Hoyt Library, Kingston, Pennsylvania; Ruth Reid, Historical Society of Western Pennsylvania, Pittsburgh, Pennsylvania; Hilary Richrod, Hoquiam Timberland Library, Hoquiam, Washington; John W. Roberts, Judicial, Fiscal, and Social Branch, Civil Archives Division, National Archives, Washington, D.C.; David P. Robrock, University of Arizona Library, Tucson, Arizona; Sarah P. Rubinstein, St. Paul, Minnesota; John Shannon, Congdon Orchards, Inc., Yakima, Washington; Richard O. Sielaff, Management Studies, University of Minnesota, Duluth, Duluth, Minnesota; Rita Sorkness, Wisconsin Regional Research Center, University of Wisconsin-Eau Claire, Eau Claire, Wisconsin; George E. Tener, Washington, D.C.; David Wignor, The Library of Congress, Washington, D.C.; Dick Woodin, Manager, Congdon Orchards, Inc., Yakima, Washington; Frank A. Zabrosky, Archives of Industrial Society, University of Pittsburgh, Pittsburgh, Pennsylvania.

To the personnel at the following institutions I owe a grateful thanks. I visited many of them, and each librarian, archivist, and staff person with whom I worked took a special interest in my research; I regret that I do not have the names of those persons who so generously provided me with their services and information:

Arizona Bureau of Mines, Tucson, Arizona; Cabell County Public Library, Huntington, West Virginia; City Auditor's Office, Tacoma, Washington; Department of Public Safety, Bureau of Health, Division of Vital Statistics, St. Paul, Minnesota; Evanston Public Library, Evanston, Illinois; Hunt Library, Special Collections Library, Carnegie-Mellon University, Pittsburgh, Pennsylvania; Huntington Public Library, Huntington, West Virginia; Minneapolis Public Library, Minneapolis, Minnesota; Office of Public Affairs, Patent and Trade Mark Office, Washington, D.C.; Republican Party National Headquarters, Washington, D.C.; Spokane Chamber of Commerce, Spokane, Washington; State Historical Society of Wisconsin, Madison, Wisconsin; University Archives, University of California, Berkeley, California; Yakima County Auditor's Office, Yakima, Washington; Yakima Valley Museum and Historical Society, Yakima, Washington.

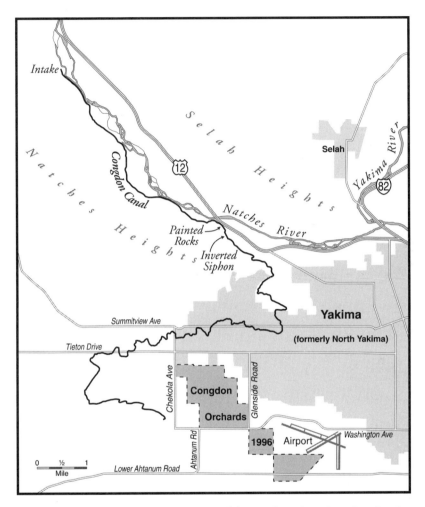

Detail of Yakima, illustrating the location of the Natches River, Congdon Canal and Orchards. Note that the canal ends prior to reaching the orchards, requiring water to be pumped the final distance.

Introduction

DURING THE FALL AND WINTER OF 1900–1901, THE LIGHTS IN THE Pittsburgh offices of Carnegie-Oliver Steel Company burned almost around the clock. Company officials knew they were about to embark upon one of the most adventurous moves in the history of American business. Chester Congdon, as the attorney for Henry W. Oliver, was consulted frequently. The success of the venture relied upon the most painstaking attention to detail. The excitement of sweeping change quickened the pace of all employees; in fact, the entire industry waited anxiously to learn the details of the new business arrangement.

This electrifying atmosphere also pervaded the John D. Rockefeller offices in New York City. Shortly after the discovery of iron ore in northeastern Minnesota, Rockefeller had quickly entered the iron ore business and had come to control not only a great many of the mines but also the railroad and ships by which the ore was shipped down-lake to the steel furnaces. It was the potential threat of Rockefeller's entry into the iron ore business which prompted the new alignment. During this new flurry of activity, Frederick T. Gates, the financial wizard who served as Rockefeller's business manager, looked after the millionaire's interests.

Any move by the steel giants would be felt throughout the industry. Smaller steel companies, if not fully aware of what was about to happen, instinctively knew that forthcoming developments would impact directly upon their operation, indeed, their very existence.

J. Pierpont Morgan served as the catalyst for this bustle of activity. Head of the largest banking house in the United States and one of the wealthiest men in America, he had been financier to a large part of the steel industry. Morgan believed that competing steel companies would only destroy each other. He came up with the idea of a single trust which would merge the iron mining and steel producing companies, maximizing efficiency and profits while reducing risk. His dream was to form the largest corporation in the world by bringing together the men whose names were synonymous with steel. The name of the new organization should reflect the size of the enterprise, and Morgan thought that United States Steel would be appropriate.

Henry W. Oliver, whose mining operations on the Mesabi produced more ore than anyone, was not present at the creation of the giant corporation. He was on a holiday cruise in the West Indies. As the merger plans proceeded, Oliver's office staff in Pittsburgh became apprehensive over how the new arrangements would affect the company. One particular clause in a contract dating from pre-merger days was especially unnerving. It required Oliver to absorb one-sixth of all ore produced by his mining company—roughly five million tons annually and increasing steadily. Oliver, however, had sold all of his furnaces and could no longer utilize this ore. Recognizing this problem, he had signed a fifty-year contract with National Steel Company by which he agreed to sell the ore to them. National Steel, however, would soon become part of United States Steel, and there was nothing in the forthcoming merger which would prevent the new corporation from establishing such a low price per ton that Oliver would suffer a large financial loss. Oliver's office cabled him suggesting he return home at once and renegotiate with National.

Upon receipt of the cable, Oliver remained remarkably serene. "There is no need to worry," he assured a business companion, "my contract was carefully considered and prepared by Chester Congdon, as good a lawyer as I have ever known. I will have no difficulty."

Oliver's confidence was well placed. A clause in the contract protected the steelmaker in price as well as iron ore tonnage. Thanks to Congdon's foresight Oliver's company was safe.

A Lake Superior Lawyer

1

The World of Chester Adgate Congdon

THE DECADES BETWEEN THE END OF THE CIVIL WAR AND THE BEGINNING of World War I witnessed a profound change in American society. The rapid growth of population was matched only by expansion of the economy. The opening of the West, the construction of the railroads, the increase of industry, all contributed to the unprecedented development. Wealth was created and destroyed almost overnight. The pace was frightening, almost dizzy in its speed; its effects touched and influenced every aspect of American life.

Americans began to realize what it was like to be a "people of plenty." This new light shed upon the nation was evident throughout the land. If the lumbermen harvested the timber in New England only to witness what seemed to be an inexhaustible supply vanish before their saws, they had but to look westward to fresh resources in Michigan and Minnesota. When miners supplied the steel for northern armies during the Civil War by tapping into the iron ore deposits of Michigan's Upper Peninsula ranges, they fully expected that resource to serve the nation for decades to come. Long before the Michigan ore topped out in production, the ranges of Minnesota promised an even greater supply and a more expansive future.

For half a century following the Civil War, entrepreneurs led the assault upon the land and its bounty. Out of what seemed self-destruction and chaos, industrial leaders devised modern business strategies which pointed the way to surer wealth and power. In the struggle for survival, individual competition yielded to combination, and combination led to the corporation with its many variations. The new corporations became the playing fields of industrialists, tycoons, and magnates—a new kind of capitalist able to dominate the modern business world.

The railroads led the way, pushing into all corners of the nation to provide a transportation system second to none. Congress, in a single decade (1862–1872) granted to the carriers 200 million acres of land. In addition, the national government extended cash loans in excess of 64 million dollars. As the railroads grew, carrying people and products, their political power expanded as well. If rail construction and operation sometimes became synonymous with corruption, the misdeeds were often excused in the name of progress. The amount was considered insignificant. No one cared as long as the tracks were laid and the land with its bounty opened for development.

One only had to look at comparative statistics to recognize American industrial superiority. Within twenty years of the Civil War, America surpassed all countries of the world in the production of foodstuffs and manufactured goods. Quality matched quantity, and American goods were recognized as superior in workmanship to foreign competitors.

The labor force also underwent change. Prior to the Civil War, immigrants from northern and western Europe (the English, Irish, Germans, and Scandinavians) supplied the labor for the factories and the farms. As the turn of the century drew near, new immigrant groups came to America in ever increasing numbers. These were the people of southern and eastern Europe (Italians, Greeks, Russians, Poles, Finns, and Slavs, to name only those nationalities which came in the greatest numbers). If those in power knew that wages and the extension of social welfare to these workers lagged behind the growth of industry, it was because industrialism served a higher cause—the god of bigness.

The society was not without its flaws. Periodically, the economy was plagued with devastating financial depressions. The prevailing optimism, however, was so great that even in times of hardship, market aberrations were accepted as errors of judgment which could be avoided in the future. Depressions might even serve the economy by eliminating weaker business rivals. Thus, hard times could be considered a blessing, pointing the way to a better and more secure tomorrow by eliminating unsound businessmen and companies that lacked solid financial foundations.

In the post-bellum period, America became a magnet for European investment, and by 1871 over $100,000,000 of American securities were marketed in London. Even the depression of 1893 failed to dampen the European optimism in the American market. With the availability of foreign capital, American companies could now direct their resources toward rapid expansion.

The turn of the century marked a new high in technological innovation and industrial enterprise with business firms constantly looking for more efficient machinery which would give them a competitive edge. When the Minneapolis flour miller, Cadwallader Washburn, learned that Hungarian mills turned out a flour superior to his own, he sent an industrial "spy," Walter de la Barre, to Budapest to discover the secret. At first denied admission into the mills, la Barre disguised himself as a workman and with the help of a mill-wright entered the plant. After learning what he needed to know he withdrew and left for Vienna. There he drew the plans for the installation of the machinery in the Washburn mill. The Hungarian process was soon installed at Minneapolis along with a newly developed American-made "middlings purifier" which removed the unsightly bran from the flour. Minneapolis mills rose swiftly to the top in world competition.

The same zeal spurred on the development of iron mines on Minnesota's Mesabi range. If not for two inventions, the steam-driven diamond-faced drill and the Thomas-Gilchrist steelmaking process, it is possible that development of the Mesabi would have been delayed for years, but the diamond-faced drill, which removed a core-sample of earth, replaced the tedious and uncertain pick and shovel work of test-pitting. Using this powerful new drill, miners could know what lay far below the surface within a short time.

The texture and composition of Mesabi ore presented the second problem. The ore was granular in composition which presented smelting problems, and it also contained a high amount of phosphorus which at best produced inferior steel. The Mesabi range, however, was the largest iron ore deposit in the world, and it could not and would not long go undeveloped. In 1879, two Englishmen, Sidney Gilchrist Thomas and his cousin Percy C. Gilchrist, discovered that at a very high temperature the phosphorus in molten ore was attracted to lime. It remained but to place lime in a converter along with the ore, heat it to the proper temperature, and skim off the lime and phosphorus as it rose to the top. A year later, it was Andrew Carnegie who bought the rights to the Thomas-Gilchrist process and introduced it in his mill at Homestead, Pennsylvania, thus giving the Scotsman the competitive edge he sought in steelmaking.

New business organization followed technology, and again it was Carnegie who rode the wave of change. In addition to the large corporation, the pool, and the trust, the Pennsylvania steelmaker came to believe strongly in verticality, i.e., control of a business from the source of raw materials, through their processing, to a finished consumer product. Owning the iron mines, the coal mines, the steel furnaces, and the means of distribution gave him complete control of his steel business.

A changing America was about to throw off the outdated ways of doing business, and with them the social and economic conventions which controlled businessmen of the past. Examining this emerging order, Herbert

Spencer, British philosopher, linked the biological determinism of Darwin with the economic relationships of industrial America. Where Darwin had observed an inevitable requirement of biological adaptation to environment, Spencer announced that man's social (particularly economic) relationships were no less rigidly controlled—survival was the only goal, success its own vindication. To deny these social "laws" or to attempt to change them only led to certain disaster. Proof of Spencerian logic was undeniable, if only for its believers. It was enough to witness that success came to some persons whereas others failed. Thus, Spencer was interpreted as justification of the industrialist who, by doing well for himself, could also claim to be doing a service for America. Spencerian "science," later identified as "Social Darwinism," came to America with the sociologist William Graham Sumner, who left no doubt that the new economic determinism was inextricably linked with progress. American industrialists, particularly steelmakers, thoroughly embraced Spencerian logic.

One part of America that was greatly affected by the social and economic changes was state government. When the states drew their original political boundaries, little thought was given to regional economic equality. If the issue came up at all, it was after the boundaries were in place. The new emphasis on natural resources for industrial growth frequently meant a struggle for power in the legislatures where representatives of the people sought to protect their economic wealth. The inequality which often resulted caused no end of regional infighting.

Minnesota was no exception. At the time Minnesota Territory was pressing for statehood, the question arose as to the boundaries of the state. There was no question that the territory, which contained all of the present state plus the eastern part of the Dakotas, was too large to admit as a single political unit. Forced to choose between an east-west or a north-south boundary split, Minnesotans chose the latter. The result left political power, based on population, in the southern part of the new state, with the economic power, based on mineral resources, in the north. At the time of Minnesota statehood (1858), the rich deposits of iron ore in the northeast lay undiscovered—but not for long. The Vermilion Range was opened in the early 1880s, and the Mesabi was discovered in 1890. Both ranges were well to the north of political power. Nevertheless, since the iron deposits were within the border of the state, southern Minnesotans argued that the wealth should be shared by all. This attitude was anathema to the sparsely populated northeastern counties whose people saw no reason to divide the wealth along population lines. The battle was joined, and the controversy appeared in various forms for several decades. As a member of the Minnesota state legislature, it fell to Chester Congdon to lead the battle to retain the wealth in the northeastern part of the state for its residents.

Lastly, northeastern Minnesotans saw the world through the eyes of the Upper Midwest. When residents of this heartland traveled abroad, as Congdon did in 1914, they judged foreign society by the standards at home. Previously, Americans had been reluctant to cast their eyes beyond the Pacific and Atlantic shores. At the turn of the century all this was about to change and over a short period of time. Some of the new globalism came from the Spanish-American War; some of it came from a new interest in international trade. Whatever the causes, America relished its new role in the international community.

The forces of change which were at work at the turn of the century were immensely powerful. None acted exclusively of another, and most were mutually dependent upon the others. All contributed in varying degrees to one of the most exciting periods the nation had ever experienced.

This was the world of Chester Adgate Congdon.

2
Congdon Ancestry

THE CONGDON ANCESTRY TRACES BACK TO NEW ENGLAND AND before that to England. Benjamin Congdon emigrated from Pembroke, Wales about 1630 (1650?) to Rhode Island, but the family was not Welsh. They had originally resided in central England and had first moved to Wales before coming to the American colonies. For two generations Benjamin's descendants lived in New England. It was Hannibal, Chester Congdon's grandfather, who began the next "removal."[1]

At a time when movement westward held the promise of greater prosperity, Hannibal and wife, Mary, moved from Rhode Island to settle at Rhinebeck, Dutchess County, along the Hudson River. The couple had only one son, Sylvester Laurentus, born January 26, 1826.[2]

History has little to offer regarding the boyhood of Sylvester Congdon, Chester Congdon's father. Although schools in this area held infrequent classes on a seasonal basis, he acquired a good education despite these adverse conditions. By age seventeen, now on his own, he moved to Elmira in the central part of the state, and it was there he joined the Methodist Episcopal church. This is not surprising considering the religious inclination of the population with whom he lived.[3]

Elmira lay in the center of a broad belt of land (a "psychic highway" as one historian calls it) which stretched through New York westward from the Catskills and Adirondacks. Within its uneven dimensions there developed a population whose religious fervor and intensity seldom has been witnessed in American history. Some people spoke of the area as "Burnt" or the "Burned-over District." Charles Grandison Finney, the greatest Congregational evangelist of the day, assured the popularity of the term when he described the inhabitants of the region as hardened, or "burned-out," by zealous Methodist circuit riders against "proper," i.e., Congregational, religious tutelage.[4]

Although by the time Sylvester Congdon came to Elmira, the fires of religious fervor had waned, there remained sufficient intensity to recruit impressionable young men. Congdon "became the subject of converting grace" and joined the Methodist Episcopal Church. He undoubtedly felt very deeply about his commitment, but membership alone was not enough to satisfy his religious inclinations. By 1847, he decided to leave Elmira and begin his training for ordination.

Preparation for the Methodist Episcopal ministry did not require formal seminary schooling. Candidates of suitable quality were assigned to work under the tutelage of an established minister, and Congdon was "received on trial" in the Genesee Conference to work with the minister in Mecklenburg and Hector, both small congregations served by a single pastor. Two years later, he was transferred to churches in Jefferson and Tyrone, again to work under the regular minister.

Prior to ordination, prospective ministers were expected to relate in full detail the path which had led them to the church, and many years later Congdon's colleagues remembered "distinct[ly] . . . the clear and edifying experience" narrated by Congdon regarding his call to serve God. Having lived up to the expectations of his Methodist elders, Congdon was "received into full connection" and ordained a Deacon in 1849 in the same church at Elmira where he had first professed his intention to become a member.

Sylvester Congdon's ordination meant larger churches and greater responsibilities, and he was assigned first to the community of Barrington and then to the Rochester North Street Church. At the latter, he remained for two years. In 1851, at the age of twenty-five, he was ordained as an Elder and moved to Clifton and Manchester.[5]

Congdon's ministerial status provided somewhat greater stability, and in the year following ordination he married Laura Jane Adgate, daughter of Chester and Hannah Adgate, both from the Hudson River Valley. The marriage vows were solemnized by the Reverend J. N. Brown in Lodi, New York. Like Congdon's, Chester Adgate's ancestors could be traced back to New England and before that England. His wife, Hannah, was Dutch, a daughter of the well-to-do Van Horns, partners in the New York banking house of Phillips and Van Horn.[6]

Between 1852 and 1858, Congdon served a number of churches: Rochester's Third Street, Port Gibson, Trumansburgh, Sodus, back to Rochester at Frank Street, then on to Elmira, and Hedding. Three children were born to the couple: Chester Adgate on June 12, 1853; Laura Sophia on February 15, 1855; and Albert Sylvester on December 4, 1857.

Congdon's rise within the church was rapid, and between 1859 and 1863 he served as Presiding Elder of the Bath District. The following year he became a delegate to the church's General Conference. From 1863 to 1867, he was appointed Presiding Elder of the Elmira District. Three more children were born: Edward Herbert on May 30, 1862; Walter Hibard on June 16, 1864; and Helen Augusta on March 22, 1867. The city of Corning lay within the boundaries of the Elmira District, and the citizens of that community, familiar and respectful of Congdon's work, requested that he transfer to their church. In accordance with the congregation's wishes the change was approved, and the family moved in the autumn of 1867.[7]

Tragedy struck the family in the late spring of 1868. The children came down with scarlet fever, a particularly dread and often fatal disease for young people. Congdon and his wife tried to serve as doctor and nurse, but the disease persisted. Indeed, there was little that could be done. In a letter written after the ordeal passed, the father described their anguish. "Terrible were the days and nights when we watched for the 'angel of death', when we turned from the 'tenantless house' to watch the slow ebbing of life in another, without a hope to cheer the gloom." Between April 27 and May 2, the three youngest children died. Chester was critically ill but within a week seemed better. Exhausted from their ordeal, the family called in nurses for Albert whom they thought several times would surely succumb. His wrists and neck were badly swollen, and the prevailing treatment called for lancing the afflicted areas to relieve what was perceived to be intense pressure. The child survived the "cure," but for rest of his life carried deep scars over impaired muscles. Among the children, Laura was the only one who escaped the scourge of the disease.[8]

Hoping to overcome their loss, the family tried to resume their life and work in Corning. Once again, however, they were to experience profound sadness. Physically worn down from the family's ordeal with scarlet fever and emotionally stricken by the loss of his children, Sylvester Congdon never fully recovered. Although he continued his pastoral duties, his health seemed to waiver. Just before the children had become ill, he had intended to take a two week vacation, but the fever had interrupted his plans. Now his work seemed especially burdensome. On May 27, 1868, he suffered a heart attack and died a few hours later. At his passing, the church honored his service with an appropriate memorial: "He was eminently evangelical and practical. He made no effort at rhetorical display. His aim was not to please a fastidious taste, but to present the truth clearly that it might be seen, and forcibly that it might be felt. In this he seldom failed." At age forty-two, he left behind a widow and three children.[9]

The church offered condolences and sympathy, but pitifully meager financial support. Fortunately, some time before his death (and probably with an eye to their future retirement), Laura had encouraged her husband to invest in a forty-acre farm near Ovid, New York. There remained a sizable mortgage, but at least it would provide a home. It was here that Laura moved with the two youngest children. Chester remained in Corning to work at the local lumberyard. It separated the family, but his employment there was simply too valuable to give up. Not having the family together must have been heart-rending for them. The boy remaining behind was fifteen years old, had just lost his father, two brothers and a sister, and now he would be living alone.[10]

The correspondence between Chester and the family reveals his homesick and lonely existence. Both children in Ovid wrote regularly, probably at the mother's prompting. Albert's ("Bertie") letters are full of those matters most important to a young boy—the garden, hens with chicks, tadpoles which he and Laura had found, and school ("my piece for Tuesday is Barbara Fietchie [sic] and Laura is to give an analysis of cammels [sic]"). To the children's letters the mother added her comments: the neighbors had been kind and dropped by, the taxes on the farm had been paid (although not without some financial difficulty), and she had hired out some of the plowing because her health would not permit long hours of hard work. Mainly, she was concerned about Chester's welfare. He was rooming alone, doing his own cooking, and she was worried. "I hope you will get your full quota of sleep," she wrote, "You have a very nervous temperament and it is greatly necessary that you have all you can get. Eight hours at least. I want you to develop into a full, strong, man both physically and intellectually."

Regarding Chester's spiritual welfare, she "hoped he would get his 30 lines [of Scripture] a day," and frequently cautioned her son to act in accordance with what his father would have wanted. "Do not feel homesick if you can help it," she pleaded, "for I know by experience that it is a wretched feeling. Be as happy as you can, and try everything you do, to do it as if your Papa was near and watching over and round about you. I often feel that that is the case with us here at home."

On her son's attempts at baking, she thought perhaps he was "mistaken about using a table[spoon] instead of a teaspoon for the baking powder," and added, "inquire of Mrs. H[eermans]." The Heermans were longtime Corning residents, Methodists, and former parishioners of Congdon's church. The father was active in city government and had developed the water system for the municipality. Their son, Harry Clay, was a year older than Chester, and the two had become close friends—an association that would last throughout their lives. It was not long before Congdon took a room with the Heermans— much to his mother's relief.[11]

In the fall of 1870, Chester moved to Ovid both to be near his family and to enroll in the college preparatory curriculum at the East Genesee Conference Seminary. The intellectual environment was suited to the young man, and he embarked upon the academic discipline with enthusiasm and vigor. When graduation exercises were held in August 1871, Dr. C.W. Winchester, head administrator of the Seminary, awarded a certificate of completion to Congdon who was valedictorian of the class. The logical advance for this promising student was enrollment in an institution of higher education.[12]

3
Syracuse University

CONGDON'S CHOICE OF COLLEGE WAS LIMITED BY FINANCES. HE WOULD have preferred Yale, but tuition and expenses ruled it out. There was another option, and Congdon was very interested. A few miles northeast of Ovid, a new Methodist school, Syracuse University, was ready to accept students, and sons and daughters of clergymen were admitted at half tuition—$10 per term.[1]

Syracuse University had only recently moved to the city for which it was named. Formerly called Genesee College and located in Lima, New York, the institution's trustees had made the move which they felt was necessary in order to build an expanded university with a national reputation. The New York State Legislature approved a new charter on March 30, 1870.[2]

At the first faculty meeting held in the late summer of 1871, the president of the University entrusted to "these intellectual stewards an historical curriculum of the classics and sciences." But, he also added, proper respect must be given to modern educational trends, and the faculty must be capable to "apprehend, thoroughly sift, and utilize for the benefit" of the student body, "all revelations in science." There was to be no discrimination at Syracuse with regard to women, race, or national origin. "Brains and heart," the president declared, were to have a "fair chance, and we propose no narrow-minded sectarianism on the one hand, nor infidelity on the other."[3]

It was clear, therefore, the "new education" would be pursued and respected at Syracuse. The aim of the curriculum was not to prepare students for the trades and professions; rather, it was to develop a well-rounded person with a liberal arts education in the classical sense, a graduate culturally well-developed and drilled to the most efficient use of his or her intellectual capabilities.

Into this academic environment the first class of forty-one students, seven of whom were women, gathered at the college chapel on the morning of September 4, 1871. Included in the student body were Chester A. Congdon and his future wife, Clara Hesperia Bannister.

Clara Bannister's family were originally from New York, although they had been living in California since 1850. Her father, Reverend Edward Bannister, a graduate of Wesleyan University, previously had served on the faculty at Cazinovia Seminary in New York, but the Methodist church had sent him to California where he was entrusted "to look after educational interests" [and] "to begin a College or University by founding, first an academy. . . ."[4]

Shortly after his arrival, Bannister, in compliance with his instructions, founded San Jose Academy, an institution not directly connected to today's University of the Pacific but "may fairly be regarded as a forerunner." Bannister's services, however, were soon needed in a college founded under the authority of the Methodist Episcopal Church. The name of the institution was California Wesleyan College and was located in nearby Santa Clara. A debate arose over the word Wesleyan in the title, and at the first meeting of the Board of Trustees the name was changed to "The University of the Pacific." Edward Bannister was elected as one of twenty-four Trustees. Bannister was also appointed Principal of the University Preparatory School. The historian of the institution credits Bannister in his role as Principal and later as President of the University (he was appointed in 1859) with being the "first real head" of what is today the University of the Pacific.[5]

From the beginning, California Wesleyan, like Syracuse, took an advanced stand on coeducation, and the trustees formally adopted a resolution that "the college shall be open to such females as may desire to pursue a college course." Consequently, a "Female Collegiate Institute" was begun in 1853. Elizabeth Bannister became its first Preceptress. In addition to her educational duties, Elizabeth cared for her family, now expanded to five children: two sons and three daughters. Clara Hesperia, the second daughter, was born in San Francisco on April 29, 1854.

The years ahead were trying indeed. Financial difficulties continued to plague the small college. In 1861, Bannister, now president, reported to the trustees, "I have nothing to recommend in respect to buildings, faculty, etc., because we have no funds for improvements," and he added, "the professors are in arrears to the amount of nearly half year's salary."

In November 1867, Bannister presented his resignation which the trustees reluctantly accepted. Following his departure from the school, Bannister served a four-year term as Presiding Elder of the San Francisco District of the Methodist Episcopal Church. From here he was reassigned to Marysville in the Sacramento Valley where he continued his ministerial work until his death on September 27, 1871.[6]

Soon after her husband's death, Elizabeth returned to New York. She decided to live in Syracuse largely because her brother-in-law taught at the university, and her oldest sister, Mary, a school teacher, had promised to assist the Bannister girls in gaining admittance. Only one of the sons accompanied the family to New York, and only for a short time before he returned to California.[7]

Prior to the move to Syracuse, Clara's education had been, according to her own description years later, "somewhat irregular." Her most formal training had been at the San Francisco Girls' High School, and this schooling had been supplemented with "some home teaching" as she later characterized it. Once in Syracuse, her family urged her to attend the university, and she enrolled in the fall of 1871.[8]

Requirements for admission to Syracuse were formidable. Entering students were required to pass examinations (varying slightly depending upon the degree program) in the subject areas of English grammar, geography and history of the United States, arithmetic, algebra to equations of the second degree, and plane geometry. Students had to be thoroughly familiar with Harkness' Latin grammar, four books of Caesar's *Commentaries*, six books of Virgil's *Aeneid*, six select orations by Cicero, Sallust's *Catiline* and his *Jugurthine War* or the *Eclogues of Virgil*, the first and second parts of Harkness' *Introduction* or the first fifty exercises of Arnold's *Latin Composition*, Hadley's Greek grammar, three books of Xenophon's *Anabasis*, one book of Homer's *Iliad*, classical geography, and Greek and Roman antiquity studies. Needless to say, students came to Syracuse well versed in the classics.[9]

Syracuse University was prepared to offer three fields of study, each four years in length: Classics, Latin-Scientific, and Science. Classics students received an A.B. degree (later designated a Bachelor of Arts), while those in the Latin-Scientific program were awarded a Bachelor of Philosophy. Science students earned a Bachelor of Science. Regardless of the program, during the freshman and sophomore years there were no electives, although upperclassmen were permitted a limited amount of curricular latitude. Each student was expected to carry an academic load of seven courses, each of which met daily. In addition to the regular course load there were weekly exercises throughout the year in "General Grammar, the Art of Composition, and Declamation." Congdon chose the Classical Course and the Bachelor of Arts, while Clara opted for the Bachelor of Science.[10]

Despite the rigors of academic life, students found time to engage in activities outside the classroom and library. Events and items of interest were published in *The University Herald*, the student newspaper. In later years, only juniors and seniors were allowed to work on the staff, but in 1872, Congdon joined the paper and in 1874, served as president of the Herald Association, the newspaper's governing body.

Some of the men formed a baseball team, the only intercollegiate sport supported by the University. Congdon served as Vice President and Field Director, a sort of player-manager. Team members were not assigned a specific position, and Congdon alternated between left and center field, shortstop, and first and third base. They played schools from the surrounding area (the game scores may indicate each team's ability): Cornell 25, Syracuse 12; Syracuse 20, Cornell 14; Hamilton 31, Syracuse 28. In the 1873 game with Hamilton, the Syracuse nine must have presented a comical sight as they took the field. *The University Herald* reported that, "Our men were in their new uniforms, which unfortunately had been built without respect to persons, and fitted like amputated meal bags. . . ," and quipped that defeat was so common that the attitude of the players was like the "old woman who used to skin her eels alive. When accused of cruelty, she said, 'There's nothing like getting used to a thing. I've skinned them like this for the last fifteen years, and they don't feel it a particle now.'"

The University Herald reported on the most pressing issues of student life. The most controversial topics were: coeducation, evolution versus divine creation, required courses versus electives, and the value of intercollegiate athletics. Recreational events (some of which later became part of the traditional annual "class day") were scheduled, although at times the determination of just how a particular exercise was to be conducted presented new problems. One ritual, for example, called for a ceremonial Indian pipe to be smoked and passed along with ivy and evergreens by representatives of the senior class to the juniors. The Class of '75 committed the *faux pas* of omitting senior women from the ceremony. "So long as ladies are admitted into the college and bear the same burdens and share the same toils, why may they not stand upon a level with their brothers in all that pertains to the class as such?" the *Herald* chastised, but it also added, "In the pipe ceremony we should not have wished to see them [the women] participate, but the presentation of the ivy and evergreen would certainly not have lacked in grace and impressiveness at the hands of a lady."[11]

With such a small student body, it would have been unusual for students not to become acquainted almost from the day of entrance, and many years later Clara's daughter recalled that her parents met in a mathematics class. "My mother seems to have caught my father's fancy the first day he saw her," she wrote, and added, "She [Clara] knew her lessons always. And he liked that." Beyond this brief remembrance, there are no documents which describe the relationship between Chester and Clara while they attended Syracuse. Undoubtedly, they saw each other frequently, and what began as mutual respect blossomed into a deep and abiding affection. Although there was no engagement announced, there developed between the two (in their second or third year) an "understanding."[12] University students, especially those whose economic well-being was as uncertain as Chester and Clara's, rarely considered marriage until the man was firmly established in his career. Considering Congdon's circumstances, it appeared that their marriage might be years away.

Finances were always difficult for him, and in February 1874, between his junior and senior years, he accepted a position as administrator in a girls school in Mauricetown, New Jersey. The break in his studies meant that he must work doubly hard in order to graduate in four years, but he had no choice. Again, in May, at the completion of the academic year in Mauricetown, he took a job in Rochester where he worked until the fall term began at Syracuse.[13]

During their senior year, each member of the Class of '75 prepared a thesis on a topic of their own choosing. Chester chose "Coeducation in Higher Schools," and Clara wrote on a "Comparison of Grecian and Gothic Architecture." As planning for graduation proceeded, the Class of '75 formed a committee, composed of Congdon and two other students, to petition the administration to "abrogate commencement orations [by students]. . . and substitute, as has been done at the University of Michigan, an address by some prominent scholar of the country, or any other exercise which may be deemed best by the faculty of the college." Congdon's introduction of the petition illustrates his penchant (which grew into a lifelong characteristic) for seeking advice from those persons best qualified to give it. The selection of an outside speaker would also duplicate a practice (and perhaps establish a precedent at Syracuse) employed by older and more prestigious institutions. The request was granted, and while the suggestion for an outside speaker of considerable reputation was not employed, the University Chancellor gave the graduation address.[14]

On graduation day, June 23, 1875, fifteen students were awarded the A.B. Degree, Chester Adgate Congdon among them, and five students, Clara Hesperia Bannister included, received the Bachelor of Science. The cloistered years of the academic world were behind them, and they were anxious to take their place in society. Regardless of their academic success, however, they were no closer to marriage. That must wait until Chester could find a position with sufficient income to support a wife.[15]

4

After Graduation: An Uncertain Time

UPON LEAVING SYRACUSE, EMPLOYMENT OPTIONS FOR BOTH CONGDON and Clara were somewhat restricted. Despite their church-related backgrounds, neither felt inclined to follow in the footsteps of their fathers. Wholesale or retail business offered opportunities, but required a certain amount of capital which neither possessed. Teaching, then a profession for which a specific degree was not required, presented one possibility for immediate employment, but the financial rewards were meager and the opportunity for advancement was limited. The legal profession was attractive, but this required additional preparation and more financial sacrifice. Clara was even further restricted since many professions were closed to women. One thing, however, was certain: whatever choice they made, their life together must be postponed.

Despite the time required for additional training, Congdon chose to "read for the bar," and he acquired a position with the Syracuse law firm of Hiscock, Gifford, and Doheny where he remained for the next two years. Reading for the bar with an established law firm involved duties which were similar to that of an apprentice-clerk. After a tutorial period of service, and at a time usually defined by the mentors, the aspiring candidate took the state bar examination. Passage meant the right to practice in that state. Reciprocity by other states was rarely granted.[1]

Clara continued her academic training at Syracuse for an additional year in order to be near Chester. She studied in the College of Fine Arts working under the tutelage of Professor George F. Comfort, Dean of the College and Professor of Esthetics and Modern Languages. Although the year was pleasant and rewarding, at the end of her studies she left Syracuse to accept a position of Instructor in Art and Assistant Preceptress at Alexandra College in Belleville, Ontario. Alexandra was a small ladies college, the counterpart of Albert College, a men's school at the same location. Situated on the north shore of Lake Ontario, it was not far from Syracuse, and Chester came to visit when he could.

Her employment at the Canadian school continued until 1878 when she accepted a position at Wyoming Seminary, a Methodist college preparatory school in Kingston, Pennsylvania. Although it was farther from Chester, the church relationship appealed to her.[2]

By the fall of 1877, Congdon was ready to take the New York bar examination. His apprenticeship had prepared him well, and on October 13 of that year he received notice that he had been admitted to practice law in the state of New York as Attorney and Counselor-at-Law. This was only the first step. Law practice would have to wait until he possessed the means to become established. Hiscock, Gifford, and Doheny was only a small law firm and advancement with them was unlikely. Besides, Congdon hoped to begin an independent practice.

In the interim, while he was looking for an opportunity, he accepted a teaching position with the Marion Collegiate Institute while also serving as Assistant Principal. Congdon had no intention of continuing with the job, and he remained at Marion only one year. His savings were still not what he had hoped, however, and when a teaching position opened in New Jersey, he accepted, but again for only a year. A teacher's pay, in Congdon's judgment, was insufficient to begin either a career or a marriage.[3]

Congdon had prepared for the law, and he was determined to find a position in the legal field. Accordingly, he began to cast about for a suitable location. Rather than open an office in one of the larger cities where he was sure to face competition from older and more established firms, Congdon decided to explore possibilities in some of the smaller towns. Among his inquiries was one directed to a friend from Syracuse who was already in practice in Fairport. The reply was not encouraging. Nearby Clifton Springs, population 800–900, his friend warned, held little promise since most of the legal work centered around a local sanitarium, and that business was already taken. The residents were "quarrelsome enough," the writer noted, but they were "too poor to employ anybody to do their fighting for them." Fairport, the letter continued, offered greater potential, especially for a young man who needed to make acquaintances. It was ten miles from Rochester, and some of the attorneys in the surrounding villages "have a desk in some office [in Rochester] if nothing more." At the moment there were, in addition to himself, four attorneys practicing in Fairport—"one a gutter drunkard, one a thief, and the other a man who does all the business." The latter, so the acquaintance thought, "would . . . take some one [sic] into his office." But, his friend concluded, "If you hear of a place where there are no lawyers[,] keep away for had there been any good picking there would have been someone on the ground. Pitch in where there is a crowd. When you see a lot of crows hovering around you may know that there is a rich feast of carrion near."

Needless to say, neither Fairport nor Clifton Springs appealed to an ambitious young lawyer. The small town possibilities nearby had not worked out, and Congdon returned to Syracuse to set up a temporary practice.[4] The larger firms in Syracuse dwarfed his small office and controlled most of the business. Congdon's independent spirit had already turned his mind to alternatives. With little to lose by relocating, he began to look farther afield.

In the spring or early summer of 1878 Congdon again chose teaching as a temporary means to replenish his finances, this time farther from home than he had ever been. He accepted a job as principal of the Second Ward [High] School in Chippewa Falls, Wisconsin at an annual salary of $900. While at Chippewa Falls he could travel about and survey the opportunities in the Upper Midwest.[5]

In addition to his own expenses, Congdon felt an obligation to send money home to assist with the farm mortgage. Anxious to maintain as much financial independence as possible, he explained to his mother, "I don't want to borrow any money just now, as I may have to borrow . . . $200 [the amount of the farm mortgage note]. . . for January, and I want to keep the bank in good humor." An appeal to the president of the school board resulted in the promise of a $100 increase at the end of the term, $75 of which Congdon promised to his family.

Over the Christmas holidays, Congdon planned an exploratory trip to St. Paul and Minneapolis. Careful to keep his mother from worrying about the mortgage, he wrote, "I shall not leave here until that note is attended to. That is the first job on my hands now." He also added a word of encouragement saying, "Don't worry . . . we will revel in luxury some day [sic]," and added optimistically, "If we don't get any harder up than we now are, we will be infinitely better off than the large majority." He closed with, "But thats [sic] a weak sort of consolation, and I want to be *better* off than every body [sic] else."[6] It was clear that the young attorney had envisioned a future which held great promise for advancement and success.

Although the school year was but half over, in February, Congdon, impatient to be on his way, resigned his job in Chippewa Falls. A legal position was open in Burlington, Iowa, and it was offered to him. In an off-hand remark, the Burlington lawyer disdainfully commented that nothing much lay west of the Mississippi river town, but Congdon wanted to see for himself. He again thought about St. Paul and Minneapolis, but chose instead a circle tour which took him to Topeka, Atchison, Omaha, and back to Fort Dodge on the Chicago and Northwestern Railway. Throughout his itinerary, he met and discussed the future of each area with farmers, laborers, bankers, judges, and school teachers. He was singularly unimpressed with anything he saw or heard. His reaction to Fort Dodge was typical—a sad disappointment in both the people and the city. "I *shall not* practice law [in Fort Dodge]," he wrote home. Following a visit to the city's local court to witness a trial in session, he declared the building little more than a stone barn and the jury an unkempt lot. "This is awful country," he determined. Some businessmen were barely eking out a living, but a "lawyer would starve. I am satisfied that the west is talked to death," he judged. "It may be an Eldorado for some people but not for lawyers," but, he added, "Me, I had rather be head here [in the West] than tail in Syracuse, but I dont [sic] propose to be tail anywhere."[7]

Congdon thought Dakota Territory might be worth examining. The isolated and sparsely populated area, however, suggested a boom-or-bust economy and matched his negative impression of the West. Besides, it was a long way from home and Clara.

He decided to visit St. Paul. The city produced a very favorable impression. It was a growing, bustling community which served a broad hinterland. While it was far removed from New York, the city looked prosperous and inviting. The thought of Clara's joining him was exciting. Continued support for his family would be improved. Also, in view of his dwindling finances he felt obliged to make an immediate decision. In St. Paul he would establish a home and practice.

5
St. Paul

WHEN CONGDON ARRIVED IN ST. PAUL HE HAD $31 IN HIS POCKET.
To his friend, Harry Heermans, in Corning, he wrote, "I was in the midst of
about the hardest grind I ever saw, and I have seen a good many." On the other
hand, he had found the place where he wanted to practice, and the prospects
for advancement looked better than anywhere he had seen.[1]

Before Congdon could begin a law practice in Minnesota, it was necessary
to take the bar examination. Bar examinations were administered only twice a
year, but Congdon was fortunate to have arrived in time for the one given in
early winter. On January 9, 1880, he was informed that he had successfully
passed and would be admitted to practice.

The next step presented a dilemma: should he open an office independent
of any commitments to a fellow attorney, or should he try to become affiliated
with an already established firm and avoid what might be a long start-up
period? For Congdon, whose finances were almost exhausted, the second
alternative seemed the only possibility. He approached and was accepted into
the law firm of Pierce, Stephenson, and Mainzer. It was a practice devoted for
the most part to routine affairs: land transactions, business arrangements,
and abstracts, broken only by an occasional divorce case. The work was monotonous, but at least Congdon was receiving a regular wage, and he was
working in a professional position where he could gain experience.

His financial obligations to his family were still pressing, and the remit-
tance sent home each month to New York was essential to their welfare. His
mother had moved to a small farm just outside Syracuse when Albert, Chester's
younger brother, enrolled at the University. The family's financial condition
remained precarious. Mrs. Congdon had leased out part of the land, but payments from the tenant farmer failed to meet her expenses. Maintaining a farm
proved too much for her, and she (presumably with Congdon's acquiescence)
made the decision to sell and move into town.[2]

The change became more complex than she had anticipated. Over the years,
the house had fallen into disrepair, and both outside and inside badly needed
refurbishing with paint and plaster. The farm did not sell, and it became a

source of worry. "I am unwilling to leave the house empty," she wrote her son, "for fear it might be set on fire." Gradually, she disposed of her belongings: two pigs for $4.00, the chickens for $10.00. The cow, "Daisy," went to the neighbors. Eventually the sale was completed, but the proceeds brought very little. Nevertheless, Congdon's mother wrote her son that, "I can send you some money. Won't it be splendid."[3]

Congdon regularly wrote home describing his new surroundings and business associates. His job grew increasingly distasteful, and he developed a particular dislike for one of his employers, Jacob Mainzer, whom he considered lazy and who was referred to in his letters as "that German." It was evident that he was both disappointed and discouraged with the monotony of the work.

His mother tried to brighten his outlook. "Do remember," she counseled, "the old lady's scripture that was so much comfort to her, 'Grin and bear it,' you will come out all right—yet only be patient, patient as you can be." Congdon had been preparing his own meals, and she was also worried about his dietary habits. Adding a cautionary note, she advised, "I think that I would not board that way any longer than necessary. Your living on crackers for 2 meals and then eating very heartily at dinner may disturb or derange your stomach and induce dyspepsia."[4]

Congdon's austere life did not improve. He remained aloof and reserved. Rev. Charles W. Bennett, Congdon's former instructor from Syracuse with whom he maintained a correspondence, offered words of encouragement. "I am certain you will go through, if work will do it," he wrote, and then proceeded with some professorial advice regarding Mainzer: "Tie [yourself] to your partner and listen to his suggestions for some time. Give him your entire confidence in the business. My reasons are—he is older, more experienced, better acquainted with Minnesota law, and with Minnesota practice, and is richer and more influential. Don't let there be a shade of a shadow of a reason for any alienation. If some things are not just as you would have things, bite your lips, pocket your indignation and bide your time. This will be good discipline for you and be wisdom as well." Fearing that Congdon's conduct might swing the other way, Bennett concluded with an admonition on gentlemanly decorum for young attorneys. "The bar is more and more insisting on politeness and high gentlemanly bearing in the courts. . . . Roughness and bravado will surely count for nothing in the higher courts, and I am sure that cultured manners in the courtroom and elsewhere will be commanded by the highest and best." Sensing the near-poverty level of Congdon's life, Bennett enclosed a "little draft which may just now ease over hard places a bit and give the difference between hardship and *bearability*."[5]

Congdon was inclined at times to periods of melancholia and self-doubt, a result of his frustrated ambition. He often gave the impression of being abrupt and brisk to the point where business associates mistook this trait for a negative aloofness. He wrote Bennett alluding to this problem, and his former mentor replied with "a few plain things in my plain direct way. You do not pursue the right course to make friends," Bennett cautioned. "You isolate yourself too much . . . . you do not seem to identify yourself with the high moral questions of the day. . . . you are not true to the best interests of your being. . . . you indulge too much in cynicism."[6]

Neither his mother's encouraging words nor Bennett's advice brought peace to Congdon. The separation from his beloved Clara was constantly on his mind. Their prolonged engagement had stretched to five years, and their eventual marriage seemed as distant as ever. Whereas Congdon became increasingly morose with the drudgery of his work, Clara tried to cheer him by being buoyant and hopeful over the possibilities of her fiancée's new position. During Clara's recent visit to Syracuse, Congdon's mother had observed that she was "sprightly and animated and seemed cheerful and looked forward to the future with a wonderful satisfaction." While walking to the streetcar, Clara had confided with assurance to Congdon's sister that she "would be married this school year." She had saved some money, she explained, and openly discussed "her little plans and arrangements." Bennett's appraisal of the relationship between the two lovers only added to Congdon's mental anguish. "Her heart is on you," Bennett wrote, "and as a pure woman—as now she is—she cannot transfer affection to any other one in kind or degree which she has poured out upon you. Her future *must be* [Bennett's emphasis] bound up in your future—united or parted."[7]

A turn in Congdon's career bolstered his spirits. In 1881, he was offered the job of Assistant United States District Attorney. A professional friendship had developed between Congdon and the United States District Attorney, William W. Billson. Billson, six years older than Congdon, was a native Illinoisan who had come to Winona, Minnesota in 1867 to establish a law practice. A year later he moved to Duluth where he joined forces with a fellow attorney, and in 1870 formed the firm of Billson and Egan. Politics held an interest for Billson, and in 1872 he ran successfully for the Minnesota Senate. This was followed by an appointment in 1876 to the post of U.S. District Attorney for Minnesota and a change of residence to St. Paul. He met Congdon shortly after the latter's arrival, and the two men became good friends. When Billson offered the position to him, Congdon agreed without hesitation. The job was only temporary, but it was a change from the monotony of Pierce, Stephenson, and Mainzer, and better still, the position offered a small increase in salary. It was enough to encourage Congdon to begin planning his marriage.[8]

He decided to take the initiative and borrow enough to return to New York, marry Clara, and bring her back to Minnesota. He appealed to Heermans, now employed with his father in the development of the municipal waterworks for Corning. Congdon decided he would not ask directly for the money, but, instead, he would simply describe his situation and intentions. Heermans might volunteer to make the loan, but if he were not comfortable with advancing the money, perhaps he might suggest an alternative.

Congdon wrote,

> Did I ever write you without asking a favor?" "I think this letter will be no exception to the rule. . . . Can you tell me where I can borrow $300 or $400 of someone? I want it because more than you can ["conceive of" originally penned in but crossed out] imagine, I desire to marry—for more than 7 years has the girl who has promised to become my wife, patiently waited for me, and for 10 times 7 yrs will she wait for me, if needs be. I only want enough to get her here and to [set] up a little home of two or three rooms; and for that purpose have I been saving and scraping for nearly 2 yrs; but every time I get a little ahead something happens to absorb it; and the consummation of my hopes is repeatedly postponed.

Congdon went on to describe his family financial obligations—care for his mother and medical bills for his brother. Although he would enter marriage with an additional debt, he explained to Heermans, "it is my duty to do so." Besides, he added, "I have a responsible position and one which promises to be a lucrative one; indeed, I can almost say that my professional success is assured." The loan, Congdon explained, would be "a business transaction" secured by a recently acquired life insurance policy. "I realize the difficulties of my request," he concluded, "and can only plead. . . in my desire for a home of my own at once."[9] Heermans reply was prompt. He had consulted with his father, and together they agreed to arrange a loan for $300 at 6 percent from S. C. Robertson, the local banker.[10]

Chester Adgate Congdon and Clara Hesperia Bannister were united in marriage by the Rev. Charles W. Bennett on September 29, 1881 in Syracuse. There was no time (or money) for a honeymoon, but neither had anticipated anything beyond being together. On the afternoon of their wedding day, the couple boarded the train for St. Paul where they lived and took their meals "for a few weeks" at Chester's boarding house.

Work at the office had occupied his time prior to marriage, and he had not had time to find other housing. The newlyweds, however, wanted their own lodging, and in the winter of 1881 they moved to 65 Wilkin Street near Irvine Park, a pleasant part of the city. Here their first child, Walter Bannister Congdon, was born on November 5, 1882. The family required more space, and the following May the Congdons moved to occupy the bottom floor of a house at 325 South Franklin—another family lived upstairs. The location was farther west from the business district of the city, but a horse drawn car line provided transportation.[11]

Two more children were born while the family lived at the Franklin residence: Edward Chester on March 1, 1885, and Marjorie two years later on January 12, 1887. Clara divided her time between managing household affairs and administering to the needs of the children. Her letters to her sister in Syracuse are full of anecdotes of her children accompanied by a description of the family's life in St. Paul.[12]

Perhaps it was the need for more room, or it may have been that they found more comfortable accommodations, but in midsummer of 1888 the family moved to 546 Selby on the west bluff overlooking the city. It was here that their fourth child, Helen Clara, was born on February 16, 1889. John, the only Congdon child to die in infancy, was also born while the family lived on Selby; he passed away two years later.[13]

The entries in Clara's journal contain typical information about the family: the children's weight at birth and at intervals thereafter, dates of their first steps and words (Walter's were "papa" and "kitty"), vaccination record (Edward's and Marjorie's "took"), and childhood diseases ("Edward came home with the measles; all the family had them"—Walter brought home chicken-pox which spread to each child, as did Helen's whooping cough).

When Walter became quite excited while Uncle Bertie sang "Drumming, drum drum" and bounced the child on his knee, Grandmother Congdon, visiting at that time, observed that "there was quite a lot of the old Adam in him [Walter]."[14]

Meanwhile, Congdon's work as Assistant United States District Attorney had become increasingly more demanding. The number of cases involving land fraud and perjury under the pre-emption laws continued to pile up faster than they could be processed. Even with an increased staff, the load was more than they could handle. At the end of Congdon's appointment, Billson had wired the Washington, D.C. office requesting an extension. Although it was approved, the St. Paul office still failed to keep up with the staggering case load. In the summer of 1883, Billson resigned, and D. B. Searle, his successor, obtained a second extension for Congdon. The office made some headway, but the case load was only slightly reduced. It seemed that they would be inundated by a never ending docket. The future held little but more of the same.[15]

By April, Congdon had decided to resign as of May 1, a regrettable step in the opinion of George B. Baxter, the second person to head the office since Billson's resignation. "There is more to do in the office than I can properly attend to," Baxter pleaded. But Congdon had already made up his mind. The only future in the Assistant's job was a promotion to head of the office, and Congdon had been passed over twice by Washington, D.C. which had sought out its own men. The decision to leave his job temporarily cut off his income, but by this time he was confident that his family's financial stability would not falter.[16] Upon leaving the government office, Congdon established a private practice where he remained for the next six years. The work was challenging and rewarding. He had broadened his legal knowledge and had gained experience while serving as Assistant United States District Attorney. Once he opened his own practice, his list of clients expanded rapidly. He traveled, not frequently, but enough to become acquainted with Minnesota and its people. On trips to Duluth, he visited with his friend Billson who had reestablished a practice there. Sometimes, in his travels, he combined business with pleasure. He considered the purchase of western mining stock a sound investment, and occasionally he visited Butte, Montana where he held shares in the Gold Flint copper mine. Congdon's fortunes had indeed taken an upward turn from the days when he first entered St. Paul.[17]

Clara also traveled. She and the children returned to New York to see her relatives and friends in Syracuse. Clara's sister, Mary, as well as "Grandma" Laura Congdon, returned the visit to St. Paul. Albert Congdon, Chester's brother, came regularly to see them, and the children became quite fond of "Uncle Bertie."[18]

Reverend Charles W. Bennett came to visit and baptized Edward, Marjorie, and Helen on one of these occasions. Will Bennett, Charles' brother, also a close friend of Chester and Clara, lived with them for almost two years before his own marriage. Other friends from New York came to visit including the Heermans of Corning (Harry was now also married). The Congdon household with children, relatives, and guests was a busy place.[19]

6
The Venture on Grays Harbor

As his practice in St. Paul grew and prospered, Congdon continued his business investments. Speculative opportunities, particularly land in the Pacific Northwest, were widely circulated at the time, and newspaper advertisements and brochures promised lucrative returns to investors who got in early. The promotional literature promised that excellent prospects abounded everywhere, but the most sought after land lay adjacent to the Northern Pacific Railroad which had just completed its tracks from Minnesota to Portland, Oregon. A branch line ran north to Puget Sound. As the railroad promised additional feeder lines, land values shot upward. Congdon decided that the Pacific Northwest would be his first attempt at investment in municipal land.[1]

Congdon was not alone. Caught up with the promise of great returns on their investment, his friends in New York were also anxious to become part of the speculative boom. Congdon, acting for the group, made several trips on their behalf in 1887. To facilitate their efforts, the New Yorkers formed the Ontario Land Company of which Congdon was a member. Principal investors in the company included Harry Heermans; Quincy C. Wellington, a banker from Corning, New York, who supplied the initial capital; and Matthias Arnot, a banker from Elmira, New York.[2]

The particular area which caught their attention was Grays Harbor on the Pacific coast in Washington Territory. Developers hoped it would grow into an important shipping point since it lay near the vast timber stands on the Olympic Peninsula. As a harbor on the Pacific it would also enjoy an advantage over the ports on Puget Sound, which required ocean vessels to travel extra miles to their destination. Grays Harbor lacked only municipal development and port facilities served by a railroad. Anticipation of growth on the harbor whetted the appetites of the New York investors.

Years before, the city of Hoquiam had been founded on the north shore of Grays Harbor to serve the lumber industry, but without a railroad the town remained small. Business activity centered mainly around the North Western Lumber Company. The attention of Congdon and his group of "eastern capitalists," as they came to be known, not only focused on Hoquiam but also on a strip of land which extended four miles along on the harbor shoreline west of the city. There they anticipated the development of a new town, Grays Harbor City, which they envisioned to become the largest metropolis on the harbor. The site had been selected years before by George H. Emerson, General Manager of the North Western Lumber Company, but little development had taken place until Congdon's arrival in 1887.[3]

First, some legal requirements needed attention. The laws of Washington Territory (Washington did not become a state until 1889) forbade a non-resident company (but not company officers) to acquire real estate. To avoid this legality and to cut their losses in the event that the scheme faltered, the investors formed three new companies under the laws of Washington Territory: the Grays Harbor Company, the Harbor Land Company, and the East Hoquiam Company. All three companies were administered by the same individuals. Congdon served as the president of the Grays Harbor Company, and his old friend Heermans (still a resident of Corning, New York) was president and manager of the other two. Albert Congdon, Chester's brother, served as Secretary and Treasurer of all three companies. In addition to the New York stockholders, George Emerson and John F. Soule, Secretary of the North Western Lumber Company, were added to the list.[4]

In theory, their plan was simple: develop a site for a new town, construct some buildings, improve the harbor, and sell individual lots at a substantial profit. Grays Harbor Company, organized in 1889, was to serve as the corporate entity for the development of Grays Harbor City. The partners immediately began to buy both upland (2,000 acres) and tideland (2,700 acres) property. Under the supervision of Congdon's brother, Albert, work began immediately, clearing the land by cutting and burning the timber. Surveyors followed laying out the streets. There was no attempt to level the surface, and the lots simply conformed to the contour of the land. The preparation was quick, cheap, and had the advantage of "providing effective drainage." Only the area where the town buildings were to be constructed was graded flat. Simultaneously, with the preparation of the town site, construction of a wharf was begun across the tide flats to deep water. A warehouse followed, as well as other buildings. The town boasted that its waterfront could handle ships at both high and low tides.[5]

With several speculative schemes booming at the same time, the question became one of priority for the partners. "I desire to impress upon your mind the fact that Grays Harbor City has more money behind it than all other towns in Chehalis Co[unty], combined, and that it is going to outdistance them all," Congdon wrote to Albert. "The Grays Harbor City people propose to stand by their town to the bitter end, and you had better act accordingly.... if you boom Hoquiam at the expense of Grays Harbor it will cost you money to do so," Congdon warned.[6]

Lots began to sell almost immediately. There was very little publicity. Buyers came to the site, looked over the available lands, and made their selection. A new problem now confronted the directors of the Grays Harbor Company, i.e., how much to improve their property before offering it for rent or sale. "There are a good many people who will build in G.H. [Grays Harbor City] this year and I think we ought to hurry our buildings along so as to get the first high rents," Congdon wrote to Heermans. "You are going to get rich this year in that country," he predicted enthusiastically. Revenue from the sale of lots totaled about $225,000, all of which went to pay for the initial improvements—wharf, warehouse, buildings, and street grading.[7]

The Harbor Land Company was organized in 1890 for the purpose of purchasing all the holdings of the original town site of Hoquiam. Within the city, the company bought 236 lots and 798 more lying adjacent to the town boundaries. Next, the company purchased the tidelands (151 acres) in front of the city, a step made possible by the laws of the state which gave shore owners the right of first purchase of adjacent tidelands. Funds for this purchase came from the sale of lots, but new investors were also welcome. In addition to Congdon, Heermans, the New Yorkers, and a few Hoquiam investors, stockholders from Boston were added.[8]

In order to facilitate their development plans, yet another company, the East Hoquiam Company, a subsidiary of the Ontario Land Company of St. Paul, was formed. The purpose of this company was to gain control of the lands (approximately 400 acres) lying on the east side of the Hoquiam River fronting on Grays Harbor and extending east as far as Aberdeen.

Financing for the land companies was always somewhat tenuous. Wellington's bank in Corning supplied a large part of the capital, as did Arnot's bank in Elmira. Both Congdon and Heermans provided whatever investment capital they could raise, but the requirements and opportunities sometimes surpassed their capabilities. Then, too, Wellington and Arnot had their own businesses to consider, and responsibilities at home often demanded first priority. If money in New York was needed on short notice, both bankers called in their notes. "The position Wellington takes is astounding," Heermans wrote to Albert, "he seems to demand that we pay him off—which is wholly unexpected." An additional source of investment capital had to be found, and Heermans had the answer. Acting with the approval of Congdon and Albert, he announced that he would try to place an additional large block of stock with other eastern investors. The plan worked, and while it did not entirely relieve them of financial troubles, it increased the support base.[9]

With Washington's statehood in 1889 came an adjustment upward in real estate taxes. Statehood demanded more locally raised revenue, and an increasing population placed additional requirements on the new government. Consequently, profits on land sales decreased. Property acquired with buildings on the land meant even higher taxes. "We must watch the valuations made by the assessor and get the figures down," Heermans lectured Albert, but the problem continued.[10]

Albert was the local resident manager and bookkeeper for the companies, while Heermans and Congdon lived in Corning and St. Paul. The logistics of running the business at long range presented difficulties. Telegrams were used for quick communication, and, therefore, information concerning land values and sales was open to any reader. To provide confidentiality, the partners worked out a cipher by which they could convey this information with security. The system was used infrequently, but when employed it worked efficiently. Communication was important in a number of ways. Congdon, always alert to company finances, kept a watchful eye on cash flow. Albert was not an experienced accountant, and his ledgers, while orderly and clear to him, were not always so to Congdon.

Problems were compounded when Heermans did not always agree with sale arrangements. "We must make some good money there this spring," Heermans wrote Albert, "Do not sell on long term. Our object in selling now is to get money." To obtain ready cash, funds were shifted from one company to another, including the financial resources of the Ontario Land Company and another business organization, the Heermans and Congdon Company. Sharp differences developed between the stockholders, particularly between Congdon and Emerson. Congdon considered the lumber company executive irredeemably self-serving when Emerson threatened a lawsuit for payment of a debt incurred by the company for materials.[11]

The prospect of improving land sales loomed the brightest one year before the financial panic of 1893 struck. In early January 1892, Heermans reported to Albert that $25,000 in Harbor Land Company stock had been "placed," and $1 million in bonds were on their way to a syndicate of London bankers. Also, the Boston investors had agreed to take a large block of stock in the Grays Harbor Company. Times were indeed looking up. "I think this year will see things change greatly for the better on the north shore of Gray's [sic] Harbor," Congdon confidently wrote his brother, "Things are brewing which will ultimately be of benefit to that county."

Still, there was a hint of financial uneasiness. The two Hoquiam banks had overextended their loans, and a worried Albert had pulled the company's deposits from the Hoquiam National Bank. Heermans, however, offered his reassurance that despite a momentary panic things would be all right. Conditions, however, were but a portent of worse times to come.[12]

The panic of 1893 was the most disastrous blow to the economy that the nation had ever witnessed. With its beginnings in the financial institutions of the East, the disaster spread first to California and almost as quickly to the Pacific Northwest. Banks, businesses, and railroads went under. The lumber trade, upon which the cities on Grays Harbor depended, fell off sharply. Land sales in Hoquiam and along the north shore of the harbor ceased, and purchase commitments made prior to the panic were voided. Fortunately, Congdon's lucrative law practice enabled him to wait out the disruption and maintain his holdings. His partners survived as well. Recovery would be cautious and slow, but by 1895 economic conditions had taken a turn for the better, and the partners were ready to plan their next move.[13]

Hoquiam enjoyed an advantage as a Pacific coast port; however, that advantage could only be fully realized with the development of a transportation tie to the Northern Pacific, the nearest transcontinental railroad. The investors were determined to link a rail tie with the north shore of Grays Harbor. The Northern Pacific, also recognizing the advantages of a feeder line to Grays Harbor, had built into Aberdeen but gave no indication of extending its line farther west along the shore to either Hoquiam or north into the Olympic Peninsula.

It was Heermans who pressed for the partners to build a rail extension from Aberdeen into Hoquiam. Congdon was wary at first, but by January 1895, now convinced of his partner's argument, he had changed his mind. "I have given a good deal of reflection to your suggestion about taking hold of Grays Harbor at once, and I am convinced that you are right," he wrote, "I am satisfied that now is the time to do it [build the extension], and that we shall suffer a serious loss if we postpone doing so." To delay would mean, Congdon thought, that companies building on the harbor would choose Aberdeen. Once the western terminal was fixed at Aberdeen, any plans to promote corporate growth in Hoquiam or Grays Harbor City, despite their superior harbor advantages, would be futile.[14]

Won over by the economic advisability of the proposal, Congdon, ever the financial conservative, agreed to Heerman's proposal but urged caution against over expansion. Having won Congdon's approval, Heermans ambitiously viewed the railroad extension into Hoquiam and Grays Harbor City as the first step toward additional development of their own properties. The tidelands in front of both cities could be improved into desirable building sites, and a twenty-mile spur line could run up the Humptulips River into timber country where the partners would acquire large tracts of land. "While such schemes would doubtless be profitable," Congdon wrote, "it would involve some risk, and take a good deal of capital, which would necessarily be earning nothing for some time." Unwilling to dismiss completely Heermans projections, however, he added, "I would have the whole plan in mind, and aim towards it, but I would go at it piecemeal, and would not put a dollar down until it was demonstrated to a mathematical certainty, not only that that dollar would bring interest from the time it was put down, but would itself come back and bring another dollar with it." Here, as well as in the entire Grays Harbor enterprise, Congdon and Heermans had each demonstrated his investment philosophy. Congdon was cautious, unwilling to commit investment funds over a long period of time, but amenable to speculate on a short-term basis providing there was assurance of a respectable profit. A dollar invested must return the original investment plus profit. Heermans was more speculative, willing to invest resources over a long period in hopes of greater profits in the future.

Congdon, however, was willing to begin the transportation plan with the immediate incorporation of a railroad to be known as the Grays Harbor Terminal Company. In fact, as he contemplated the full development he became more enthusiastic. Spurs could be constructed leading to "every factory in Aberdeen west of the Wishkah [River], and to every mill in Hoquiam." The plan was to eventually sell the railroad to the Northern Pacific; consequently, Congdon argued, the road bed must follow the best route into Hoquiam, "so that when the N.P. or any other railroad is in a position to buy it, they will gladly pay the price asked." With these plans in mind, Congdon added, "The N.P. will have to buy it when they go beyond Aberdeen, and will pay at least what it cost and interest." If, upon completion, the Northern Pacific wanted to lease the line, an arrangement, he calculated, could be worked out at 6 percent of the construction cost.

The estimated cost of the railroad was somewhere between $45,000 to $50,000. If the higher figure were not exceeded, Congdon felt that the rails ought to be extended to Grays Harbor City as far as the wharf "so that everything would be in readiness for mills and factories to be built along the water front on the tide flats." Again, with characteristic caution, Congdon added a caveat, "I would not improve the tide flats at present. Let a few mills be built on them at first, located in accordance with an approved plan." In this way, local development would increase the demand for timber. Only then should the partners extend a line up the Humptulips River where it could be "immediately operated at a profit." Meanwhile, the value of the land in Hoquiam would increase in value. Again, stressing the desirability of the plan, Congdon concluded, "In view of these facts it seems to me that the question for us is not whether it is desirable for us to put the railroad at once into Hoquiam, but whether we are able to do so."

In the months that followed two things became clear. First, the Northern Pacific had no intention of building a line from Aberdeen to Hoquiam, and second, they resented the intrusion of any other railroad on what they considered to be their domain. Congdon wrote from St. Paul that John W. Kendrick, General Manager of the Northern Pacific, "would do all he could to prevent such extension." The General Manager, hearing of the partners' plan, had commented that the construction cost estimates were far too low. Congdon was not dismayed. Recalling an earlier investment, Congdon cited to Heermans an incident where the estimate had been especially high as a way to discourage development. Kendrick's estimates were made, Congdon judged, "simply to prevent our taking hold of the scheme."

Rejecting the Northern Pacific estimates, Congdon informed his partners that he had personally visited with W. D. Roberts, the chief officer of the Northern Pacific, who had told him that the estimates were based on outdated costs and prices and that the work probably could be done for one-third to one-half less. The higher estimates, Congdon thought, should not be entirely dismissed and would serve a purpose: the partners intended to ask the residents of Hoquiam and Grays Harbor City for a bonus to assist in financing the railroad, and the upward costs would serve as the figure presented by Congdon and his partners to the communities in case the estimates proved inaccurate.[15]

A few short months later in March 1895, the Northern Pacific filed for bankruptcy, the railroad went into the hands of receivers, and Kendrick was out of a job. This change brought about a different attitude from railroad officials regarding a monopoly on transportation in the Grays Harbor area. From St. Paul, Congdon wrote Heermans that "the receivers of the N.P. will cooperate in every manner within their power to facilitate the construction of such extension.... they will either make a traffic contract, or will take the road and operate it, giving the builders all the net profit." This was, indeed, good news, and Congdon encouraged his partner to move ahead with all speed. "As soon as you are ready to formulate a definite plan I will at once [see N.P. officials] . . . and arrange that end of the deal. It seems to me that with the cooperation of the N.P. it will be impossible for us to sustain any loss on the railroad extension, if we build it economically."[16]

The financial condition of the Northern Pacific at that time, however, was not such as to allow any expansion, and Congdon and his partners were hesitant to move on their own. Some kind of working arrangement between the land companies and the railroad was necessary. The delay went on for two years while the Northern Pacific reorganized; at last, in 1897 negotiations began again. Once back on sound financial ground, the Northern Pacific took a more positive view toward the Hoquiam extension and decided they would build the line provided the Grays Harbor investors supplied some of the construction costs.

The railroad, well aware that the land companies needed its services more than the railroad needed theirs, drove a hard bargain. First of all, the Northern Pacific demanded and was given a right-of-way from Aberdeen west to Hoquiam as well as free depot sites; second, the amount of money necessary for the construction of the railroad was to be deposited in the First National Bank of St. Paul. From this fund the railroad could draw money to meet construction costs. The railroad agreed on a repayment plan whereby a percentage of the freight and passenger revenues each month from traffic over the new extension would go to repay the fund. No return was to be made on the right-of-way or the depot sites. To meet this financial obligation, the Grays Harbor Company put up $60,000 in cash with a stipulation that $27,000 more would be forthcoming if needed. To obtain this right-of-way (essentially, waterfront property on the Wishkah River in Aberdeen) and depot sites, the citizens of Hoquiam raised $10,000. To raise the capital, the Grays Harbor Company, the Harbor Land Company, and the East Hoquiam Company bonded their lands for $100,000 ($60,000 in first mortgage bonds and $40,000 in second mortgage bonds) and sold them at sixty cents on the dollar. Wellington and Arnot took the first mortgage bonds, and Heermans, Congdon, and Emerson guaranteed payment.[17] The railroad was completed in 1898.

The railroad extension did not create the expected land boom. Property values remained fairly constant, while taxes continued to rise. Heermans was forced to spend four to six months of each year in Hoquiam attending to the management of the properties. To a disgruntled stockholder who wrote asking when the companies would declare a dividend, he explained,

> Almost every land company similar to ours that I know of has gone into the hands of a receiver and been closed out. We proposed and tried [at] every point to sell our properties at fair value but not at sacrifices. I am anxious with you to secure dividends on my stock in the company but believe it will take say a couple of years to pay off our debts so that dividends can be made. The real estate market has been a phenomenal disspointment [sic] to all interested in the business during the last ten years. . . . There has been no speculation whatever by capitalists.[18]

With the railroad question settled, the partners could concentrate their efforts on land sales. In spite of the lack of financial impact from the railroad, in Heermans mind, there was no hesitation about improving property to increase profits.

In Corning, Heermans had been one of the men who built and owned the water works for the city. Heermans was a civil engineer, and the water system which he had developed was highly efficient and served as a model for surrounding communities. Real estate developers in Corning were always quick to point out to their clients the advantages of a safe and dependable water supply. If it would work in Corning, why not Hoquiam? In 1898, Heermans incorporated the Hoquiam Water Company. The incorporators were, besides

Heermans, Emerson, Soule, J.O. Stearns, and Heermans brother, John. Water came from the Little Hoquiam River diverted through an intake about five miles north of the city. First one and then two reservoirs were constructed, and the city enjoyed a daily supply of 8 million gallons. Heermans predicted that even with the anticipated population growth of the city, this amount would adequately serve the residents' needs. Congdon was not impressed by the development of the water works, and he preferred to wait and see what the effects would be. "I have known a good many town site companies that did great work for the community, but I never did know one that made money for its stockholders, but I presume there are such," he wrote Heermans.[19]

As Heermans predicted, population grew—no doubt due in some part to the desirability of a wholesome and generous water supply, but it never approached Heermans prediction of 40,000. By 1900, the city's population had reached 2,608, and by 1910 it was 8,171.[20]

An unforeseen development was about to interrupt continued expansion. The Washington State Supreme Court in 1909 ruled that "no franchise will be granted by a city to a private water company purely for domestic purposes excluding manufacturing uses." This decision began the slow but inevitable passing of utilities to public ownership. "The decision of the Supreme Court seems to be an absurdity and if not reconsidered will work great hardship in many ways in the development of this state," Heermans protested to a friend.[21]

Heermans was also the developer of an electric light plant for the city of Hoquiam. In view of the growing trend toward municipal ownership of utilities, it was probably not the wisest investment. Once again, Congdon reminded his partner that, "Anything that the community as a whole may want, such as water works, electric light plants, street railways, water fronts, etc., will be difficult to hang on to, and are therefore not desirable investments." As desirous as these civic improvements were, there was only a modest reflection in real estate prices.[22]

Despite the attempt to attract cargo shipments (both incoming and outgoing) that otherwise were routed to Puget Sound, Hoquiam remained dependent upon the lumber trade. By 1908, there were twenty-seven mills operating on Grays Harbor, eight of which were clustered about the city of Hoquiam. But even with the growth of the lumber trade, population remained small.

There seemed to be no end to problems. Clearance for vessels over the bar at the entrance to the harbor frequently impeded ship movements. The partners, largely through the efforts of Heermans, successfully lobbied the federal government for funds to dredge the bar and the channels leading to the various ports. The government response was a $1 million appropriation, which financed a dredge allowing ships with a twenty-seven foot draft to pass safely into the harbor.[23]

Heermans had always spent at least half, if not more, of his time each year attending to the real estate business on Grays Harbor, but even then a large part of the transactions had to be conducted at long distance. Albert could handle some of the details of the business, but a great deal more required Heermans attention. Also, in 1905, Heermans, still determined to manage a utility, purchased the municipal water works in Olympia, Washington, a decision which, in view of the growing shift from private to public ownership, seemed ill-advised. By 1908, business demands upon the New Yorker's time were so great that he decided to make a permanent move to the Pacific Coast. In that year, he sold his interest in the Corning Water Works and moved to Hoquiam where he and his family took residence in the Hotel Hoquiam, a recent acquisition by Heermans. Congdon approved of Heermans' move. It would provide immediate attention to business.

Although somewhat cramped in their new quarters, the advantages of proximity to his work more than offset the living inconveniences. Residence at the hotel, however, was short-lived. In July 1910, while Heermans and his wife were visiting New York, the hotel was destroyed by fire. Luckily, the Heermans' children were unharmed, but their entire household belongings were lost. Partly because of his investment in the Olympia water works, and partly because Heermans felt that Olympia was a more desirable location in which to raise a family, a move was made inland. From that time forward, Heermans resided in Olympia and commuted to Hoquiam.[24]

Real estate values continued to fluctuate over the years. Rather than cut his losses and get out, Congdon continued to hang on if only in loyalty to Heermans. Revenue from land sales seemed to move downward more than up, but even when business was doing well Heermans thought it prudent to sound out Congdon before completing a transaction. The partners were caught in a typical speculator's dilemma: sometimes they sold only to find that afterwards the property increased in value; at other times they hung on only to find that the value went down. "We have been waiting [a long time], and I would dislike to give this property away at the beginning of the great growth which the Grays Harbor country is going to have," Congdon cautioned his Hoquiam partner. "You will remember, we sold our Yakima property [another investment] as soon as things commenced to move, whereas if we had waited a year or two longer we could have gotten five times as much for it. Do not let us repeat that operation on Grays Harbor." The sale was postponed, but the profits were modest.[25]

The investment risk did not always lie with the temperamental market. When the state passed legislation to take control of the tidelands, thus removing them from private ownership, Congdon vented his frustration in a letter to Heermans, "The prophecy which Mr. de Tocqueville made nearly one hundred years ago in his celebrated book entitled *Democracy in America*, is now at the point of being fulfilled. He said, you remember, that there were so many more people who would have little or nothing than there were who would have much, that it was inevitable that the ultimate result in the United States would be that those who had nothing would take from those who had something whatever they had. That process is now going on, and it is up to you [Heermans] to figure out a scheme to hang onto what you can as long as you can, and put your property into such shape that you can hang on to it."[26]

In spite of everything, Heermans retained his characteristic optimism. Responding to Congdon's wariness about continued investment in real estate, he wrote,

> I have no reason to change my life-long opinion and experience about real estate as a general proposition. The greatest fortunes in the world are founded upon real estate holdings, and the safest fortunes are those consisting of real estate. Such investments are least affected by panics, catastrophies, and other unforetold and unforseen conditions which affect nearly every other class of investments. Of course, we have ups and downs in the real estate market, and real estate is off at the present time, but the prices will return and advances will be made in values. We have good properties that will ultimately all pay out.[27]

From time to time, Congdon made personal loans to the companies at Grays Harbor. The role was always a delicate one, since it placed him in the role of a creditor as well as a stockholder. Congdon, as always, was a stickler for keeping his relationship with the companies on a businesslike basis, and when notes were not paid on time he resented this tardiness. Sometimes, in lieu of payment, Congdon accepted stock from the company to which the loan had been made. In reality, this trade-off was the best of both worlds. To Heermans, he wrote at one point (unknowingly expressing his own role), "unless the [land company] changes its condition in the next twelve months, its creditors [Congdon had loaned money to the Ontario Land Company which in turn had loaned money to the other land company] will own it and not the stockholders. I do not know as that will be a bad thing for its creditors, but it will be for its stockholders." But, if the companies prospered, Congdon, as both creditor and stockholder, was in a favorable position.[28]

Speculative real estate in the Pacific Northwest was undoubtedly the least lucrative investment into which Congdon entered. Despite the cautious approach advised by Congdon, the investments continually absorbed more funds than they paid out. Grays Harbor, despite its favorable location when compared with other Pacific coast ports, never became an ocean-side Puget Sound. Transcontinental rail traffic, which the partners anticipated would be forthcoming, terminated at Portland, Seattle, and Tacoma. The vast timber resources of the Olympic Peninsula found only a partial outlet through Grays Harbor, and the lumber towns on the harbor remained small communities.

The Grays Harbor experience had been difficult for Congdon. Operating a business partnership at long distance had been frustrating. Speculative real estate at best was not without its problems. Without a direct transcontinental rail link and a more accessible harbor, Grays Harbor would always remain second to Puget Sound.

7
Raymond

Despite the losses incurred on Grays Harbor, the expectation of great profits from western land investment, especially in town development, continued to be tempting. Congdon never lost faith in the Pacific Northwest as an area of great potential economic growth. The rich timber resources on the Olympic Peninsula would someday stimulate industrial and population growth, and to be in on the ground floor of this development was the dream of many investors.

In the fall of 1905, Heermans, returning from a short vacation/business trip and in a buoyant mood, wrote Congdon, "A new town site is being located in the South Bend country on the Willipa [sic] River about four miles east of the old town of South Bend and the new place is to be called Raymond."

"The promoter of this enterprise," Heermans wrote, "is a former State Fish Commissioner, a very popular fellow and hustler and a man of large acquaintance throughout the State." The New Yorker went on to explain that the ex-commissioner, A. C. Little, had taken an option to buy a large block of property adjacent to the tidelands for the low figure of $3 to $5 per acre. Little had run out of money, however, before he could conclude the deal. Pressed for capital, Little had approached Heermans, offering to sell him a quarter interest for $2,500 providing Heermans loaned Little's organization, The Raymond Land and Improvement Company, $5,000. Little, Heermans explained, had already located two saw mills and two shingle mills on the property and was about to place two more saw mills close by. Heermans had been encouraged by Frederick Weyerhaeuser's chief woods foreman, R. A. Long, when the latter had informed him that "more timber would be cut at South Bend than on Grays Harbor."

The possibilities were enticing, and, to say the least, Heermans was enthusiastic. "I do not see any possible chance of loss and everything points to some rapid money making," he wrote with typical optimism. Although Heermans had not visited the Raymond town site (he planned to go in a few days) he proposed to have the Ontario Land Company make a loan of $5,000 to the

Raymond Land and Improvement Company, a debt which, he explained, "will be repaid within 12 months."[1]

Upon receipt of his partner's letter, Congdon immediately sent off a wire indicating that the Ontario Land Company could indeed provide the money, but, he added, "The important question is will this furnish sufficient funds to enable the enterprise to go through beyond question." The brief telegram ended with, "See letter." In the follow-up correspondence, Congdon, in his usual fashion, came immediately to the critical questions: was the town site location feasible? How firm was the commitment from the mill owners to build? Were there competing town sites? And then, to the most telling question of all, "how quick a deal is it?"[2]

If the Ontario Land Company loaned the Raymond Land and Improvement Company $5,000 and the scheme collapsed, the partners would lose their investment. Why not, Congdon suggested, have the Ontario Land Company go in with Little "on an even keel, that is, take a half interest on the same basis that his [Little's] half interest cost him." If the enterprise needed more money, Congdon concluded, "we could consider the question of making loans to it." It was this arrangement that was concluded. The Ontario Land Company loaned the Raymond enterprise $5,000 at 8 percent. Always cautious, Congdon warned his partner, "You will remember that where we fell down in our Grays Harbor speculation was that after we got a nice little slice of it, and the boom got to going fairly well, we bit off a very large chunk, more than we could masticate. I strongly suggest that we do not repeat that error in Raymond."[3]

The loan of $5,000 was followed by a request for an additional $4,000 to be used in "paying up of a mortgage now outstanding on 62 acres of land." More loans of various amounts were extended, and, much to Congdon's consternation, they were not always followed by prompt repayment. To Congdon's fears of pending bankruptcy, Little responded that "the money was all used to buy additional property and to pay off some mortgages" which would enhance the value of the current holdings. Also, "surveying, street improvements, and additional purchases of tideland and other property have been heavy," but "only a small amount of this outlay has been expended in such a way that it is not now an asset of the company." It was the same problem which Congdon and Heermans had faced on Grays Harbor. Additional purchase and development increased the value of the land, but how much should the speculator purchase and develop before converting his investment into a profitable sale?[4]

By now the Ontario Land Company owned 325 shares of stock in the Raymond company, and Congdon wrote Heermans asking for an appraisal of their investment. Heermans continued his characteristic optimism. He reported that, in his estimate, the shares were worth $200 each, and that the future of Raymond looked very bright. In addition to three lumber mills in full operation, nine more were being "located," along with three shingle mills, a "big" shipyard, two machine shops, one box factory, an electric power plant, and a street railway. The evaluation was a typical Heermans "paper" assessment. A. C. Little also fueled the optimism of the venture. Writing to Congdon, he calculated that, "The property of our corporation will sell for more than four times as much as it would when Mr. Heermans bought the interest. . . ."[5]

By the middle of 1907, Raymond had enjoyed a modest growth. The Northern Pacific had opened a new depot at the end of a spur line which terminated in the town. Four large lumber mills and a variety of ancillary stores were in operation. In addition, the Raymond Land and Improvement Company had purchased a second mill and expected to have it operating that summer. From this mill the town promoters expected to obtain lumber for a plank street and graded roads, improvements which would enhance property values. Capital for additional improvements, however, was still lacking, and Heermans estimated that an additional $15,000 must be raised to meet their needs.[6]

In spite of his many misgivings, Congdon again supplied the necessary capital. Heermans wrote appreciatively, "We are greatly obliged to you for favoring us in this manner," and enclosed in his letter a financial statement of the Raymond company. The money went for additional land purchases. Congdon was not satisfied. "The statement on its face certainly looks good," the Minnesota partner wrote, "but I cannot resist the conviction that the officers of that corporation are deceiving themselves. . . . You may have a first class town at Raymond and I believe you will, but since you[r] caompany [sic] will have to carry the load and pay the cost of getting that town, the land Company may become insolvent even though the town succeeds." Noting that the real estate boom had ended in both New York and Los Angeles, he closed with a warning, "I predict that unless the Raymond Land Company changes its condition in the next twelve months, its creditors will own it and not its stockholders." Heermans remained confident. "There is nothing in the State of Washington to indicate a collapse of real estate sales at the present time," he replied, but then admitted, "but neither at Raymond nor at Hoquiam have we had any boom."[7]

Against his better judgment, Congdon continued to be the financial bene-
factor for his friend's venture. Regularly, he responded with loans and payment of interest on existing notes. Gradually, however, their speculation began
to sour. When the Raymond Land and Improvement Company failed to repay
one of Congdon's loans, Heermans tried to persuade him that in view of Congdon's income from his legal business he did not really need the money.[8]

With relations strained between himself and Congdon, Heermans turned to
another source of finances. To meet business debts, he began to borrow funds
from the Ontario Land Company and the East Hoquiam Company, a practice
thoroughly disapproved of by his partner. To add to their problems, the legislature of the state of Washington embarked on a statewide road-building effort, all of which demanded additional tax revenues. All lands on the Olympic
peninsula were inspected, re-evaluated, and taxes raised accordingly. Both
Heermans and Little lobbied against highway appropriations, but their efforts
were in vain. Relief from additional taxes came only when the legislature adjourned. "We believe. . . that the end has come for the wild cat [sic] visionaries
to plunge the people in debt," Heermans wrote Congdon. But the increased
taxes remained.[9]

To make matters worse, a regional depression was beginning to force the
shutdown of several lumber and shingle mills. By the fall of 1914, the real
estate market and financial conditions were rapidly deteriorating, and the
Raymond Land and Improvement Company was fast running out of funds.
The Ontario Land Company had been continually tapped, additional bonds
had been issued (most of which had been purchased by Congdon), and
Congdon had time and again bailed the company out of financial difficulties.

Heermans wrote Congdon that, "The Company must raise some money
by December 1, 1914 to prevent the sale of property for improvement taxes."
Stockholders were anxious to divest themselves of Raymond Land and
Improvement Company holdings. Later in December, Heermans appealed to
Congdon for another loan of $20,000 at 10 percent per annum. Congdon re-
sponded with the funds, but the end was becoming evident.[10]

By midwinter of 1915–1916, 80 percent of the manufacturing enterprises
were closed, and unemployment skyrocketed. Hourly wages for workers still
employed were drastically reduced. With all available cash going to essentials,
regular payments by those people who owed money to the land company
stopped. Always one to see the glass half full, Heermans predicted that the

depressed conditions would be short-lived. "It is my conclusion," he wrote Congdon, "that the disastrous conditions prevailing at Raymond during the past year will be fully overcome and the most encouraging outlook is now in sight that has existed for the past three years." In the meantime, Heermans thought, the investments of the Raymond Land and Improvement Company could best be protected by holding on to their properties. Disposal under the prevailing conditions would exacerbate the woes of the remaining stockholders who would receive only a fraction of their money back.[11]

Economic conditions during the middle of 1915 through the first quarter of 1916 brought the Raymond Land and Improvement Company to its knees. Delinquent taxes forced the sale of some of the choicest lots owned by the company in the business district for as little as $200. Protesting all the while that he knew nothing of the sale, A.C. Little was forced to resign. Additional sales were anticipated but did not materialize. Hoping to save the investment, Heermans came to Raymond from Olympia as quickly as he could, but events were already moving on an unalterable course. Nevertheless, his report to Congdon contained the usual optimistic tone. "With Mr. Little out of the way and expenses reduced to a minimum, it is my belief that this proposition can be safely carried through without the advance of much additional money."[12] Although Congdon's answer is not known, it is highly unlikely that he was in accordance with his partner.

By 1916, it was evident that the Raymond Land and Improvement Company was no better an investment than Grays Harbor. The town of Raymond developed into a small mill community, much the same as those on Grays Harbor, without ever rewarding either Congdon or Heermans for their faith or their financial investments.

Congdon had learned his lesson, and The Raymond Land and Improvement Company was his last venture in municipal land development. There were higher yield investments in other fields where Congdon felt more at home.

8

The Mesabi: Rivalry for Ore

CONGDON'S LEGAL PRACTICE IN ST. PAUL WAS DEVELOPING VERY NICELY. He worked hard, and his client list grew steadily. The cases were interesting and varied, and it seemed that he might very well settle in to build an established office with an excellent reputation. Occasionally, his work required that he travel around the Upper Midwest, and he observed that both the economy and the population were growing. Whenever he traveled north to Duluth he visited William Billson, whose legal practice was expanding with the development of the city. Billson was enthusiastic about the future of Duluth, and his comments stirred Congdon's interest.

On one of Congdon's trips to Duluth, Billson proposed that the two men form a law partnership. It was a difficult decision for Congdon. Despite Billson's encouragement, it would mean disrupting his life and work in St. Paul. His practice was going very well, and his family had settled in and was enjoying life. But, there were several reasons why Billson's offer was attractive. During his trips to Duluth, Congdon had observed the growth of the city as the major port on Lake Superior. Billson's buoyancy reflected the optimism and activity that Duluth represented. For the past several years, the city had enjoyed a flourishing lumber business with the location of a dozen or so mills at the mouth of the St. Louis River. Several Michigan companies, their timber supply fast dwindling, had moved there. Railroads carried grain from the Red River Valley and the Dakota prairies to Duluth's harbor elevators. Real estate and mercantile industries experienced rapid growth. Duluth banks increased from three in 1885 to twelve by 1889, and loan agencies surpassed this by rising from six to fifty-three during the same period. In 1885, the city with its population of 17,685, supported nineteen practitioners at the bar. Five years later the population doubled, and the number of lawyers increased threefold. Most of all, and perhaps greater than any other cause for jubilant optimism in Duluth, was the news of a recently discovered deposit of iron ore sixty miles to the north. It already had a name, the Mesabi, from the contour of low hills which the ore body followed, and it would turn out to be the world's largest and richest deposit. The railroad carrying ore from the Mesabi to Lake Superior terminated at the docks in Duluth, where ships stood ready to transport their cargo to the steel mills.[1]

Billson's offer was too good to pass by. Despite the prospects of a promising law practice in St. Paul, in 1892 Congdon agreed to join his former associate. The logistics of moving a family of six were understandably complex, and it was decided that Chester would move first to begin his new job and to locate housing. Clara and the family remained behind and did not move until May 17, while Chester commuted between the two cities in order to be with his family as much as possible. Years later, Clara recalled that when time for the move came, Chester took the two boys with him, and she and the girls stayed at a hotel while the furniture was being shipped. Will Bennett, brother of Congdon's mentor at Syracuse, and his wife helped with packing those items not trusted to the moving company. The disruption of family life was only temporary, and the anticipation of living in Duluth made the inconveniences bearable.

On previous trips, Chester had taken an interest in the eastern section of the city, and he found an available house at 1530 E. First Street. Inclement weather made moving difficult and for four days heavy rains delayed the family's occupancy of their new home.[2]

The Congdons were not the only ones caught up in the air of excitement. News of the Mesabi focused the attention of eastern steelmakers on northeastern Minnesota. Pennsylvania furnacemen viewed the new discovery with both anticipation and apprehension. On the one hand, new supplies of ore might mean lower prices. However, Mesabi ore was granular and soft, quite unlike the hard, solid ore which they had been using. In fact, it was rumored, Mesabi ore was inferior and unsuited to steelmaking.[3]

Chief among the doubters was Andrew Carnegie, the largest steel manufacturer in the nation. At an earlier date, hoping to interest Carnegie in their mines, the discoverers of the Mesabi, the Merritt brothers, had invited the chairman of the Carnegie company to send an expert to visit the Mesabi and see for himself. After examining the soft, granular substance, the "expert" pronounced it little more than a "sample of dirt." Carnegie, of course, accepted the decision and refused to have anything to do with the Mesabi.[4]

One not so easily dissuaded was Henry W. Oliver, second only to Carnegie in Pittsburgh steel production. Oliver's background was remarkably similar to Carnegie's. Both emigrated to America at an early age, and both settled in Pittsburgh. They had even known each other as young boys when they served as delivery "runners" for the telegraph company. Each was now head of his own steel company.

With the announcement of the discovery of ore on the Mesabi, Oliver dispatched George Tener, his most trusted lieutenant, to investigate the new range. Tener's report was far different from the one which Carnegie received. While it did not unequivocally accept the new ore, neither did it present a rejection.[5]

Oliver's attention was at that moment, however, divided between the Mesabi and other matters. For several years, he had been active in the Republican Party, especially in lobbying for government protection against foreign steel. In the summer of 1892, Oliver was busy drafting the party's stand on the steel tariff, a plank which he intended to present at the national convention. In July, the Republicans convened in St. Paul, adopted Oliver's carefully worded statement as part of their platform, nominated Benjamin Harrison as their presidential candidate, took care of other matters, and adjourned.[6]

With his political work finished, Oliver invited a number of his friends to accompany him to see the Mesabi. In his private railway car, Oliver and his companions rode north to Duluth. Though sixty miles south of the Mesabi, the city was already recognized as the capital of the iron range and the port on Lake Superior from which the ore would be shipped.

At Duluth, the party learned that travel to the Mesabi would be formidable indeed, and sensing that some of his guests were less than enthusiastic about continuing, Oliver turned his car over to them for their return home. Then, Oliver, George Tener, and Captain Edward Florada (a mining supervisor from Michigan) pushed on up the north shore of Lake Superior to Two Harbors. Here they boarded the Duluth and Iron Range Railway which took them north to Mesabi Junction where the railroad crossed the eastern end of the range. From this point Oliver and his party took a buckboard west for thirty-six miles over the "Mesabi Trail," an almost impassable route. After jolting and bouncing for hours, they arrived at their destination. The Merritts were on the site and had located several mines, all of which interested Oliver. The Pennsylvania steelmaker, in the words of one historian, "saw in a flash that he had found what he was looking for, a vast body of high grade ore cheaply mined." He was determined to obtain a lease on as much iron ore property as possible.

Oliver returned to Duluth and began negotiations with the Merritts. On June 20, the arrangements were signed. Oliver agreed to mine 150,000 tons annually at a royalty of fifty-five cents per ton plus an advance payment of

$25,000. Leonidas Merritt, negotiator for the Merritts, held out for sixty-five cents per ton since twenty-five cents was earmarked by Minnesota law for the School Fund. Oliver consented. Following an embarrassing moment when Oliver, in order to cover the initial payment on the lease, had to mortgage one of his ships, the arrangements were concluded.[7]

Oliver had been put at a disadvantage in his first Mesabi negotiations by not having the advice of legal counsel. The Merritts had not dealt with him unfairly, but he was determined to find a local attorney who could represent him in future business dealings. Upon inquiring, he was informed that the best legal mind in Duluth was William W. Billson. Oliver proceeded to Billson's office and asked to see the attorney. Informed that Billson was out and not expected to return very soon, Oliver agreed, albeit reluctantly, to see Billson's partner, Chester Congdon. It was a most fortuitous meeting. The two men hit it off immediately, and Congdon was retained as Oliver's legal counsel in Duluth. But, more than that, a firm relationship, both business and personal, was forged between the two and remained throughout their lifetimes.[8]

Confident that Congdon would handle legal representation of his interests in Minnesota, Oliver returned to Pittsburgh where he formed the Oliver Mining Company. The acquisition of additional mine leases demanded more capital, and it was to this task that Oliver next turned his efforts. Eighteen ninety-three was not the best time to attract investment money. What had been a rising economy suddenly and without warning plummeted to a condition which the newspapers described as "panic." The collapse of the Philadelphia and Reading Railway, with its close ties to several influential Wall Street financial houses, touched off a severe credit contraction. On May 3, the stock market crashed.

With some reluctance, Oliver made a decision to approach Andrew Carnegie. Surely, the Scotsman knew the steel business and would realize that the time to purchase leases was when the market was low. But if Oliver were to form an alliance with Carnegie Steel he would have to succeed where the Merritts had failed. Following the discovery of the Mesabi in 1890, Leonidas Merritt had tried to interest Henry C. Frick, Carnegie's General Manager, in leasing the mines, but Frick, following the advice of the company's expert, had rudely turned the Duluthian away. Oliver went to see Frick, and this time the results were different. Frick was receptive to Oliver's proposal, but it remained to convince Carnegie.[9]

Between the time Leonidas Merritt and Oliver approached Frick, several changes had taken place in the iron ore mining and steel production businesses. On the Mesabi it had been determined that due to the composition and formation of the ore bodies, the mining cost per ton would be quite low. In addition, the Carnegie company had changed its operational strategy. Heretofore, Carnegie had been unconcerned with leasing the ore supply and had been content to remain primarily a steel manufacturer. Recently, Carnegie's partners had tried to push the Scotsman in the direction of corporate verticality, i.e., the ownership and production of raw materials, the conversion of these materials into basic products, and, finally, the manufacture of finished articles. It was the first of these steps that changed Frick's mind about the Carnegie company's investment in the Mesabi.[10]

Frick's conversion also may have been prompted by the terms which Oliver offered. In return for a $500,000 mortgage loan, Oliver agreed to turn over to Carnegie one-half interest in his new mining company. It was simply an offer too good to turn down, and Frick enthusiastically informed Carnegie of the opportunity. Carnegie, however, stubbornly had made up his mind not to have anything to do with Oliver.

Writing from Rannoch Lodge in Perthshire, Scotland, Carnegie refused to acknowledge the advantages of the Mesabi leases. With bowed determination, he wrote Frick,

> Oliver's ore bargain is just like him — nothing in it. If there is any department of business which offers no inducement, it is ore. It never has been profitable, and the Messaba [sic] is not the last great deposit that Lake Superior is likely to reveal.[11]

Still, Carnegie's business sense told him that the Oliver offer was worth taking. Again, in correspondence with Frick from Sorrento, Italy, he grudgingly admitted that.

> Oliver hasn't much of a bargain in his Mesabi, as I see it, but in view of threatened combination it is good policy to take the half as independent of its intrinsic value; it gives us a wedge that can be driven in somewhere to our advantage in the general winding up. In less strong hands Oliver would be squeezed. . . . Still, I favor *taking* the Oliver half.[12]

Carnegie's acceptance of the merger may have been brought about in order to hedge his domination of the steel industry; that is, rejected by Carnegie, Oliver might ally himself with another funding source, leaving Carnegie at a disadvantage. Still, Carnegie continued to grumble. To his Board of Directors, he wrote,

> The Oliver bargain I do not regard as very valuable. You will find that this ore venture, like all our other ventures in ore, will result in more trouble and less profit than almost any branch of our business. . . . I hope you will make note of this prophecy.[13]

Frick, supported by other Carnegie officials, was not to be dissuaded and successfully completed the negotiations with Oliver. From now on the two steel companies would join forces—Oliver to mine the ore, Carnegie to manufacture steel.

The addition of Carnegie's money to his own eased Oliver's financial difficulties and made expansion possible. With Congdon heading the legal work, Oliver leased the Lone Jack mine in August 1893. Within eighteen months this addition was followed by leases on six more mines.[14]

Meanwhile, John D. Rockefeller had entered the iron ore mining business. When the Merritts needed funds they had approached the oil king, and he had responded first with a half million dollars and then by forming a business alliance, the Lake Superior Consolidated Mines, with the Duluth family. The depression of 1893 had caused the Merritts to default on payment of a loan from Rockefeller, and this, combined with a failed lawsuit brought by the Merritts against their partner, resulted in Rockefeller's taking control over all mines, railroad, and docks listed under Lake Superior Consolidated Mines.[15]

Competition for mining properties was intense, and Oliver constantly urged Congdon to be aware of economic conditions and to acquire additional iron ore land whenever opportunities arose. In fact, some people believed that Oliver, a prime consumer of ore, manipulated the market to drive small operators under. Congdon, however, was convinced that market fluctuations were the work of Rockefeller's greed.

As the drive for iron ore grew, Oliver and Congdon, as well as Carnegie, viewed the oil king's entrance into the mining business with great apprehension. At best, it meant another competitor; at worst, it meant the creation of a new Rockefeller trust similar to the one he had created for the oil business.

Should the latter develop, it would erupt into a devastating battle between the two mining giants.

To offset the possibility of an industrial war with Rockefeller, Oliver proposed a "gentlemen's agreement," a truce and a bargain to be struck between Carnegie-Oliver and Rockefeller. Oliver proposed that the Carnegie-Oliver company lease all of the iron ore included in Lake Superior Consolidated and refrain from acquiring any more leases or purchases without Rockefeller's permission. Rockefeller, in turn, would agree not to enter the steel manufacturing business. Carnegie's outlook brightened as he contemplated what this arrangement would bring. He wrote,

> I think we should ally ourselves with Rockafellow [*sic*] — Oliver showed me yesterday a sketch of alliance which is good. Will get Mesaba [*sic*] ore most[ly] Bess[emer]. . . . Hope it will be closed this week.[16]

The agreement which Oliver and Congdon had put together was beneficial to both Rockefeller and Carnegie-Oliver, but the old rivalry was not that easily put aside. Despite a clause which bound each party to a fifty year commitment, both sides began to break the accord before the ink was dry.

Congdon was certain that Rockefeller was at fault. According to the bargain, Oliver had been promised Lake Superior Consolidated ore at prices competitive with everyone else. When Rockefeller violated this provision, Oliver felt no compulsion to keep his end of the deal, and he instructed Congdon to push aggressively forward in acquiring additional mine leases.[17]

The feud was not entirely Rockefeller versus Carnegie-Oliver. Loyalties were divided inside the Carnegie-Oliver camp. That Carnegie did not own more of the stock in Oliver's mining company bothered the avaricious Scotsman. Several times, Carnegie had hinted to his partners that he was really entitled to more. Finally, Carnegie could stand it no longer. As the price for having acquiesced in the Rockefeller deal, Carnegie demanded that Oliver sell him a large block of company stock. Oliver was hardly in a position to resist, and, in 1897, transferred a large number of shares to Carnegie. The amount, combined with stock already held by Carnegie, meant that the Scotsman now owned five-sixths of the Oliver company. As a businessman, it was hard for Oliver to live with only one-sixth, but considering the amount of ore mined on the Mesabi, he was still a very wealthy man.[18]

9
Family

LIVING IN DULUTH WAS ALL THE CONGDONS HOPED IT WOULD BE. With a promising career before him, Congdon was ready to settle into the community. Billson had established a practice into which Congdon adapted very quickly. There was an abundance of legal work, and Congdon's experience in St. Paul with land legislation provided him with ample background for dealing with mining cases. The Oliver Iron Mining Company was expanding rapidly, and each acquisition of ore land demanded his supervision over a myriad of legal details. Between 1895 and 1910, Duluth enjoyed an unparalleled growth. The discovery of new ore bodies almost daily accelerated the excitement. The eastern part of the city expanded with the construction of large and stately mansions owned by the iron mining wealthy.[1]

Clara's time was occupied with the family, and her social life revolved around the Methodist church. Charles Bennett was now teaching in Chicago, and the entire Congdon family attended the marriage of his daughter to William Dyche, with whom Chester would later travel to the South Seas.

Two children were born in Duluth. Elisabeth Mannering on April 22, 1894, and Robert five years later on September 4, 1898. Clara kept a journal of the family's activities recording those dates and events which were most important. A great deal of the journal describes the events in her children's lives: Walter's graduation from grammar school, his first music recital, his first pair of long trousers. As they grew older, the boys went on camping, canoe, and fishing trips to nearby lakes. The usual childhood illnesses—measles, appendicitis, and a bout with typhoid—periodically delayed their activities but left no lasting effects. Marjorie and Helen tried their hand at cooking dinner, but "it did not pass." A second attempt produced better results, and each was rewarded with five dollars.[2]

Occasionally, Chester and Clara hired a "live-in" to stay with the children while they traveled on sightseeing trips (Yellowstone, New England) or to visit family and friends (usually to California to see Clara's brother or to New York to see both Bannisters and friends). Sometimes, Chester combined business with one of these excursions. As the children grew older and traveled more easily, there were family trips to historic sites and national expositions — Seattle, Chicago, San Francisco, and Portland.[3]

In the fall of 1895, the family made their second move in Duluth when they bought a large brick house at 1509 E. Superior Street. With a Flemish gable set in a sandstone front (the rest of the house was red brick), it was one of Duluth's most elegant and fashionable residences. Built by Oliver Traphagen, a Duluth architect, for his own family, the house was put on the market when its owner decided to move to Hawaii. It was well suited to an active family. This would be the Congdon residence until 1908.[4]

The children took their early education in Duluth, but went east for their preparatory and college work. Walter and Edward attended The Hill School, a preparatory school in Pottstown, Pennsylvania, and Robert attended The Taft School in Watertown, Connecticut. They each went on to take a degree from Yale. Elisabeth and Helen attended Dana Hall School in Wellesley, Massachusetts and then graduated from Vassar.[5] Marjorie attended Dana Hall School before going on to Florence, Italy and Miss May's School.

For some time, Chester and Clara had been interested in building a house farther east in the city on the north shore of Lake Superior. The view of Lake Superior was spectacular, and the couple had always dreamed of designing their own home. On August 3, 1901, Clara noted in her journal, "First plans of the new house," although "plans" did not refer to architectural drawings but rather to the general ideas of what they had in mind. In 1903, Chester began purchasing the land, just over twenty-one acres, a little over three miles east of Duluth's city center. The property was bordered on one side by the lake and stretched a quarter mile back from the shore. On the west side there was a small cemetery begun many years before, and on the east only a wooded area. The isolation appealed to the couple. Clara is reported to have remarked about the bordering cemetery, "I will have quiet neighbors."[6]

Two small streams, Tischer's Creek and Bent Brook, flowed through the property. Tischer's Creek would eventually provide sufficient flow for the house humidification system as well as for irrigation and a garden pool. The city provided water, gas, and electricity.

Plans for the house developed slowly. Both husband and wife were busy with other things — he with business matters in Duluth and the Pacific Northwest, she with family responsibilities and church affairs. From time to time they journeyed out to the site to speculate on building location and grounds design.

On July 28, 1903, Clara recorded in her journal, "Chester and I went to Tischer's Creek to measure the place for home, etc." They decided that the building would be constructed between the two streams in the center of the property.[7]

The next job was to select an architect, and the Congdons chose Clarence H. Johnston, Sr., an architect for the state of Minnesota who, in addition to his government duties, did private contract work. Johnston had graduated from the Massachusetts Institute of Technology, and he had traveled and studied in Europe. Very likely it was Johnston who suggested a Jacobean style architecture. The pleasing lines of the exterior and the comfort and warmth of the interior living space appealed to both Chester and Clara.[8]

Site preparation began on May 5, 1905 with the construction of an entry road over which the building materials could be transported onto the property. On June 15, excavation for the house foundation began, 42 by 140 feet, running parallel with the lake. The cornerstone was inscribed, "CAC A.D. 1905." Construction ceased with the onset of winter, but the exterior walls of the ground floor were in place, and those of the first floor were underway.[9]

The family residence was only one of several buildings scheduled for construction. There was a carriage house, complete with its own apartment (later made into two). This building contained room to store several carriages and sleighs, along with the cow stanchion and horse stable areas. A gardener's cottage and four greenhouses were also constructed. At lakeside there was a boathouse with an attached pier. On the grounds a bowling green, tennis court, vegetable garden, cow paddock, and groomed section of land by Tischer's Creek were developed. A reservoir built on Tischer's Creek supplied water for the grounds.

Duluth winters are especially harsh, and the late spring of 1906 delayed the bricklaying until April, but by October all three floors and the attic of the house were finished. The iron-beam supports for the roof were installed in late November and the work of laying the roof tiles was begun only to be halted by the cold weather. Meanwhile, work progressed on the carriage house, and by the end of the year the exterior walls were up and the interior finishing was underway.[10]

The residence was to be heated by radiators with steam provided from centrally located boilers. Once these were in place the interior work could progress without concern for the weather. Throughout 1907, workmen installed a network of pipes, metal air ducts, and an electric system. Plasterers, brickmasons, and interior wood finishers all went about their respective jobs.

The boat house and pier presented a challenge to Johnston's engineering talent. Originally, the boat house was to be constructed spanning the mouth of Tischer's Creek. This location, however, was abandoned, and both boat house and pier were constructed on the lake front in line with the house. In early May of 1907, while the shoreline was still ice-bound, workmen cut holes to measure for the pier footings. Precast cement blocks were laid on top of submerged wooden cribbing to provide a solid foundation which could withstand the force of Lake Superior storms. It was slow work, and although the boat house was not as large as some of the other buildings, the problems with construction delayed its finish until the fall of 1908.[11]

Landscaping was contracted to Charles Wellford Leavitt, Jr., a professional civil and landscape engineer, whose offices were in New York City. Leavitt was well-known and had an excellent reputation. He had been the chief contractor for some of the most elaborate landscape projects, both public and private, in New York and throughout the United States. A year before construction on the buildings began, Leavitt was at work designing a plan for the grounds. He, like the Congdons, was concerned about protecting the natural beauty of the site. It was probably Leavitt who suggested building the main house in the center of the property between the two creeks, and it may have been his recommendation to move the boat house from the mouth of Tischer's Creek to a location more in line with the residence. Although Leavitt probably recommended it for esthetic reasons, the relocation was a wise move. The water level at the mouth of the creek is constantly changing. The lateral drift of Lake Superior's wave action deposits large quantities of gravel at the creek's mouth where it remains until an increased flow of stream water after a heavy rainfall washes it out. In future years this would have impaired the use of the boat house.[12]

Retaining the natural environment of the property meant leaving as many existing trees and shrubs as possible. In addition to the natural vegetation, trees, shrubs, and plants were introduced to enhance the grounds. The land sloped gently down to the lake shore, and Leavitt designed a series of stepped terraces which not only allowed the excavated earth from the house construction to be moved a minimal distance but also would prevent erosion. Upon the brick-supported terraces rested a fountain and formal, symmetrical gardens. Bent Brook was lined with stones cemented-in to hold the soil.[13]

Birthplace of Chester Adgate Congdon, Jay Street,
Rochester, New York.

The Congdon farm, Ovid, New York, 1899.

Chester Congdon's parents, Sylvester Laurentus and Laura Adgate Congdon.

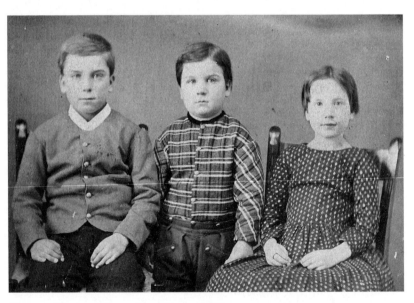

Chester, Albert and Laura Congdon, ca.1862.

Chester Adgate Congdon, ca. 1870.

Clara Hesperia Bannister, 1870.

Clara Congdon and Walter, ca. 1883.

Edward and Walter, 546 Selby Avenue, St. Paul, Minnesota, ca. 1888.

Chester Congdon with Marjorie (top) and Helen
(bottom), 1894.

Helen, Walter, Edward, Marjorie and John, 1892.

Chester Congdon with Robert and Elisabeth, Minnesota Point on Lake Superior, ca. 1902.

Glensheen, Duluth, Minnesota, 1908.

Front Hall, Glensheen, 1908.

Hesperia, the Congdon family yacht, ca. 1910.

Glensheen and grounds, 1908.

Walter, age 22, 1904.
Edward, age 19, 1904.
Marjorie, age 19, 1906.

Helen, age 15, 1904.
Elisabeth, age 10, 1904.
Robert, age 5, 1903.

Bannister family reunion, Glensheen, July 1909. Back row (from left): Alfred E. Bannister and Walter. Middle row: Alfred Bannister, Elmer Buckman, Helen, Marjorie and Elisabeth. Seated: Edward, Mary Bannister, Emma Bannister, Chester, with hand on Robert, Bertha B. Buckman, Dorthea Bannister, John Race, Alice B. Race and Clara.

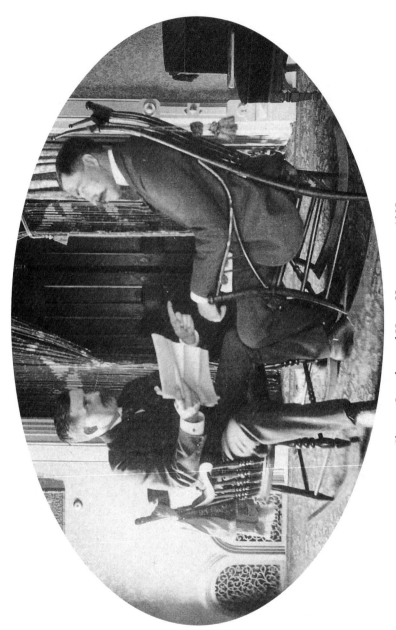

Chester Congdon and Harry Heermans, ca. 1885.

Chester Congdon camping, Baja, California, ca. 1902.

Clara Congdon, 1906.

Chester Congdon, 1906.

Chester Congdon, Glensheen, 1909.

The Congdons hoped to make the estate as self-sufficient as possible and this meant there must be ample room for a vegetable garden and a cow barn. These were located to the east of the main house. Also, the original soil on the property consisted mainly of clay and rock, a mixture hardly conducive to gardening and the kind of landscape architecture envisioned by Leavitt and the Congdons. Consequently, five hundred loads of rich black earth were spread over the old soil in order to provide a more fertile base.[14]

Beginning in 1907, Leavitt supervised the planting of hundreds of trees, shrubs, and plants. He was familiar with the best nurseries throughout the country and was determined to secure only their finest stock. Leavitt, knowing that Congdon expected top quality, was demanding, and his orders for merchandise illustrated his precision. Regardless of quantity or supplier, Leavitt's letters were the same. He wrote,

> Make out bill in duplicate to Mr. Congdon and send them to me to be checked . . . Unless invoice is sent in duplicate to this office when shipment is made, I will not check same or receive stock. There is to be no substitution without orders from this office. If you are unable to supply any of this stock, please let me know at once. All orders accepted must be for stock in your own nurseries or if you purchase any stock outside, I must be notified where the stock is to come from, so I can inspect it, and my consent must be obtained before shipment is made from other stock than your own.

Leavitt was a professional who demanded, and received, the highest quality professional service. As the work progressed, Congdon developed an interest in landscaping and paid close attention to Leavitt's progress.[15]

Four greenhouses were constructed on the estate, and it was here that seedlings and plants were started for later transplantation. In the years following construction, it was Congdon who, in conjunction with his full-time gardener, supervised the upkeep and maintenance of the grounds, a job that he handled with precision reminiscent of Leavitt.[16]

Furnishings and design for the interior of the house were contracted to the William A. French Company of St. Paul. On February 17, 1908, a representative of the company brought a crew of carpenters to finish off the interior. Edward F. Caldwell and Co. from New York installed the silver electrical fixtures in the dining room. Each room was individually designed and appointed; yet there was a continuity throughout the house. The first load of furniture arrived on December 22, 1908, to be followed by many more.[17]

The Congdons did not wait until all construction on the house had been completed before they moved in. Clara recorded in her journal that on "November 21, 1908, Ned slept in his room," and three days later, "November 24, we moved in and all spent [the] night there." Only a small amount of finishing work needed to be completed, and family and workmen did not intrude on each other. Three years and nine months from the beginning date of construction, John C. Bush, supervisor of the work, wrote in his day book, "February 1, 1909 — end of house construction."[18]

There remained only to bestow upon the estate a suitable name. The property was christened Glensheen, derived from a combination of the Congdon family's origin in the village of Sheen in Surrey, England and the wooded setting of the house. Needless to say, the family immensely enjoyed the new facilities. The library grew to well over a thousand volumes, including a wide variety of subjects from history and government to literature, economics, and science. These were not decorative pieces placed there to adorn the shelves and impress visitors. Each volume indicates the care and attention given to a much-used library. The family subscribed to about twenty-five periodicals and newspapers which reflected a variety of tastes and interests. One end of the ground floor of the house was turned into a "Little Museum," and it was here that mementos and souvenirs from trips all over the world were displayed. In every sense of the word, Glensheen became the center for the Congdon family. Visitors from far and near were welcome guests. Clara's journal entry in 1913 perhaps sums up the family's activities: "Very social and busy summer; many social and house guests."[19]

Spurred on, perhaps, by his working on Glensheen, Congdon expanded his interest in the environment. He became particularly interested in preserving the natural beauty along the north shore of Lake Superior. For many years, the lack of transportation along the shore had discouraged developers, and only a few fishermen lived there. It was evident, however, that with the expansion of Duluth and the surrounding area it would not be long before the beauty of the north shore would be taken over by private builders and lost to the public forever. Congdon was determined to preserve for public benefit at least part of this spectacular scenery.

He developed a plan to offer the city of Duluth a gift of funds sufficient to purchase the right-of-way for a public highway which would extend from the edge of the city's eastern boundary to the border of St. Louis County.

Specifically, Congdon proposed that the city purchase, with his gift funds, a strip of land extending along the lake shore for approximately thirteen miles. The gift, however, contained a proviso that the land be preserved in its natural state and never used for any purpose other than a highway. The gift specified that negotiations for purchase of the property and the construction of the highway were the responsibilities of the city.[20]

On June 2, 1913, Duluth's city government authorized the purchase of the land and construction of a highway from the mouth of the Lester River (the eastern city limit) to the county boundary. A second ordinance, adopted by the City Council on June 2, 1915, formally accepted Congdon's gift.[21] Preservation of this land in its natural state assured that the public would continue to enjoy some of Lake Superior's most picturesque shoreline.

Chester Congdon passed away before his plan could be completely realized, but his wife and children continued to work for the development of the highway by contributing generously to the cost of construction. The highway which today follows the north shore of Lake Superior from Lester River to Stony Point is known as "Congdon Boulevard"—a lasting tribute to the man who conceived the idea.

10

Agricultural Development in Yakima

INVESTMENTS ON GRAYS HARBOR REQUIRED CONGDON TO TRAVEL there several times. On his homeward journey in 1887, the Northern Pacific train passed eastward over the summit of the Cascades and down the heavily timbered slopes of the mountains where it routinely paused at North Yakima. Whether Congdon intended to stop off here or acted from some impulse will probably never be known, but whatever prompted his action resulted in a decision to spend some time investigating the city of North Yakima and the valley which stretched southeastward to the Columbia River.

The valley is divided into two sections linked together by the Yakima River, which has its origins in the slopes of the Cascades. The upper valley begins at Selah Gap, a notch cut by the river in the high rolling hills, and widens out to a broad floor. About five miles downstream, the Natches River, largest tributary of the Yakima, flows in from the west. At the confluence of the Natches and the Yakima rivers lay the city of North Yakima. The valley which stretches on either side of the two rivers extends southeast through another cut in the hills known as Union Gap. Below this opening lies the lower valley, a much wider and longer expanse of level agricultural farmland which stretches for sixty miles to the Columbia River. Rich volcanic loess, ranging in depth from a few inches to thirty feet, lies on the floor of the entire valley, and it is this soil which gives the land its fertility.

Irrigation is the key by which agricultural development in the Yakima valley was opened, and settlers as early as the 1850s devised all sorts of schemes to water their crops. Several small dams, ditches, and flumes of various kinds drew water from streams which crisscrossed the valley floor and distributed water to farmlands.[1]

Although several small communities were scattered along the river, the largest city, North Yakima, lay in the upper valley. In 1887, the city served its inhabitants and the surrounding area with goods and services. Sixty-two commercial buildings, all "usually occupied," constituted the downtown and included a variety of establishments ranging from two banks to a hand-laundry. Nine attorneys handled the legal work, and five real estate firms advertised residential as well as agricultural property. Two major hotels (one two-stories tall, the other three) dominated the commercial district and served as the hub of activity. The other buildings and stores were occupied by agriculturally oriented merchants. Two years after Congdon's visit the city would establish a municipal water system which tapped into the Natches River four and one-quarter miles above the town's center, but talk was already going around about the advantages which this service would provide. Residents were also looking forward to new city lighting. North Yakima held all the promise of a growing and prosperous community.[2]

There is no documentation regarding the length of Congdon's stay or his impressions of the city and valley, but there is no question that he came away determined to become economically involved in the area. Most surely, he traveled the length and breadth of the upper valley (and perhaps the lower, as well) and visited with a variety of people. Maps were readily available from real estate offices, and he acquired some of these. When he returned to St. Paul, his report to the New York investors was very favorable. Opportunities abounded for investment and development in this part of the Pacific Northwest.

During the next several years, Congdon revisited the Yakima valley with agricultural investment in mind. On one of those trips he purchased 640 acres of prime land on the southwestern edge of North Yakima at a location known as Wide Hollow. A small creek, the Ahtanum, ran through the property, and when the valley was first settled water from this source had served for irrigation. But the Ahtanum was far too small to meet Congdon's needs. The only available water must come from one of two sources: the Yakima or the Natches Rivers. Either alternative posed several problems. To draw water from the Yakima would require a large and expensive pumping system. To acquire water from the Natches meant transporting it by gravity flow through ditches or flumes over rough topography including a formidable canyon which must be crossed.[3]

Immediate development would have to wait. Congdon's law practice placed heavy demands on his time, but he continued to think about agricultural development in the Yakima Valley. Land acquisition began to take on a new dimension for him. His friends in New York preferred to speculate for a quick turnover and profit, but Congdon decided to keep the property himself and develop it into a horticultural enterprise. It might become a pleasant diversion from his law practice, and with the proper attention it could be a profitable venture.

In 1894, Congdon was back in North Yakima, this time with two specific purposes in mind. First, he needed to appropriate water for his land. He had ruled out the Yakima River. A pumping system for that distance would be too expensive. A diversion of the Natches River would have to do. By constructing an intake several miles upstream, water could be transported to his land by canal.

The next step required Congdon to secure a water rights claim for the amount he intended to use from the Natches. Water rights and usage in the semi-arid West has always been a thorny question, and the state of Washington in drafting its constitution in 1889 had not made the issue any clearer. Riparian rights (rights assumed by owners of land which lay adjacent to water) remained ambiguous. The constitution contained only a single sentence on the subject: "The use of the waters of this state for irrigation . . . shall be deemed a public use." The first legislature, however, provided legislation whereby landowners might appropriate water from lakes and streams. Parties claiming water rights were directed to file sworn statements of their claims. Later legislation specified the procedure by which persons, corporations, and associations could file for water rights. Claimants were required to post a notice at the point of diversion or storage specifying the amount, purpose, and place of use. A copy of the notice must be filed with the county auditor within ten days of the posting, and work on the project had to be started within six months. Failure to meet these requirements nullified the claim.[4]

Consistent with state water appropriation law, Congdon, on March 7, 1894 "posted" his claim to 150 second feet of water (the unit of flow which will produce one cubic foot of water in one second of time) to be diverted from the Natches River.[5] On March 29, 1894, this water claim was finalized by the Yakima County Auditor and officially registered in the Water Rights Book for Yakima County. After careful consideration, Congdon realized that 150 second feet of water was excessive, and four months later, on July 28, 1894, he reduced his claim to 50 second feet.[6]

The second step in moving the irrigation project forward was to create a formal corporate organization by which the work could be carried out. Over the time Congdon had visited North Yakima he had become acquainted with several individuals who were familiar with the area, who knew something about land investment, and who were interested in local agricultural development. They were Edward Whitson, William B. Dudley, Alfred B. Weed, and James M. Gilbert, all of whom were residents of North Yakima. Whitson, in fact, had been responsible for the installation of North Yakima's first water system. On May 23, 1894, this group incorporated the North Yakima Canal Company.[7]

Having created an organization for overseeing the construction of the canal, the next step was to hire an engineer to do the surveys. Congdon approached Alfred Bannister, Clara's brother, now a civil engineer residing in Alameda, California. Congdon included a description of what he wanted to do and concluded by asking Bannister to take charge of not only the surveys but the construction of the canal as well.[8] Bannister, however, was reluctant to give up his work in California and accept these responsibilities. In a follow-up letter, Congdon tried to persuade his brother-in-law. "I am very anxious that you should make the survey," he wrote, "we wish to have an estimate upon which we can rely."[9] Still, Bannister hesitated.

Congdon, anxious to proceed with the project, hired a local engineer. The reports were not favorable; they focused on the difficulties of construction and high cost of building a canal which would be required to carry a large amount of water over a long distance. Congdon doubted the validity of the report and again sought Bannister's assistance. Enclosing a copy of the engineer's report, Congdon explained, "This report shows the cost of the ditch to be twice as much in the aggregate as well as twice as much per acre as [the engineer for the company] was positive it could be built for," Congdon wrote, and added, "For many reasons I doubt the reliability of this report, and I suspect it was made for the purpose of inducing me to drop the scheme." Look it over, Congdon requested of his brother-in-law, and let me know whether we can build a ditch to water that amount or a little more land for less money. Our plan, stated Congdon, is to build this ditch and "get some mortgages from the land owners who would buy water of us at the rate of $33 per acre, not only to pay for the cost of the ditch, but give us a profit of about 100 percent beside[s] sufficient water for our land." The right-of-way from the intake on the Natches River to Wide Hollow, Congdon thought, could be obtained "for practically nothing" by running the ditch behind the land already occupied. Congdon was persistent about Bannister's taking charge of the ditch, and, at last, he agreed to Congdon's request.[10]

In June 1894, Congdon impatiently wrote Bannister, offering funds to off-set his expenses, and urging him to arrive in North Yakima as soon as possible. By now, the company had increased the projected irrigated area to an additional 1,500 acres on top of the original 3,000. Anticipating a rise in real estate prices if company plans were leaked, Congdon cautioned Bannister that it would be better "if the people of North Yakima did not know for whom you are doing the work there," but then thought better of his advice and added there was no "need to go to unnecessary trouble to do that."[11]

Despite the lateness of the season, the decision was made to begin construction, and members of the company along with Congdon urged Bannister to proceed in all haste. Congdon, always ready to offer advice and unwilling to leave decisions entirely in Bannister's hands, wrote his brother-in-law, "You will not finish before it freezes up unless you put on more men. Why do you not increase your number as soon as you get your camp at Cowychee [sic, Cowiche], and string them along the whole distance? After it freezes up and storms commence, expenses will increase materially, as it already has by reason of the short days. In my opinion you should put on as many men as you can possibly work with economy. Of course, if you have as many men as you can handle economically, that is sufficient; but it seems to me that more men could be handled." Congdon wanted to see for himself, and he announced that he would arrive in North Yakima within a few days.[12] The records do not indicate whether additional laborers were hired.

The operational plan for the canal was relatively simple. An intake was to be constructed on the Natches River about five miles above its confluence with the Yakima. From the diversion point the water was to be carried by gravity flow to Wide Hollow where it would be routed into lateral ditches and distributed to agricultural lands.

If the operational plan was easily conceived, the actual construction was an engineer's nightmare. The key to the operation was to keep the water "on grade," i.e., gravity flow, between the intake and the distribution point. The terrain between the intake and Wide Hollow covered some of the most formidable topography in the upper valley.

Construction for the first couple of miles past the intake presented few problems. But from that point, the ditch had to be excavated and blasted out of the rocky sides of the canyon. A few miles below the intake, a trestle, eighty-five feet above the valley floor and constructed in the same timber-supported manner as a railway bridge, was required to run the canal (a wooden flume) around a sheer rock cliff, known as Painted Rocks (prehistoric Indian pictographs remained on the rock surface). Once around the cliff the water had to be transported across Cowiche Canyon, a U-shaped drop of one hundred feet. The plan called for an "inverted siphon," a thirty-two inch pipe (designed and patented by Bannister) which would carry the water down the side of the rock face to the canyon floor and up the other side. The pipe was constructed from two-inch thick California redwood staves held together by steel bands and rods. Once across the canyon the canal continued to Wide Hollow. The water was carried "on grade," for the entire distance.[13]

One hundred fifty men were employed, and the ditch slowly began to take shape and form. Work began on the canal in the late summer of 1894 with Bannister in charge. At the intake, a wooden box was constructed with a gate to regulate the amount of water admitted into the canal. A few yards downstream, a revolving water wheel was installed to frighten fish from entering the canal.[14]

Residents of the area, through local newspaper accounts, were kept informed of the workmen's progress. The trestle around Painted Rocks created the most interest. It was spectacular, indeed, and journalists at the *Yakima Herald* kept readers abreast of the construction. "Around the giant cliffs which form the Painted Rocks the flume will tower, clinging to the rest of the sheer wall whose pictured sides have been made famous throughout the valley of Yakima and little trickling rivulets may burnish the granite front that nature's wildest storms have long assailed in vain." It was, indeed, a magnificent structure both in journalistic description and actual construction.[15]

With the canal well under way, the officers of the company began to sell water rights. Each share of stock sold for $25 cash or $30 on a five-year contract and provided enough water for one acre of land. Stock owners were exempt from any additional payments except those which might be levied for canal maintenance. Some of the local farmers had once doubted that the canal would be successful, but as the construction progressed their worries receded and sales increased.

At the same time, a right of way for the canal had to be obtained from those landowners over whose property the water would flow. Congdon had anticipated that he could skirt most of the occupied land, but a few purchases were necessary, and these rights were obtained from the owners.[16]

By March 1895, the canal, trestle, and "inverted siphon" were completed and ready for testing. The ditch was "puddled," that is, a small amount of water was turned in to settle and seal the sides and bottom, and a few last minute repairs were made before beginning full operation. Water for 3,000 acres was ready for delivery along fifteen miles of canal.[17]

Despite precautions, troubles developed but were dealt with accordingly. Water eroded away the sides, and the earth from above slid down into the canal damming its flow. By May, however, Bannister felt satisfied that he had finished his job and could return to California.

More troubles lay ahead. Recipients of the water had given mortgages on their land as payment security. New breaks in the canal occurred, and each brought immediate protests from the farmers. With Bannister gone, James Gilbert was in charge, and he was unable to keep the ditch in operation and the water users satisfied. Congdon feared that the whole plan was slipping away. "Oceans trouble Yakima," he wired Bannister. "Mortgages repudiated. Gilbert away. Can you go there immediately and make ditch carry water. Otherwise we suffer great loss. Answer quick."[18] Before he could receive an answer from Bannister, a letter arrived from Ed Whitson. The Board of Trustees of the company had held a meeting, he explained, and had concluded that it was time to advise Congdon of the true state of affairs. First of all, Whitson wrote, there were only 500 acres under cultivation, and there was not sufficient water to serve even these users. When the flow was increased the sides of the ditch washed out. The flume around Painted Rocks leaked, and the escaping water eroded away the base of the supporting timbers. Whitson reported that even if the flume could carry full capacity, it was doubtful that the amount would be sufficient to meet the needs of those farmers who held a contract with the company. To complicate matters, water had been turned into the ditch too late in the season, and despite the reduced flow, farmers demanded their full amount. Moreover, it was impossible at this time of year to shut down for repairs. Farmers in the valley have lost faith in the company, Whitson complained to Congdon, and several have considered legal action to recover damages to their crops. It was essential, his partner urged, that Congdon come to Yakima.[19]

But 1895 was an extremely busy year for Congdon. His legal work made it impossible for him to get away. Congdon thought that Bannister could handle the problem, and a wire was sent informing him of the crisis. A reply telegram from the California engineer only served to exacerbate the situation. "Impossible to go," wired Bannister. "Ask Hiller and Burbank [a local construction firm] to put in two thousand feet [of] ditch lining where Whitson designates." But Congdon was not satisfied. "Your reputation [and] our investment at stake. Can't you possibly save enterprise by going immediately? Contractors not equal [to] situation which constantly grows worse."[20]

Congdon had anticipated that Bannister might not be able to go to Yakima, and he sent a telegram to Heermans, now a resident of Olympia, asking if he might investigate the situation. Heermans was familiar with water transportation problems from his New York days, and Congdon trusted his judgment. Heermans agreed, and it was with great relief that Congdon received his friend's assessment of the ditch problems. The reports on the status of the canal, Heermans reassured Congdon, are "absurd and foolish." He too, once arrived in Yakima, had heard the tales of gloom and doom about insufficient water, canal breaks, flume inadequacies, and farmers near revolt. However, Heermans continued, upon investigation the canal was working quite well, in fact, nearly up to full capacity considering the amount of water which it was carrying. True, some bad leaks had been discovered, but they had been repaired in short order. Heermans assured Congdon that water was flowing "the *entire length* of the canal and furnishing an ample abundance." He described how he had ridden "along the canal . . . and saw the water on the fields doing fine service, the crops looking fine, and about 500 acres under cultivation." "*Our managers have no sand*," he concluded. They forget that the ditch is new, Heermans wrote, and that some problems are bound to occur. "I do not take any stock in the opinions of these parties," he stated independently, and concluded, "From all that I saw I think the engineering work as well as the grades and flow are very well done. The quantity [the full capacity of the ditch] has not yet been settled, but I shall stand by Bannister against the whole crowd."

Undoubtedly with a great feeling of relief, Congdon wired Bannister of the good news, and sent a follow-up letter denouncing his Yakima business partners. Congdon vowed not to trust their judgment again and pleaded with Bannister to make himself available should problems arise in the future. But, from that time forward the canal continued to function with remarkable efficiency. In 1897, Congdon's brother, Albert, moved to North Yakima to become president of the irrigation enterprise, the name now changed to the

Yakima Valley Canal Company. Congdon felt much better with the chief administrator in family hands.[21]

The original canal served the company for seven years, but by 1902 the sides were badly eroded. Repairs were needed, and the company trustees decided that as long as major reconstruction was required the length should also be extended. Seven miles were added (for a total of 22) to the Wide Hollow end of the canal, and an additional 1,000 acres (for a total of 4,000) were served by its waters. The cost was estimated at $35,000, a considerable total. Legal work in Duluth demanded a great deal of Congdon's time, and he had resigned as trustee of the company in 1899, but now he offered to loan the company the entire cost of the expansion provided Bannister would again serve as the chief engineer. Bannister presented a proposal to the company by which he would undertake the job at a salary equivalent to 10 percent of the total cost which he estimated not to exceed $35,000. Congdon also demanded, as part of his loan agreement, that the company issue 500 new shares of stock at $30 per share at 8 percent interest. Congdon's loan would be secured by his holding stock in the amount of the loan. "I believe that under this plan," he wrote, "we can secure as good a ditch as can be built with ample water to irrigate the best land in the county, and in a manner which will burden no one." It was true that while Congdon was no longer a trustee of the company, he was, in reality, investing in an expansion which could not help but to improve the value of his own land.[22]

The last major improvement on the canal was started in 1910. Edward Bannister, Alfred's son, had recently moved to Yakima from California, and Congdon had given him a job surveying for new pipe lines on his ranch. At the completion of this work, the trustees of the canal company asked the young man to do a study of the ditch with the idea of reducing erosion in the canal and replacing the wooden structure with something more permanent. Also, the company was anxious to examine the possibilities of lengthening the canal and thereby increasing both water users and revenue.

Bannister spent the summer of 1910 analyzing the entire canal, and by fall he was ready with several recommendations: line the old open ditch with reinforced concrete, replace the wooden flume at Painted Rocks with reinforced concrete and anchor it firmly to the rock cliff thereby eliminating the need for the timber supported trestle. The only time, however, when the work could proceed was in winter when farmers did not need the water. It took two years to complete the job, but in the end the canal was the most durable of its kind, an example of the most advanced engineering.[23]

Between 1905 and 1912, Congdon accumulated additional land, half of which was planted to orchard while the remainder served for open grazing. The entire acreage drew water from what had now come to be known as the "Congdon ditch." Congdon's property now contained seventeen workers' homes, a large bunkhouse, barns capable of stabling forty horse teams, a hop house, a carriage house, grain tanks, and a silo.[24]

Although a resident manager was employed, the ranch was essentially run by Congdon from his office in Duluth. Every phase of operation came under his close scrutiny. Planning, both immediate and long range, was discussed by correspondence with the local manager. No detail was too small or insignificant for Congdon's perusal. He subscribed to and read voraciously from agricultural bulletins, journals, and books, the information from which he frequently dispatched as a recommendation to his manager. His library, both in Duluth and Yakima, grew to several hundred volumes on various aspects of agriculture. His suggestions were not dictatorial, but if the resident manager entertained another opinion Congdon demanded an explanation.

Congdon's comments were usually sound, and ranch managers seldom found reason to quarrel with his judgment, not because he was "the boss" but because his advice was based on reliable operational principles as well as a canny sense for profit. When Speyers (the local manager) wanted to hire a man to dig a well for the house, Congdon had a better plan: since the contractor would have to purchase new equipment, why not, he suggested, buy the well-digging rig, hire a man to operate it, and sell him the equipment when the job was finished. On the subject of spraying equipment, Congdon sent Speyers an agricultural bulletin from the Missouri State Fruit Experiment Station with the comment that, "I know nothing about this kind of machinery, but it seems to me that they discuss the whole question more intelligently than anything I have ever read before." When Speyers wrote that a particular tract of twenty-two acres would produce 190 boxes of apples, Congdon replied that a six-year-old orchard should do better, and he wanted to know the reason for the short yield. Regarding the control of insect damage, Congdon also drew upon his extensive reading. Aphids, in particular, were a perennial and devastating pest, and Congdon strongly suggested a spray mixture of "Whale

Oil Soap and Mc.Dougall's [sic] Insecticide" recommended by a Canadian experiment farm.[25]

A portion of the ranch was devoted to experimental horticulture. From Stark Brothers Nurseries in Missouri, Congdon obtained two varieties of nectarine seedlings which, unfortunately, upon arrival were unidentified. To the nursery he wrote, "I would be greatly obliged if you would inform me how I can distinguish [between] the two varieties so that I may know which I am getting in my orchard." He explained, "I am planting a great variety of trees there for the purpose of determining which varieties do the best in the Yakima Valley." Not all the trees were revenue producing—at least immediately. Congdon instructed Speyers to plant walnut trees to provide shade along some of the driveways and, perhaps, someday to be profitable.[26]

No subject received more attention than ranch finances. Speyers was the resident manager, but he was accountable to Congdon for each expenditure, no matter what the amount. Correspondence between the two included regular financial statements which Congdon scrutinized with great care. To Yakima, Congdon sent the forms upon which the accounts were kept, and his letters regarding expenditures read like lessons on accounting procedures. "I note your barn expense was $69.14 for the week." Congdon analyzed, "I suppose this included the cost of making hay. Is this correct?" Other expenses were similarly studied and reviewed.[27]

The ranch foreman and workmen received frequent attention. Congdon paid the "going wage" for employees, and for that compensation he expected a full day's work. When Speyers wired that Barrager, the ranch foreman, threatened to quit unless he received more money, Congdon was irate, "Disregard question of salary, and wholly because of his stand and deliver attitude, I think Barrager better quit." In a follow up letter he explained the difference between ownership and hired help,

I reach this conclusion without paying any consideration whatever to the question of wages, but wholly because of his attempt to hold me up. I will not permit any man to do that. . . . The kind of man I want for a foreman, is the kind that will stay with the men, and see that they are doing the work which they are sent to do, and that when they go to the field in the morning they are equipped properly for the work, so that they will not have to return to the barn from the field, as I saw happen repeatedly this spring. I do not want a man so fine that he cannot look after the men closely, and cannot himself take hold and work if needs be. What we need there now is not a business manager, but a man to work with and over the men.

It was not long after that Speyers found an acceptable replacement for Barrager.[28]

Hops grow especially well in the soil and climate of the Yakima Valley, and Congdon's ranch included several acres of the vines. Hops, of course, were used in making beer. There is a bit of family history which has it that Clara Congdon, as a member of the Woman's Christian Temperance Union, objected to hops grown on the family ranch. Congdon, in deference to his wife's views, gave the order, and the vines were removed.[29]

Throughout the Yakima valley ranchers had organized a number of processing, storage, and marketing associations. Until 1913, Congdon marketed his fruit through the Horticultural Union, a local Yakima fruit ranchers association. "We have not as yet learned the ropes," he explained to Speyers. Moreover, he went on, "I do not think we should attempt to sell our own apples until we can produce each variety in carload lots. In the meantime, by selling through the Union, we may learn how the job is done." Unwilling to be associated with anything less than a first class product, Congdon inquired of Speyers, "If we sell through the Union, do we have to label our boxes? I should prefer not to do so until our pack is gilt-edged."[30]

In 1913, Congdon constructed his own fruit-processing and storage warehouse. The decision meant cutting himself off from whatever advantages might accrue from cooperative processing and marketing, but it also meant independence. In typical fashion, Congdon made certain that the building housed the most modern equipment. The structure, although not excessively large, was massive in frame and aroused considerable comment from carpenters regarding its construction. Other buildings were added as demand grew. The operation of the warehouse also meant using his own brand label, a mark of distinction for the Congdon orchards.[31]

Transporting fruit from the ranch for shipment on the railroad presented a problem. It was five miles to the Northern Pacific's loading platform in North Yakima, and the boxes had to be transported over a rough road. The delicate fruit, however carefully packed and loaded on wagons with spring axles, was inevitably bruised. Congdon endured this situation for a time, and then he determined to do something about the problem. The solution was obvious: have the Northern Pacific extend a spur line into Wide Hollow where it would serve not only the Congdon ranch but also the nearby Nob Hill and Broadway areas. Congdon went to see the Northern Pacific officials in St. Paul about the matter, and the railroad officials concluded that the rail extension would serve the ranchers' interests as well as their own. The track was completed in 1915.[32]

Congdon tried to visit the ranch at least twice a year and sometimes more frequently depending upon his legal schedule in Duluth. In late 1914, he made the decision to build a residence for himself. Kenyon and Maine, an architectural firm from Chicago, was chosen to design the house. Stone quarried in Cowiche canyon near Painted Rocks served as the building material. To supervise the construction, Congdon hired Hans O. Lovald, a Duluth construction supervisor who had proven his capabilities on several prominent buildings. Lovald moved his family to the Yakima ranch and remained there for almost two years while the work was carried on. The location was on a small bluff overlooking the Congdon land. At one end of the house there was a square tower—a feature which caused local people to identify the structure as "the castle" (a nickname still used). Congdon's name for the dwelling was more formal, and he called it "Westhome." Construction on the house began in 1914 and was completed in 1916.[33]

There is a sequel to Congdon's acquisition of land in the Yakima valley. When Washington was admitted into the union in 1889, one of the major questions to be resolved was the location of the state capital. Olympia had served as the territorial capital since 1853. While it might have been prudent at that time to have the administrative headquarters of the state located on the western side of the mountains, by the time of statehood residents on the eastern side of the Cascades were quite certain that a more geographically central location would be more appropriate.

If the capital were to be moved from Olympia to a location east of the Cascades, the choices were narrowed to two: Ellensburg (in the Kittitas Valley) or Yakima. The competition would be fierce, and obviously Olympia, with the advantage of prior designation, possessed an advantage. But, perhaps Yakima could provide some additional enticement: Congdon offered a gift of land upon which the buildings could be constructed. The designated area was located on the western edge of the city. In September 1889, Congdon presented to the cashier of the Pacific National Bank in Tacoma a deed for the land. Acceptance of the gift required that the Yakima site be selected for the state capital and that the next session of the state legislature so designate its location. Failure to meet these requirements meant the land would be returned to its owner.

The election in October 1889 to approve the new state constitution included a choice where voters could indicate their preference for a capital site. The results were inconclusive. None of the cities received a majority of the votes cast, and the question was deferred to the general election in the fall of 1890. This time, Olympia received a clear majority. The voters had made a decision, and the Congdon land reverted to its owner. In a magnanimous gesture, however, Congdon offered the land to the city of Yakima for use as a park. The city deliberated for some time, but at last concluded that the location was too far removed from the residential area. The offer was declined, and the land remained in Congdon's possession. It was later subdivided and sold.[34]

11
The Western Mesabi

THE YEARS BETWEEN 1895 AND THE FIRST DECADE OF THE NEW CENTURY witnessed the greatest change ever to take place in the iron ore and steel business. Oliver's partnership with Carnegie continued, and even though he retained only one-sixth of the business, the mining company became a vital part of the relationship. With Congdon acting as the Carnegie-Oliver agent, mine properties on the Mesabi expanded rapidly despite Carnegie's continued reluctance about owning iron ore. Their purchases were not confined to the Mesabi but extended to the Vermilion and the Michigan Gogebic ranges as well.

The rivalry with Rockefeller grew more intense as the giants jockeyed for position. When the oil king increased the shipping rates on his railroad, Oliver and Congdon responded by incorporating a new line, the Virginia and Ely Railroad, which, they announced, would terminate on Lake Superior at Grand Marais. The railroad never developed beyond the planning stage, and whether the two men were serious in pursuing its construction remains speculative. Rockefeller's next move was to raise rates on his shipping line. Oliver's response was to order ten new whaleback ore carriers for Lake Superior—only to have Rockefeller, the principal owner of the shipyard, cancel the order. Oliver fought back and purchased the ships from another company. Every move and countermove among the rivals had a dramatic effect on the industry as a whole. The war went on, each side seeking to gain any advantage over the other.[1]

It was J. Pierpont Morgan who put a stop to the conflict. Morgan had too much at stake to watch the leaders of the industry slowly destroy each other. Over the years the New York banker had financed many of the smaller steelmakers, and he was not about to let Carnegie or Rockefeller or anyone else jeopardize his investments. It was Carnegie who finally precipitated Morgan's grand scheme. After numerous skirmishes—such as when the Scotsman announced plans for a new steel-tube plant at Conneaut, Ohio which would compete with a Morgan steel firm—Carnegie finally decided to retire and devote his time and fortune to philanthropy. This opened the door for a merger that would end the steel industry's wars.

Morgan dispatched his representatives, who visited with each of the steel producers, both large and small. Gradually, the smaller companies were persuaded that the competitive struggle within the business was ruinous. A combination of enterprise would better serve them all. The large companies, Carnegie-Oliver and Rockefeller, were the last to come in, but with Henry Frick and Charles Schwab serving as negotiators, both were induced to sell their holdings. With Morgan's victory came the creation of United States Steel Corporation, America's first billion-dollar conglomerate.[2]

At the time of the negotiations, Oliver was on a vacation. When he arrived home the formation of U.S. Steel was completed. The only piece of the steel business missing was Oliver's one-sixth share of Carnegie-Oliver. Carnegie, having completed his sale, was ready to depart for a vacation in Scotland leaving Oliver to work out his own sale arrangements. Oliver went to see Carnegie at his home in order to find out the price which the Scotsman had received. Henry Oliver Evans, Oliver's biographer, relates the following anecdote regarding this meeting. Confronted by Oliver, Carnegie readily admitted selling his five-sixths interest but refused to disclose the price, saying that he had taken a vow of secrecy with Morgan. When Oliver reminded Carnegie that they had a previous informal agreement to sell at the same time, Carnegie denied that such an agreement, written or unwritten, ever existed. Oliver left without the information.

Following the meeting, however, Oliver arranged for his friend, Thomas M. King, to sail on the same ship as Carnegie and during the journey to twit the Scotsman about selling too cheaply. King had also sold his steel company to U.S. Steel and had received a substantial payment — information with which Oliver planned to prod Carnegie, hoping that the latter's ego would overcome his promise of secrecy. The plan worked, and Carnegie revealed to King the price he had received — information which was relayed to Oliver when the ship docked in Liverpool.

With this information in hand, Oliver drafted three letters offering to sell Morgan his one-sixth interest. Each letter was identically worded except for the asking price — $9,000,000, $9,250,000, and $9,500,000. On the following day, Oliver intended to present whichever asking price he thought Morgan would accept. Following his meeting with Morgan in New York, Oliver sent a telegram to his Pittsburgh office: "Found party very receptive. Have sold nine and one-quarter tons." The sale had been concluded at the middle price.

In 1894, Oliver had optioned his stock in Oliver Mining Company at $16.67 a share. By the time of the formation of U.S. Steel six years later, each share of stock had sold for $9,250, an increase of 555 per cent! Although not in the same financial league as Andrew Carnegie or John D. Rockefeller, he was a very wealthy man. His sale of stock to U.S. Steel, however, put him out of the mining business (although U.S. Steel continued to use the name Oliver Mining Company as the mining component of the corporation) and ended his need to retain legal counsel in Duluth. Over the years Oliver's relationship with Congdon had made the Duluthian one of the wealthiest men in Minnesota, but now both men were removed from the iron ore and steel businesses.[3]

A few months following the formation of U.S. Steel, Congdon, who was in New York on private business, met Oliver in the famous "Peacock Alley" of the Waldorf Astoria Hotel. Oliver inquired about Congdon's future now that he no longer represented the mining company. For himself, Oliver admitted, "I feel like Othello, my occupation is gone." Congdon's reply was more positive. "Well," he said, "I'm going back to Duluth and practice law and get a few ore leases on the side."

Oliver had not expected Congdon's optimism regarding the iron ore industry, and he asked, "Why do you think there will be any market for ore? It seems to me that the [U.S.] Steel Company will cover the field so [completely] that there will be no market."

The Duluthian's answer was both philosophic and pragmatic. "I believe that the tree never grows to the sky," Congdon replied, and then added, "At any rate, getting leases won't cost me anything but a little time and I'll have plenty of leisure, I guess, before I get back into the swing of office practice."

Congdon's plans were based on more than fanciful speculation. Heretofore, Oliver Iron Mining Company had acquired only those mines with the richest ores, principally on the central Mesabi where the ore tested 60 percent at a minimum. This practice was continued by U.S. Steel which had shown little interest in the leaner western deposits. Literally, dozens of sites, particularly on the western Mesabi, had been examined and evaluated only to be rejected because of the low iron content and/or a high ratio of silica (sand).

Congdon had learned a great deal about the iron ore mining business during his days with Oliver. Now, anticipating the day when the mining industry must turn to less desirable ore, Congdon, acting on his own, had already obtained a number of leases primarily on the western Mesabi.

A short time after their conversation in New York, Congdon received a telegram from Oliver asking if the Duluthian would meet him in Hot Springs, Virginia where Oliver was vacationing. Congdon, without inquiring about Oliver's purpose for the request, made the journey east. The two men spent several days enjoying the resort. Oliver offered no explanation why he had requested Congdon to join him. Finally, on one of their horseback trips into the hills, Oliver got down to business. "The last time I saw you," he said, "you said you were going to get some ore leases. Have you done anything about it?"

Congdon produced a small card containing the details of the leases which he anticipated obtaining. This information he reviewed with Oliver, identifying the mines and supplying the essential information on each one. Congdon had guessed Oliver's intentions. The Pennsylvania steelmaker, already worth millions but without a company in which to invest his money, was lost without involvement in the business which had been his whole life. Congdon had come east hoping to realign himself with Oliver. Each man was waiting for the other to make the first move.

Oliver took the card, looked at it, and thoughtfully remarked, "This will take some money, won't it? How much do you think you will need?"

Again, Congdon was ready. He had already totaled the capital required to finance the leases, and he answered, "$600,000." It was a large sum of money, but he explained to Oliver that he was well on the way to raising that amount. Several of his friends had already agreed to become part of the investment. Congdon mentioned that he also planned to approach several of Oliver's Pittsburgh friends.

It was then that Oliver came to the point of his meeting with Congdon. "You're looking for partners then? How would I do for a partner?" Congdon had guessed right; Oliver wanted back in. Congdon feigned surprise at the steelmaker's offer, "I never thought of you in that connection because I understood you didn't think there would be any market for ore."

Oliver replied, "Well, I've thought it over, and I believe you're right, as you usually are. How would it be if I would furnish the money you require and take one-half of the stock and you the other one-half, [and] you make such provision for other partners out of your half?"

The maneuvering was over. Indeed, Oliver's offer was more than Congdon had expected, and he responded quickly, "I couldn't want a better partner than you." No written contract or agreement between Congdon and Oliver was ever signed. A handshake sealed the pact.

Congdon returned home to organize the Chemung Iron Company, the organization by which the mines would be acquired. By the fall of 1902, Congdon wrote Oliver laying before him a summary of their economic position and recommending a plan for leasing the mines. In the lawyer's own distinct, direct, and forthright style, he began by summarizing the Chemung Iron Company's undeveloped ore assets in tonnage and dollar value. Congdon anticipated that if a depression should hit the mining and steel business, the Chemung Iron Company would be "attacked by bandits [specifically, U.S. Steel, Rockefeller, and James J. Hill (builder of the Great Northern Railroad)] who would attempt to wrest this property from us." And, as Congdon viewed the future of the iron ore mining business, the "crest of the prosperity wave has already passed." The best course of action, Congdon argued, in view of this uncertain situation, would be to sell their properties before a downward swing in the market could occur.[4]

Oliver's reply was prompt. "I am giving your . . . letter . . . my closest attention," he wrote. Acknowledging Congdon's comprehensive analysis, he continued,

> Surely neither of us, when we do reach a settlement, will reflect that our action was taken without deep thought and careful consideration. I think I am on the right line but will not commit my plan to paper. In the meantime unless you see some very great objection, I desire that you immediately proceed to take out a charter for a railroad, covering . . . our different properties and terminating at, say, Duluth. I suggest that you title it Minnesota and Pittsburgh, or Minnesota and Consumers' Iron Ore Railroad Company. If you think best, go to the expense of having some other lawyer or law firm in Duluth do the work, so that it will not imperil your interests with the big company [U.S. Steel].[5]

On the same day he wrote Congdon, Oliver left for New York to see James Gayley, Vice President in charge of iron ore for U. S. Steel. Negotiations for leases on Chemung properties to the Steel Corporation were started immediately and successfully completed a short time later. The details were worked out in a series of telegrams between Oliver, his representatives in Pittsburgh, and Congdon in Duluth. By gathering all these secondary mining sites into one package, Congdon and Oliver had made it possible for U.S. Steel to add a long-term base to its reserves. The Chemung Iron Company proved to be an extremely lucrative venture for both men.[6]

The Chemung Iron Company was not the beginning for Congdon on the western Mesabi. As early as 1899, Congdon had formed a partnership with Guilford G. Hartley, a fellow Duluthian, who also had an eye for obtaining leases on less-than-desirable iron ore properties. As an entrepreneurial team, Hartley and Congdon were a perfect match. Hartley, a Canadian by birth, had emigrated to the United States as a young man. During the 1870s and 1880s, he farmed in Dakota Territory before moving to Brainerd, Minnesota where he engaged in the retail lumber business. He ran for state office and served a term in the Minnesota House before being appointed as Registrar of the U.S. Land Office in Duluth, a post he held until 1886. In that year he resigned to become general manager of the Duluth Street Railway. In Duluth he became involved in a variety of personal business and civic affairs not the least of which included investment in iron ore lands. The discovery of ore on the central Mesabi alerted Hartley to the potential development of the western end of the range, an area where his knowledge was extensive stemming from his lumbering days in the Brainerd area.

In 1904, Congdon incorporated the Canisteo Mining Company (he served as president) and Hartley joined him shortly thereafter. The company served as the corporate vehicle for the exploration and lease or sale of mining property on the western Mesabi. To conduct the exploration, Congdon and Hartley hired Edmund J. Longyear to do test drilling. The results showed five ore locations. While they indicated a presence of iron, they also revealed that the ore was mixed with silica (sand), a waste product. Nevertheless, the partners continued their acquisition of ore properties.[7]

Near the town of Marble two mines had been opened in the early 1890s. The first of these, the Diamond, had at first created a great deal of local enthusiasm and speculation, but the remote location of the mine presented shipping problems; in addition, the ore was contaminated with a large amount of silica. Excavation proceeded—until the shaft and drifts flooded. Attempts to reopen the mine proved futile, and it was closed in 1899. Five years later the use of advance technology showed that the mine could be reopened. This was enough to encourage Congdon and Hartley, and they proceeded with the acquisition.[8]

The second mine, the Arcturus, was located just east of the Diamond and the ore also contained silica. John Mallman, mining superintendent, had stockpiled some of the ore, realizing that the silica would have to be removed before it would be marketable. In 1897, Illinois Steel Company of Chicago decided to try using the ore, and the first shipment was delivered to their plant. The results were disastrous, and the company severed all connections with the Arcturus. Shortly afterwards, the financiers of the mine declared bankruptcy.

The technical challenge of the Arcturus attracted the attention of Congdon and Hartley. A mining engineer was hired to construct a small washing mill which would remove the contaminating silica. The operation of the mill was expensive and a great deal of iron was lost with the waste, but the effort showed enough promise to continue. Further research and large amounts of capital would be required in order to construct similar mills on the western Mesabi. In addition, the development of the mines would require the construction of a rail line to transport the ore to Lake Superior. Both Congdon and Hartley were fully aware of the financial and technical effort needed to continue with full mining development; nevertheless, they decided to move ahead with the acquisition of these low grade mining properties.[9]

Aid came from a most unexpected source — Thomas F. Cole, president of the Oliver Iron Mining Company, the mining subsidiary of United States Steel. Cole, a Michigan native, had spent most of his life in the mining business. Under his leadership, the headquarters of Oliver Iron Mining Company was moved to Duluth where he became acquainted with Congdon and Hartley.

Both men began to educate Cole on the potential of the western Mesabi. The mining executive agreed that it was shortsighted for U.S. Steel to pass over the leaner deposits and that use of the less-desirable ores of the western Mesabi would serve to prolong the life and sustain the profits of the mining company. In the spring of 1904, Cole visited the Arcturus and the Diamond mines, examined the drill samples, and agreed with Hartley and Congdon that the ore could be made marketable. With this decision, he committed himself to expansion into the controversial western Mesabi.

As forceful as was Cole's determination to mine the ores of the western Mesabi, the decision still needed the approval of the Board of Directors of U.S. Steel, especially its chairman, Judge Elbert Gary. To venture into mining the leaner ores marked a change of policy for U.S. Steel, and Gary was not easily convinced. Cole's reputation was "on the line" in his discussions with Gary and the Board of Directors. The Oliver president's recommendation meant an outlay of $10 million, a sizable investment that would not return a profit for a long time. Only after prolonged and heated argument was Cole's proposal accepted. It was the successful washing of Arcturus ore that proved to be the most persuasive factor in changing Gary's opinion. Western Mesabi iron ore could be successfully and profitably mined, and this opened the way for the purchase of both the Chemung and Canisteo mining company leases by U.S. Steel.

In 1910, United States Steel financed the construction of the first large washing plant (a process called "beneficiation") on the western Mesabi at Trout Lake. Within a short distance of the plant, the company built the planned "model" city of Coleraine, named in honor of its progenitor, Thomas F. Cole.[10]

It was on the western Mesabi that Congdon first met Harry C. Dudley, a mining engineer employed by U.S. Steel. The two men hit it off immediately. Dudley, a native of Connecticut, began his college education at Stanford, but transferred to take a S.B. (Bachelor of Science) degree in economic geology at Harvard. Prior to his coming to the western Mesabi, Dudley had worked as a mining engineer for Cleveland-Cliffs on the Gogebic Range in Michigan. In 1905 Dudley was hired by John C. Greenway, general superintendent for U.S. Steel on the western Mesabi. With Congdon's and Hartley's investments in iron ore properties it was inevitable that Dudley should become acquainted with the two Duluthians.[11]

Dudley, writing years later, remembered Congdon as "one of the great American business lawyers of his time, as well as one of the great developers." The mining engineer recalled that one of Carnegie's partners paid Congdon the ultimate compliment, saying, "When our Pittsburgh and New York lawyers could not pull us out of trouble, and we had a lot of it in those days, we sent for Congdon, who never once failed us."[12]

It was from Congdon that Dudley recalled some advice given him on hiring a person to a professional position. The Duluthian's advice was: tell the person what was expected of him, and "fire him if he asks how to do it." Dudley had good reason to recall these words when he later resigned from the Oliver company to accept an assignment from Congdon. A meeting between the two men took place in Duluth in March 1911. For some time Congdon, along with some of the "Old Crowd" from Pittsburgh (as Congdon liked to call them) had been interested in Brazilian iron mining, and it was with this speculation in mind that Congdon had asked Dudley to meet with him. Dudley recalled that he asked Congdon for instructions on what to do in Brazil. "There are none," replied Congdon, "You have been picked for the job. You are working for the Old Crowd. You will receive ten percent interest in anything you purchase. Figure yourself a salary. $10,000 will be deposited to your account at the Mechanics and Metals Bank in New York. You can spend one million dollars. Cable us in time to round up more money if the venture will take more. You don't have to write any reports, but we will read every word you write. If you ask how to do anything at all, we will get someone else."[13]

With those terse instructions, Dudley left for Brazil. After several months of weary and fruitless exploration and after investigating various potential sites, the geologist was convinced that "the Gogebic magnetites, only twenty-three miles from Lake Superior, have a greater potential value for the distant future than such ore in the jungle of Brazil." This information was forwarded to Congdon.

By the date of Dudley's message the price of ore delivered at Sparrows Point (the receiving port on Lake Erie) had dropped to where the cost of importing ore made the enterprise unprofitable. Congdon and his associates read the report thankful that they had not rushed headlong into Brazilian mining. Had Congdon and his friends invested in Brazilian ore the cost of production and delivery would have been prohibitive. Congdon told Dudley that the latter's evaluation of the Brazilian ore fields plus his recommendation that an investment closer to home would be more profitable had saved the would-be investors $1 million.[14]

From that day forward, Congdon and Dudley worked together as a team in assessing and leasing iron ore lands. Rarely did Congdon reject Dudley's advice, but more often Dudley's recommendations were acted upon with profitable results. Of Congdon's investments (in particular, an iron ore mining venture called the Marengo Company), H.C. Frick, Pittsburgh mining executive, commented, "Congdon, you've done it again. You won't make any money yourself on them [the ore bodies], but your children and your grandchildren will receive large returns for a very long time." In Dudley's opinion, Congdon's claim to wise and prudent investments rested on the practice of heeding the advice of professionals when he was dealing with unfamiliar matters.[15]

12

The Legislature of 1909: The Tonnage Tax

WITH THE MESABI'S PRODUCTION GROWING STEADILY, THE MINNESOTA legislature of 1909 planned to increase state revenue by levying a tonnage tax on iron ore. A tonnage tax had been previously enacted in 1881 and lasted for fifteen years before it was declared unconstitutional and repealed by the legislature. At the present time the only tax derived from ore was levied by local governments in those counties where the mining was located.[1]

That the northeastern part of the state should produce such vast wealth and solely benefit from taxes placed on it, piqued residents in other parts of the state—particularly in southern Minnesota. The entire state, so the argument ran, should benefit from its "natural heritage."

Additional resentment was created by the fact that the iron ore was shipped to the steel mills in the East where, according to some people, the "Steel Trust" reaped vast profits. If the entire state were not going to benefit from its natural heritage and enormous profits were made from iron ore, then a tax must compensate for the loss.

A third argument known as "diminishing value" was also presented as justification for the adoption of a tax on iron ore. Proponents of diminishing value maintained that in thirty years the iron deposits of northeastern Minnesota would be exhausted and the mines deserted; consequently, iron ore production should be taxed more heavily than other property—for example, farmland which constituted a more permanent source of revenue.

In response to continued pressure, the legislature of 1905 passed a constitutional amendment which permitted a broad application of the tax laws to mining property. While the amendment did not specify a particular tax, most people expected it to be on ore tonnage. By law, constitutional amendments must be approved by the voters, and the proposed new amendment was scheduled for consideration at the next general election.[2]

To be on safe ground, the legislature requested an opinion from the state attorney general on the constitutionality of the amendment. His reply was encouraging. It read, "The effect of this amendment would be to greatly enlarge the power of the legislature with reference to taxation. . . . Should this amendment be adopted, all property of every kind in the state would be subject to taxation, according to the method the legislature saw fit to adopt. . . ."[3]

In the general election of 1906 the amendment was approved by the voters. Though the way ahead seemed clear, a new hurdle appeared. A mix-up in printing the ballots for the 1906 general election resulted in a suit in district court against the state claiming that the placement of the tax amendment on the ballot confused voters; thus, the plaintiffs argued that the election results, including the approval of the amendment, must be set aside. The case went almost immediately from the district court to the Minnesota Supreme Court which agreed to review the balloting process.[4] Proponents of the tonnage tax knew this would take more time than they were willing to grant.

A new strategy evolved. Unsure how the Supreme Court might decide the case of the misprinted ballots, advocates of the tonnage tax decided not to wait for the Supreme Court to act. They drafted a second constitutional amendment, almost identical to the first. The amendment was passed by the legislature, and was submitted to the voters in the general election in 1908.[5] This meant that two amendments, one pending the decision of the Supreme Court, the other up for voter approval, would determine the fate of the tax on ore.

In the general election of 1908, not only were Minnesota voters asked to decide upon a tax amendment to their constitution but also to approve a third term for their governor, John Albert Johnson. Johnson, a newspaper editor from St. Peter, was considered a progressive, and he had first been elected governor in 1904. His charismatic personality together with his stand on reform issues resulted in a second term in 1906. While he repeatedly denied that he would be a gubernatorial candidate in 1908, the Democratic party would not be denied, and Johnson at last threw his hat into the ring.[6]

The Democratic platform, to which the reluctant candidate pledged his support, advocated the adoption of a tonnage tax on iron ore by declaring,

> . . . this amendment will open the way for the passage of a tonnage tax on iron ore . . . . We recommend the adoption of such an amendment, to the end that these interests may be required to bear their just share of public burdens.[7]

The Republican gubernatorial candidate was Jacob F. Jacobson, a Norwegian immigrant from Lac qui Parle County, who had served briefly as a minor county official. Jacobson had aspirations beyond local politics, and, after an unsuccessful bid for the Republican nomination for governor in 1906, he emerged in 1908 as the party's candidate. The Republican platform of that year "favored the adoption of the tax amendment," and urged the "revision and amendment of our tax laws so that all property shall contribute its just share of the state and local expenditures."[8]

For northeastern Minnesota, an additional tax would strike directly at its major industry. With so much at stake, Chester Congdon decided to run for the state legislature as the Republican representative from the 51st District. He had not made his views known on iron ore taxation prior to the election. Congdon had voted twice for Johnson, but the Democratic party's stand on the tonnage tax alienated the Duluthian. As the campaign wore on Congdon's stand became clear: he understood and approved of local taxation on iron ore, but he could not endorse a state-imposed tonnage tax because it meant that revenue from the mines would now be whisked away to serve the entire population.[9]

The election campaign of 1908 opened with a spirited address by Johnson in which he made taxation the paramount issue. After describing the need for state revenue, the governor, without naming a specific kind, advocated a tax on iron ore. If re-elected, Johnson promised, he favored deriving the state's revenue from taxation of "special interests which so largely have dodged taxation." Tax reform, Johnson warned, was opposed as "extravagant" by his opponent, Jacobson, even as he dined like "King Belshazzar" among the business elite of Duluth.[10] The dinner to which Johnson referred was sponsored by the West Duluth Republican Club and was served by the ladies of the Methodist Episcopal church in the rooms of the West Duluth Commercial Club. The Biblical image of "gold and silver goblets" from which "kings, princes, multiple wives, and concubines drank" was hardly descriptive of the occasion, but it made for lively campaign rhetoric.

Johnson's speech was immensely popular with his supporters, but, curiously, while he had endorsed his party's plank on increased taxation for the iron mines he had avoided mention of a specific tax. Some listeners were sure that he supported a royalty tax (a tax based on iron ore sales), but no one was sure.[11] Johnson also neglected to address the question of continuing local taxes on ore.

A few days later Johnson tried to define his position. He supported raising state revenue from an ore tax while at the same time he approved of a direct realty tax by local governments. "I wish it to be clearly understood," he declared, "that I oppose any system of taxation that will deprive local governments and local improvements of a liberal, reliable, and continuous source of revenue."[12] Johnson was clearly advocating two levels of taxation.

Corresponding with Frank Billings Kellogg, a St. Paul lawyer for the mining companies, Congdon described the difference between the two candidates. He wrote,

> Jacobson. . . is reputed to have the "interests" behind him. This means to many people the railroads, the liquor men, the iron mines, and all other classes who are reputed to desire an unfair advantage under the law, are supporting Jacobson, because they hope through him to secure some unfair advantage. You and I know there is nothing to this, but many Republicans believe it. On the contrary, a great many Republicans believe that Johnson is spending his life fighting all such "interests". I am one of those foolish Republicans who twice voted for Johnson under this belief, besides contributing to his campaign once and possibly twice. . . . We therefore have the strange situation, that the Republican candidate is erroneously believed by many Republicans to be the tool of selfish men, while the Democratic candidate who is in fact such a tool, is believed to be antagonizing such men. You will therefore find this campaign for this reason a difficult one for the Republicans in Minnesota.[13]

Campaign news continued to make the front pages of both Duluth newspapers. The *Duluth Evening Herald*, a Johnson organ, continued to describe the battle as a contest between the "steel interests" and the people. United States Steel Corporation remained passive about the forthcoming election. Chester Congdon considered it his responsibility to warn Thomas F. Cole about the consequences of the corporation's continued inaction. Hoping to prod the business executive into a more aggressive stand, Congdon wrote Cole saying,

> I find your mining companies singularly unappreciative of the vital issue they have at the coming election. The plan is that all state taxes shall be paid by the railroads and the iron mines. The taxes of the railroads cannot be raised without a constitutional amendment. Therefore as the money needs of the State increase, the taxes on the iron mines will be increased. A tonnage tax will be imposed on the iron mines, all of which will be paid into the State Treasury. There being no constitutional limitation on the amount of

this tax, it will expand as the needs of the State expand. . . . In addition to that, the mining companies will still have to pay all their county and municipal taxes and assessments, which now constitute about eighty-five percent of their taxes.

Congdon anticipated an adverse reaction if something were not done, and he warned Cole,

> This means a constant struggle with the communities with whom they [the mining companies] live. Instead of loyal support which the Companies now receive from such communities, they will be constantly antagonized by them; thus, in addition to a large increase in taxation, you will have constant friction and trouble with the local communities, which will cost the mining companies more than the increased taxes.
>
> All these communities are anxious to assist in the defeat of this tax amendment, but the impression prevails that your companies are indifferent, and of course they naturally argue that if the Oliver Company has no objection to the tax amendment, it must be all right, so that by this indifference you are bringing onto these companies trouble which will last as long as they do business in Minnesota.
>
> It seems to me that every possible effort should be made by your companies to defeat this amendment, and to point out its evils to the people. Of course, I understand it is the fixed policy of your corporations not to interfere with politics. . . . I do not understand it to mean that you must idly sit by and not lift your voice in opposition to laws enacted, or sought to be enacted, for the express purpose of oppressing your companies. . . . If you have any desire to prevent any such tax, now is the time to do so. . . .[14]

There is no evidence that Cole heeded Congdon's advice.

On October 25, nine days before the election, fifty-three Duluth businessmen, under banner headlines on the front page of the *Duluth News Tribune,* signed an open letter addressed to the residents of St. Louis County. The letter stressed that additional taxation would restrict the continued growth of the mining companies in northeastern Minnesota. The signers, including Congdon, were related to the iron mining and steel industry and reflected a cross section of commercial sentiment in the northeastern economy. Undoubtedly, this campaign effort was the result of the Duluth Republican Club.

Three days later the letter was followed by a second, again signed by more businessmen with civic leaders' signatures added to the list.[15]

With the exception of his appearance at the "Belshazzar" dinner, Jacobson had not campaigned in northeastern Minnesota. It was reported that he planned a northern tour in mid-October, but it was postponed. Disappointed that the Republican candidate would not appear, the Democratic *Duluth Evening Herald* repeatedly charged that Jacobson was a tool of the steel trust and was afraid of showing his face in mining country.

In Jacobson's absence, his supporters would have to fill in. At a political rally held in the Fay Opera House in Virginia, Minnesota, Chester Congdon captured the attention of the audience when he announced that he had taken a trip to St. Paul ten days previously with the express purpose of asking Jacobson where he stood on the question of the tonnage tax. Congdon reported that Jacobson had assured him that he was "in favor today as always that the tax paid by any man, corporation or community . . . be distributed the same as the tax paid by any other man, corporation or community." Jacobson's statement was at best ambiguous, thus enabling his followers to apply any interpretation to his reply. Congdon concluded, "What could be plainer than this answer as evidence that Mr. Jacobson is favorable to St. Louis county and is a friend to its citizens and has its interests at heart." The *Evening Herald* picked up the story, and hoping to embarrass both Jacobson and Congdon, accused the two men, first of collaborating to misrepresent the Republican candidate's stand on the tonnage tax, and second of sharing a confidence which should have been open to the public.[16]

Late in the campaign, Jacobson decided to visit the iron counties, and on October 31 he delivered a speech in the Duluth armory. Weeks of campaigning in other parts of the state had taken their toll, and his voice was almost gone. He appeared on the platform flanked by Congdon and the chairman of the local Republican club. Jacobson's speech was short, and he spent the bulk of it ineffectively describing his legislative career and the remainder proclaiming his independence from "the interests."[17]

It was Congdon who delivered the political address of the evening. Speaking as an opponent of the tax, the Duluth attorney came immediately to the main thrust of the controversy. He explained,

> It is not so important how the taxes are collected, it is the manner of the distribution that concerns us in this campaign. The question is whether the

taxes of one county shall be distributed in the same manner and on an equality with the taxes of other counties. It is not a question of a tonnage tax, a royalty tax or any other form of taxation, but shall we use these taxes as other counties do, or shall we be discriminated against to pay more than our share to the state. . . . It is a matter of little concern to me whether the taxes on iron ore are raised by a royalty or tonnage tax, but I am vastly interested in such tax, however raised, being properly distributed in St. Louis county the same as any other taxes. . . .[18]

The election followed in two days. Johnson won 52 percent of the total vote, while Jacobson captured just under 44 percent (the remainder went to third party candidates). Congdon won his seat in the House. His district cast its ballots in favor of Johnson by a slim margin. The tax amendment failed. Even though it was approved by a 2–1 margin of those voting on the proposal, it failed to receive the required majority of the total number of votes cast in the election, and, therefore, was lost.[19]

The contest for the tonnage tax, however, was far from over. Attention now shifted to the Minnesota Supreme Court. For more than two years the Supreme Court had deliberated the question of the "incorrectly placed" items on the ballot of 1906. If the Supreme Court found the election legal, the proponents of the tax on iron ore could proceed to draft a tax bill.

At last the Supreme Court was ready. In early January 1909, from a 4–1 split, the Supreme Court held that the district court had erred in declaring the election illegal. The placement of the tax amendment on the ballot had not invalidated the election. The constitutional path now had been cleared for the passage of a tax on iron ore.[20] The decision was received by northeastern Minnesota with great dismay. There was no question that a tax bill would be introduced, and the battle must be fought in the legislature.

The legislative session of 1909 opened shortly after the New Year holiday, and, as expected, a tax bill (H.F. No. 227) was introduced in late January.[21] The bill said nothing about local taxation, and it was clear that the intent was to enact a state tonnage tax. The "Duluth Delegation," led by Chester Congdon, five House members, and three Senators, again stood resolutely opposed to the measure and began seeking the votes to defeat it. Try as they might, they were not successful, and the House gave its approval by a narrow margin.[22] The legislation would now go before the Senate.

Although people in northeastern Minnesota usually kept in close touch with what was going on in St. Paul, organized opposition to H.F. No. 227

did not emerge until it was considered by the Senate. On March 24, the chairman of the Duluth Commercial Club, Trevanion W. Hugo, declared open war on the tonnage tax proposal. Joining him were Bishops James McGolrick (Catholic) and James D. Morrison (Episcopal), both of whom advocated concerted action by all organizations in St. Louis and adjoining counties to alert people of the imminent peril.[23]

The call to battle was answered by a cross section of public officials. Mayors across the Mesabi iron range declared their opposition, and they were supported by their constituencies. Acting as a "committee of mayors," they drafted a letter to members of the legislature describing the devastating effect which the bill would have on their communities. If adopted, they warned, it would create such an additional tax burden on the mining companies that they would severely restrict the operation of their properties. The result would mean a reduced source of revenue for the local communities accompanied by a dramatic increase in real estate taxes across the range. In Chisholm, for example, the tax would increase from $33.90 to $741.12 on a "typical" piece of property, and this illustration was true of property taxes in towns from Grand Rapids to Ely.[24]

A new element in the protest against the tonnage tax now appeared. For some time, United States Steel Corporation had been developing plans to construct a steel mill on the St. Louis River in western Duluth. This $5 million construction had first been made public in 1907 when the corporation had informed the Minnesota legislature of its intentions. Since that date the plans had been expanded from a $10 million to a $25 million development. In addition to the mill, two feeder railroads and a connecting bridge over the St. Louis River were included. An estimated 10,000 jobs directly related to the steel mill would be created, and 30,000 to 40,000 workers would be employed in businesses created by mill development. Implementation of these plans, however, depended upon the rejection of the tonnage tax. Needless to say, a steel mill would enhance the economic future not only for northeastern Minnesota but also the rest of the state. Opponents of the tonnage tax intended to use the plans for a steel plant as one of their major weapons. If northeastern Minnesota wanted a steel mill, it would have to reject the tonnage tax.[25]

For the first time since the tonnage tax controversy began, Oliver Mining Company expressed its opposition to the bill. Writing to Congdon, George D. Swift, Assistant Secretary for the company, described Oliver's objections. The argument presented in the letter did not address the question of dual taxation but was based largely upon how difficult and complex the implementation of a tonnage tax would be.[26]

Duluth's Commercial Club now took the initiative and invited members of the Senate to visit northeastern Minnesota where they could witness for themselves the area's thriving economy and hear firsthand how the tonnage tax would damage not only the area's economic well-being but also impair its future growth. In the late evening of April 1, a Northern Pacific train, with three extra sleepers and a dining car attached, departed from St. Paul with the legislators on board. The entourage arrived at Duluth early the following morning where they were joined by members of the Commercial Club. The group then proceeded north to the iron range over the Duluth, Missabe and Northern tracks.[27]

Between mid-morning Friday, when the legislators arrived in Coleraine and their return to Duluth late Saturday afternoon, the senators visited several mines, listened to descriptions of future development, visited more mining facilities, and heard from a variety of civic leaders, mine officials, and local politicians. En route, encouragement came when one senator exclaimed, "You may depend that the Senate will do what is right on the tonnage tax question," and another declared that, "If any man in the Senate believes that the tonnage tax will or should be passed, his judgment should be taken out into the back yard and reformed." If his colleagues shared these convictions, the tonnage tax would be defeated. The *Duluth News Tribune* reported that "from the time the senators first sighted the outer workings of the gigantic Canisteo mine at Coleraine until they saw the shadows from the east envelope the ramparts of the great Virginia open pit at nightfall, they appeared to be interested and profoundly impressed."[28]

The final engagement with the senators took place in Duluth at a banquet hosted by the Commercial Club. Once again, community leaders, including northeastern Minnesota boosters and opponents of the tonnage tax, led a vigorous attack on the bill. At 11:30 p.m. the Senators departed for St. Paul. In parting, several Senators expressed their intention to change their vote, but proof of their conversion would come with the vote in St. Paul.

Still anxious to put forward every effort to defeat the tonnage tax, Duluth Mayor R. D. Haven issued a call on April 7 for 300 men to depart for St. Paul to mount one last protest. The response was immediate, and the group departed for the capital on a Northern Pacific special train. Once there they gathered in front of the Ryan Hotel to form a column of twos for a march to the Senate chambers. Each man wore across his chest a broad blue ribbon emblazoned with "NO TONNAGE TAX." As the delegation filed inside the building, they overflowed the main floor and the galleries, and a few were forced to occupy an adjoining room.[29]

Chester Congdon was the group's speaker. Beginning at eight o'clock and continuing for the next three hours, Congdon delivered his last impassioned plea for northeastern Minnesota and the defeat of the tax bill. There was nothing new to add; he had articulated the same arguments before, but this time he reinforced his speech with a detailed account of what the iron mining industry meant to his region and to the state. After he had spoken at considerable length, he announced his intention to stop only to be met with cries of "Go on, go on!" and the audience interrupted his oratory with enthusiastic applause.[30]

Despite several parliamentary maneuvers to delay or kill the bill, the moment of truth came on April 16, 1909. By a modest margin, the Senate approved H. F. No. 227. Opponents of the tonnage tax had lost, and only the Governor's signature was needed to enact it into law.[31]

The last hope for northeastern Minnesota lay with Governor Johnson. He had stated repeatedly during the campaign that he would veto any measure which denied tax revenue to the local communities in northeastern Minnesota. By now Johnson had become convinced that restriction on local taxes was a very real possibility with the passage of the legislation. There was some talk that the governor would seek the opinion of the attorney general who might rehear arguments on the constitutionality of the legislation, but this seemed unlikely. Nevertheless, it was rumored that if such a turn of events occurred, Congdon would present the negative case.[32]

Johnson gave little indication of his intentions. Observers speculated on the possibility of a veto, and this rumor seemed to have substance when a state official wired the *Duluth News Tribune* that Johnson would indeed kill the bill. Still the state executive waited. He held a conference with the Tax Commission and visited with the state auditor—which only gave rise to more rumors. Meanwhile, 2,000 telegrams from northeastern Minnesota arrived on the Governor's desk, all bearing the same message. Not content to leave their fate in mortal hands, the northeastern churches prayed for divine intervention.[33]

On April 20, Johnson drafted a veto message and sent it to the House of Representatives the following day. Ironically Johnson, who had campaigned in favor of a tonnage tax, was about to kill it. He explained that in his opinion, the bill was

> in principle and administrative features a more or less uncertain and ill-digested experiment, not fully understood even by its friends and intensely feared by the sections of the state to which it [e]specially applies. . . [and that] it threatens to violate the fundamental principle of taxation, that of equality, [and] at the same time fails to meet the constitutional requirement of uniformity in taxing the same class of subjects.

Continuing on, Johnson was also wary that the legislation would strike a severe blow to the development and prosperity of northeastern Minnesota, and he was uncertain how the law would be applied. Northeastern Minnesota's claims of insufficient representation in the legislature (an issue heretofore unraised), Johnson continued, were justified, and to impose a tonnage tax on that section without giving them an adequate voice in the passage of a law was wrong. Furthermore, the veto message continued, Johnson had doubts that the bill would accomplish the desired results, and would instead impose a disadvantage on mining companies both large and small. For all these reasons, the governor concluded, he had decided to veto the bill.[34]

Needless to say, northeastern Minnesota heaved a sigh of relief. Again, telegrams poured into the Governor's office expressing the gratitude of hundreds of northeastern Minnesotans, who only days before had suffered what seemed to be a conclusive defeat. Sponsors of the tax legislation announced that they had no plans to reintroduce the bill. The last gesture belonged to 15,000 school children from northeastern Minnesota who sent to the governor a huge bouquet of red roses.[35]

Congdon successfully sought re-election in 1910. As a public servant in the legislature of 1909 he had demonstrated a capacity for leadership which rivaled even the most seasoned veterans. He had won the trust and support of those persons who opposed the tonnage tax, and his colleagues had repeatedly delegated to him the responsibility of speaking for their cause. Legislators of divergent opinions had found him a formidable opponent. Perhaps he, more than many others who were involved in the tonnage tax battle, saw the issue in its clearest light—a question involving dual taxation of ore production and the state's right to share in the profits from northeastern resources at the expense of damaging future mining development.

The defeat of the tonnage tax in 1909 would not draw the curtain on the question of revenue derived from iron ore. The issue would rise again under new conditions and with new protagonists in Minnesota's struggle to make its peace with the iron ore mining industry.

13

The Legislature of 1911: Redistricting the State

ALTHOUGH CONGDON HAD BEEN DEFEATED IN HIS EFFORTS TO PREVENT the passage of a tonnage tax (saved only by Governor Johnson's veto), he decided to run again for the Minnesota House in 1910. His record on iron ore taxation had won him the approval and respect of his constituency, and he won again by a large margin—2,893 to 809—over his nearest opponent. This time he focused on legislative redistricting. Few issues aroused as much attention and anxiety in northeastern Minnesota.[1] Residents of that area strongly believed that if the mining industry, which produced immense taxable wealth along with thousands of jobs, were to be preserved for northeastern Minnesota, they must have the votes to which they were entitled in the legislature.

The Minnesota legislature had been negligent in its response to population changes. The last reapportionment had been carried out in 1897 and was based on the state census of 1895 which showed a population of 1,574,619. The 1910 census increased that figure to 2,075,708, a gain of 32 percent. Over the fifteen year period, northern Minnesota, particularly St. Louis County, greatly exceeded the state's percentage increase. Thirty-one counties where the increase had been the heaviest lay north of a line bisecting the state approximately at mid-point. In addition, two metropolitan counties south of this line, Hennepin and Ramsey, had also experienced an increased population—slightly higher than 50 percent in each.[2]

To exacerbate the difference, the southern counties of the state had lost population between 1895 and 1910. Here the agriculturally based economy had progressed to a point where new machinery made it possible to operate farms with fewer hands, and increased efficiency permitted larger acreage. Children born to farm families no longer found it desirable or profitable to remain at home, and many of them had emigrated to the metropolitan centers.[3]

Governor Adolph O. Eberhart, successor to the governorship when Johnson unexpectedly passed away in 1909, sensed the urgency of reapportionment as a popular issue and advocated it in his message to the legislature. He was not alone. Both House and Senate were well aware of the need to redraw the state's legislative boundaries.[4]

The work of drafting a reapportionment bill was given to the Standing Committee on Reapportionment, chaired by Chester Congdon. Of the twenty-seven committee members, twenty-six were Republicans. The three most underrepresented counties (Hennepin, Ramsey, and St. Louis) contained a total of eight votes. The rest of the committee membership was distributed almost evenly throughout the state.[5]

At a joint session of both House and Senate reapportionment committees, Congdon offered a list of guidelines by which he hoped the two houses could proceed. First, he proposed a maximum in total legislative membership: 63 in the Senate and 126 in the House; second, as far as practicable, and with the exception of Hennepin, Ramsey, and St. Louis, no county would be divided in determining senatorial districts; third, following the census returns, the legislators from the affected areas would make the decisions regarding new boundaries.[6]

Opposition to the guidelines arose immediately, and it became evident that even the smallest details would be challenged. Members of both legislative bodies were anxious to have their ideas incorporated into a reapportionment bill, and requests and suggestions poured into the House committee. Not all ideas were clear or rational, but their sheer number indicated the intense pressure on the legislature. One bill, for example, called for a constitutional amendment which would limit representation in the cities of St. Paul, Minneapolis, and Duluth to one-half of the number allowed for the same population in the rest of the state.[7]

Congdon, realizing that it would be difficult, if not impossible, to please everyone, issued a statement saying that it was his intention to report out of committee a bill which would "meet with the least friction." Hoping to ward off at least some of the inevitable criticism, the Duluth legislator tested the committee's ideas on a few close colleagues in the House and found that "nearly all were favorably received."[8]

Twenty-nine days into the session, Congdon introduced the committee's bill, H.F. 477. Several compromises had been necessary, but essentially, it provided for increasing the size of the House to 126 members and for reducing the size of the Senate to 61. The underrepresented northern part of the state received hardly any increase in the Senate. Opposition notwithstanding, the House committee reported on the bill with a "do pass" recommendation with only four dissenting votes.[9]

The plan by which H.F. 477 redrew the legislative boundaries for St. Louis County brought accusations of gerrymander. Two new districts ran like narrow corridors north from the city of Duluth through the Mesabi and Vermilion iron ranges to the Canadian border. A few irate lawmakers charged that it was a deliberate attempt to make sure that St. Louis County not only received additional representation but also to "render them all safe for the iron mining companies."[10]

Congdon explained the bill, saying that while the committee had tried to leave county boundaries intact, it was not always possible to reconcile political divisions with population. Some adjustments were inevitable. In view of the difficulties, the chairman concluded, "it had been impossible to give every district its exact representation."[11]

While the bill was undergoing discussion in the House, a new issue arose. As district lines currently stood, the smaller southern counties each elected a senator. Under the reapportionment plan, seven senators were to be taken away from the southern part of the state and redistributed. As a result, several of the smaller counties would have to be joined into one senatorial district. Noting that these smaller rural counties supported a local liquor option, critics of H.F. 477 charged that its proponents were in league with the brewery interests and that their motive was not only to reduce southern Minnesota's representation in the legislature but also, by taking away their votes, to defeat the "drys."[12]

Under fire now from both the anti-reapportionists and the pro-county option legislators, Congdon and his committee, nevertheless, chose to plunge ahead. Surprisingly, H.F. 477 passed the house by an overwhelming 85–13.[13]

The bill would now be considered by the Senate. This body was the one most directly affected by redistricting. Observers expected a difficult battle with prolonged debate if not outright defeat. Governor Eberhart threatened that if the legislature did not pass a reapportionment bill he would call an extra session, the responsibility for which would fall on the obstructionists.[14]

One other issue surfaced during the debate on H.F. 477. The issue was brought, oddly enough, by progressives who heretofore had championed "one man, one vote." They attacked an increase in representation for St. Louis County simply because it had increased its population particularly in the north where the iron mines were located. With the opening of the mines, thousands of European immigrants had been hired as laborers. While they added to the total population, most of them, for various reasons, were either ineligible or neglected to vote. The progressives were sure that if the immigrants voted their ballot would be controlled by the mining companies. Therefore, the argument ran, reapportionment should be based on the number of votes cast in recent elections rather than on straight population.[15] However, this idea never reached the floor in amendment form.

When H.F. 477 came up for debate in the upper house, several Senators offered amendments, none of which passed or affected the proposed redistricting. Despite parliamentary maneuvering, the measure was brought up for final passage. By a vote of 36 to 27, H.F. 477 was defeated. A motion to reconsider suffered the same fate. It is difficult to determine an explanation for the vote, although observers who have since studied the course of this legislation believe that it was the attempt to gerrymander St. Louis County that defeated Congdon's committee bill.[16]

Congdon's House Committee on Reapportionment had opened up the war only to have its work rejected. The next offensive was undertaken by the Senate. Four senators, hoping to protect senatorial representation by counties as much as possible while restricting multiple senatorial representation in the larger counties, introduced an amendment, S.F. 360, to the Minnesota state constitution.[17] It provided (in part) that

> ... no county or any of the parts thereof shall ever constitute or be a part of more than six (6) Senatorial Districts; not more than six Senators shall ever be apportioned to any one county.[18]

After surviving several attempts at change, the amendment was approved and would now be transmitted to the House.

The amendment was clearly a blow to additional senatorial representation from St. Louis as well as Ramsey and Hennepin Counties. Congdon planned to crush the amendment when it reached the House. When S.F. 360 arrived, Congdon immediately moved to indefinitely postpone further action, and when this failed he offered a motion to table the issue. Again, the vote went against him.[19] For the next week, the "Six Senators" amendment was bantered about (without change) in the House, and it became evident that most of the legislators leaned toward retaining senatorial election in each county as well as a limit on the number of Senators within the larger counties.

Congdon was not about to give up. It was highly likely that the "Six Senators" amendment would pass. If this happened there would be a cap placed on the maximum number of senators from St. Louis County. The most immediate strategy seemed to be to change the wording to make it read as favorably as possible. In view of House sentiment, Congdon offered an amendment increasing the maximum number of Senators apportioned to any one county from six to seven. The increase of one senator was not much, but it was better than leaving the total at six.[20] Even with the senatorial representation increased, Congdon was not pleased with the bill.

By a close vote S.F. 360, with the Congdon amendment, passed the House.[21] A motion to reconsider was offered, but no action was taken. The House adjourned.[22]

There occurred at this point one of those strange and unusual parliamentary procedural questions which requires a precise interpretation and enforcement of the rules which govern a legislative body. Two members of the House refused to acknowledge the adjournment, and chose to continue their parliamentary maneuvering on S.F. 360. They rose to present a question of personal privilege claiming that the House, against its own rules of parliamentary procedure, had ignored the motion to reconsider, had adjourned, and had illegally transmitted S.F. 360 back to the Senate. Their challenge went unanswered.[23] A second attempt in the form of a petition signed by nineteen members, including Congdon (always a stickler for adhering to rules) asked that the Senate return S.F. 360 to the House. The petition was ignored.

The irregularities in the House bothered Senate members as well. Twelve senators signed a petition rejecting the idea that the Senate could legitimately take up the amended version of S.F. 360. Their action, however, was brushed aside, and the Senate approved the bill with Congdon's seven senators amendment.[24] Now the bill could move forward.

S.F. 360 was signed by the President and Secretary of the Senate, the Speaker, Chief Clerk of the House, and forwarded to the Governor. Without signing or in any way approving or disapproving the amendment, the Governor passed the measure on to the Secretary of State who wrote across the top, "Filed April 21, 1911, Julius Schmahl, Secretary of State." Schmahl now had every intent, in conformance with the law, of placing the issue on the ballot in the forthcoming general election in November 1912.[25]

Congdon and other members of the House were certain that the entire series of legislative procedures committed after the failure of the House to reconsider S.F. 360 were illegal. If their fellow legislators would not respond, there seemed to be no recourse other than to take legal action. Here was an opportunity to kill the limitation on senatorial representation by court action, and suit was brought in Hennepin County District Court. The case went before the court as *Fowler v. Schmahl.*

While the House and Senate waited, Judge William E. Hull considered the case. As presented to Hull, the case revolved around three issues: first, that the House had returned S.F. 360 to the Senate illegally since a motion to reconsider was ignored and the House had adjourned; second, that the Governor had not signed S.F. 360 but had turned it over to the Secretary of State who intended to place it on the 1912 general election ballot; and third, that S.F. 360 violated the federal constitution's guarantee to each state a republican form of government. Since, in this case, St. Louis, Ramsey, and Hennepin counties were underrepresented in the legislature the three counties did not provide equal representation as provided for in the federal Constitution.

On September 15, 1911 Hull delivered his decision. He had ruled against the plaintiffs. In an attached memorandum, Hull elaborated upon his decision. The first point, the motion to reconsider, Hull declared, was a matter for the legislature to decide. If the action defied procedure, it was up to the legislative body to make the correction. On the question of the Governor's failure to sign the bill before it was placed on the ballot, Hull decided that it was not necessary for the Governor to sign an act proposing a constitutional amendment. "Neither the statutes nor the [state] Constitution requires it. ... The Governor has nothing to do with constitution-making; for this is the concentration of all the power of the people in establishing organic law." Hull went on to explain that there was a distinct difference between constitution-making and law-making and that the Governor had no power to affect the former. He concluded that S.F. 360 was in "no sense law-making, but is a specific exercise of the power of the people," and that "the Governor could not defeat the will of the people by vetoing a proposed amendment to the Constitution." On the third point, Hull found that S.F. 360 was not an abridgment of the Constitution's guarantee of a republican form of government. If there was an injustice in Minnesota's representation in the legislature, it was up to the people of that state to rectify the situation. Hull concluded his memorandum by noting that several states (he cited sixteen) based representation in their state legislature on geographic boundaries and ignored population—all of which satisfied the guarantee of "republican government."[26]

There was no appeal to the Minnesota Supreme Court. Hull's decision had been legally persuasive. The final hurdle for S.F. 360 was to win the support of voters in the general election in November of 1912.

Congdon, now convinced that even the increase from six to seven senators was unacceptable, opened the offensive in St. Louis County. Purchasing (with his own money) a two column, twenty-inch space in the *Duluth News Tribune*, he exhorted voters to cast their ballots against the entire amendment. His wording presented a powerfully logical and emotional appeal. To constitutionally limit St. Louis County to seven senators, he wrote, was a violation of representative government. After reviewing the effects of the amendment on St. Louis County, Congdon concluded emphatically with, "Any voter in this county who thus votes away his own political franchise demonstrates his unfitness for American citizenship. Any voter in this county who does not vote NO on this amendment is the enemy of his neighbors and himself."[27]

The Minnesota constitution requires that amendments be approved by a majority of the total number of votes cast at the election.[28] In the 1912 election 349,678 voters went to the polls. Of this number, 122,457 cast their vote in favor of the amendment; 77,187 voted against it. Therefore, despite a majority of 45,270 votes in favor, it failed to pass since it fell short of the constitutional requirement—in this case 174,839 votes.[29]

True to his word, Governor Eberhart summoned an extra session of the legislature for the purpose of enacting a reapportionment law, but it was a futile effort. The momentum was gone. H.F. 18, a new reapportionment bill, was introduced on June 10 and referred to the Committee on Reapportionment. When reported out of committee, it was confronted with a motion to indefinitely postpone. The motion was approved.[30] The issue of redistricting was dead.

For Congdon, the parliamentary maneuvering and the political intricacies of the legislature brought a disillusioning end to his legislative service. The world of politics was quite different from business, and he was disturbed by his experience as a lawmaker. He would try politics only once more in 1916, and then as a member of the Republican National Committee. Unfortunately, his death in that year cut short his service.

14
Bisbee

THE IRON ORES OF THE LAKE SUPERIOR COUNTRY WERE NOT THE ONLY mining developments to interest Congdon and his associates. Available ore land worth the investment in the Upper Midwest was becoming more difficult to obtain, and as a result the "Lake Superior Group," as they came to be known, turned their attention to the copper mines in southern Arizona at Bisbee.

The Lake Superior investors were neither the discoverers nor the initial developers of the Arizona mines. The honor of discovery goes to an army scout and several "old prospectors," while the modern development of the first substantial mine, the Copper Queen, goes to the Phelps Dodge Corporation. In the late years of the nineteenth century, Phelps Dodge was a successful export-import New York company with no relation to mining. Their interest in Arizona copper began when Dr. James Douglas, a Pennsylvania mineralogist, after examining the Copper Queen along with some other mines, encouraged the company to purchase the properties. From that time forward, Phelps Dodge rapidly converted its business interests from overseas trade to mining.

If Phelps Dodge was fortunate in acquiring the Copper Queen, they were equally unfortunate in not purchasing the adjacent land to the south. Prospectors tried to sell them this property, the surface of which revealed only barren hills, but they would have none of it. In the early 1880s, however, an eccentric Irish prospector, Jim Daley, established a claim which he named the Irish Mag in honor of one of the "soiled doves" at the Hog Ranch, a local brothel. A shortage of capital prevented Daley from developing the mine, and his violent temper led him to engage in verbal battle with the owners of the Copper Queen over the boundaries with those of the Mag. A cantankerous individual, Daley's temper finally got the best of him when he beat up a Mexican and murdered a local law enforcement officer before fleeing across the border. When he failed to return he was legally pronounced dead.

With the disappearance of Daley, the ownership of the Irish Mag was contested by several claimants: a man who declared he had purchased the rights from Daley's widow, a Mexican woman with whom he had been living, a saloon keeper who maintained that Daley had sold the Irish Mag to him, and two storekeepers who laid claim by reason of a foreclosed mortgage. A ten year court battle ensued at the end of which the ownership of the Mag was awarded to Martin Costello, who had grubstaked a prospector who claimed he had purchased the rights to the mine from Daley's widow. Costello, a resident of Tombstone, had no intention of working the Mag and declared his intention to sell—for a staggering price. The mine remained undeveloped. The owner repeatedly approached the Phelps Dodge partners in New York, each time only to be politely turned away.

In early 1898, while these negotiations were going on, Captain James Hoatson, mining foreman from the Calumet and Hecla mine on the Upper Peninsula of Michigan, arrived in Bisbee. Hoatson had been employed by a Michigan stockbroker to investigate and determine the value of another mine in the Arizona mountains. While there, Hoatson was instructed to get in touch with John Graham at Bisbee. As an employee of the same stockbroker who hired Hoatson, it was Graham's job to report on mining developments in Arizona, particularly in the Bisbee area. Upon Hoatson's arrival, Graham directed his attention to the Irish Mag and surrounding properties. Learning that Costello was thinking about selling the Mag, Hoatson advised his friends in Calumet to obtain an option. Costello's title, however, was still under litigation, and, in fact, ownership was currently being decided by the United States Supreme Court. When that body confirmed Costello's title in May 1899, Hoatson negotiated a purchase on behalf of a newly formed company, the Lake Superior and Western Copper Company. The company was incorporated under the laws of the state of Michigan with Charles Briggs, a Calumet banker, as president. On November 1, 1899, the first digging began.[1]

With what he thought was sufficient funding to sink a shaft to the 900 foot level, Hoatson began operation. At the 750 foot level he ran out of money without striking ore. The Lake Superior and Western Copper Company was broke. Work on the Irish Mag shut down, and the stock dropped to a few cents a share.[2]

Hoatson's sister was married to Thomas Cole. During a visit to Calumet, Hoatson informed her about the recent attempt to develop the Irish Mag, and she related the story to her husband. Cole's interest was immediate, and he speculated there would be no difficulty in obtaining investment capital from his friends if the property were as promising as Hoatson made it out to be.[3]

To verify Hoatson's enthusiasm, Cole dispatched George Tener, one of his officers, to Bisbee. His report to Cole was not encouraging. Tener wired that he could not recommend the investment, but would gamble $5,000 if Cole would invest a similar amount. With $10,000 fresh capital the work on the Mag was renewed. It was now up to Cole, Tener, and whomever else they could interest to raise $1 million working capital. Boston was the "Wall Street of Copper," and Cole began there, but investors expressed no interest. Cole then turned to his friends in Carnegie Steel, and a favorable response was immediately forthcoming. The "Cole crowd," as it came to be known, consisted of Cole; Charles Briggs, Calumet merchant and banker; Thomas and James Hoatson, Calumet; Charles d'Autremont, lawyer and former mayor of Duluth; C.D. Fraser, president of U.S. Steel; Henry W. Oliver; and Chester Congdon. Although these men constituted the main investors, a smaller portion of the stock also went to other subscribers.[4]

The investors formed a new company, the Calumet and Arizona Copper Company (C&A) to replace the defunct Lake Superior and Western, and in March 1901 the incorporation documents were filed with the Michigan Secretary of State. To provide for a final payment to Costello, the continued development of the mine and the construction of a smelter, $1 million was needed. The funds were raised by shares divided among the Cole group.[5]

The C&A's development at Bisbee was divided into two parts: continued excavation on the Irish Mag shaft and the construction of a smelter at Douglas, twenty miles away. As the shaft at Bisbee approached the 950 foot level, a drift (a tunnel running at a right angle to the main shaft) was extended outward where it cut through 300 feet of high-grade copper ore. The richest concentration of ore ran as high as 30 percent, while surrounding deposits averaged a minimum of 15 percent. The ore body also turned out two ounces of silver and one dollar in gold per ton. It was the richest strike that Bisbee had ever seen. The C&A built a smelter in time to process the first ore in late 1902, and a few months later the company paid its first dividend. It was Cole's opinion there was "sufficient ore on this claim alone to supply a 500-ton smelter for many years to come."[6]

The success of the Irish Mag touched off a wave of speculation in mining properties. The Cole group, as well as independent buyers, feverishly began to acquire land as prices shot upward from $30,000 to $40,000 an acre. At such high stakes the small bidders could not compete, and the land

Clearing timber for Summit Avenue, Grays Harbor, Washington, ca. 1889.

Chester and Clara Congdon (on right), main shaft of Irish Mag Mine, Calumet & Arizona Mining Co., Bisbee, Arizona, ca. 1905.

Guilford G. Hartley, Chester
Congdon's partner in Canisteo
Mining Company.

Harry C. Dudley, Superintendent
of Canisteo Mining Co., and later
Chester Congdon's son-in-law.

Train load of ore taken from Canisteo Mine, ca. 1900.

Chester Congdon and John Campbell Greenway, Superintendent, Calumet and
Arizona Copper Company; Baja, California, ca. 1902.

Westhome, Yakima, Washington.

Congdon Orchards, Yakima, Washington, ca. 1915.

Congdon canal flume, Painted Rocks, 1893.

Blue Goose label, Congdon Orchards.

A NEW REP:
C. A.
CONGDON,
OF
DULUTH.
HE
POSSESSES
MUCH
ORE LAND

Caricature of Chester Congdon by Frank Wing, 1909.

Chester Congdon, Monterey , California.

The Hughes Campaign Train, Red Wing, Minnesota, en route to the Pacific Northwest. From left: Chester Congdon, Mrs. C.E. Hughes, Honorable Charles Evans Hughes, Cordenio A. Severance and Eric L. Thornton, August 9, 1916.

Chester Congdon, Yakima, Washington, 1916.

acquisition race was reduced to Phelps Dodge versus C&A. For example, while the C&A investors haggled with the owners over a half-million dollars in cash for a piece of undeveloped mining property (it became the Lowell Mine worth between $10 and $12 million dollars), Phelps Dodge paid the price without hesitation.[7]

Cole visited Bisbee in 1902. By this date the C&A had acquired more property and sunk additional shafts—the Briggs, the Congdon, the Del Norte, the Oliver, and the Hoatson. As he stepped off the train, the sight before him must have quickened his heart-beat. Before him lay the Phelps Dodge Copper Queen with its laborers busily at work in the shaft and smelter. Nearby, C&A's Irish Mag and other shafts poured forth their wealth while a train waited to transport the ore to the smelter. Several independent mines of smaller capacity were in full operation. The countryside surrounding the mines bore evidence of additional deposits. With exuberant enthusiasm, Cole quickly asked, "Isn't there any more ground that we can buy here?"[8]

And buy they did. To facilitate their operations, Calumet and Arizona formed four subsidiary companies: the Lake Superior and Pittsburgh, more commonly known as the "S&P;" the Calumet and Pittsburgh, the "C&P;" the Pittsburgh and Duluth; and the Pittsburgh Junction, better known as the "Junction." Each company had its own functions. The "S&P," for example, handled the smelting and refining of the ore, but all were directly related to the overall operation of the "C&A."[9]

For the next four years, the Bisbee district out-produced by four to one all other copper mining areas in Arizona. The reports on the C&A properties reflected this production in all their mines. Analyzing the current conditions in three of the company's mines (the Briggs, Hoatson, and Junction), the resident mining engineers expressed their optimism to Congdon. Regarding the future of the Hoatson shaft, L. W. Powell, C&A General Superintendent, wrote Congdon that, "we have every reason to believe that this shaft will eventually be one of the big producers of the camp."[10]

It was Thorald Field, one of the resident geologists who sounded a more cautious note. To Congdon, he wrote, "If the C&A is to continue being one of the great copper mining companies of this country we will have to be very careful as regards the grade and tonnage of the ore mined and the exploration work." Charlie Briggs, president of the C&A, keeping a close watch on production figures and the actions of the General Superintendent, was more direct. When the cost of production rose in the Cole shaft, he questioned the advisability of continuing the operation. "I think Mr. Powell should reduce the output and expenses at Cole as Junction and Hoatson increase. . . . [T]he . . . right of it would be to shut it down." he advised Congdon. On Powell's effectiveness he was more critical. The superintendent's overall policies, the C&A president warned, were "taking. . . all together [sic] too much risk." Congdon agreed. Powell wrote Congdon explaining his policies, but it was a weak defense. Rather than accept the General Superintendent's statement, Congdon relied on Field for a description and analysis of what was going on in Bisbee. To Charlie Briggs, Powell continued to forward ambiguously promising reports. Field's reports did not correspond with Powell's, and Congdon continued to believe Field. It was clear that the General Superintendent had lost the confidence of the C&A Board of Directors, and his dismissal was imminent.[11]

Criticism of Powell's superintendency continued. It was true that some of his decisions were commendable, but more often, in Congdon's eyes, they lacked prudent judgment. In addition to Congdon's unfavorable opinion, other objections to Powell were circulating among the C&A Board of Directors. Returning from a C&A Directors meeting in New York in July 1909, Congdon, acting on his own, wrote Powell about their concern. The board, in a "very bearish frame of mind," Congdon confided, had denounced Powell on several counts. The General Superintendent had not given "the mines [his] personal attention." The directors charged that the work was being done by subordinates, and was being performed inadequately. The negative attitude of the board, Congdon continued, had existed for some time, dating back to operation policies which resulted in high costs of production.[12]

Two weeks later, Congdon wrote Powell on a matter of a more immediate concern. To the charge of inattention to duty, Powell's loyalty to the C&A was questioned by the Board of Directors. "There are rumors going around in which you are in the midst, and I conclude that this row is in large part responsible for the stories floating around, and concerning which I wrote you. You should be particularly careful to see that there is no ground for any such rumors," he advised and added, "This rumor business looks nasty to me and ought to be stopped."[13]

By December, there was no question in Congdon's mind as to the necessary course of action. To Charlie Briggs, he wrote, "I still think the sooner we dispense with Mr. Powell's services the better for the company," and to Cole he was even more direct. "He [Powell] is inattentive to our business. . . . The fact is that property worth over forty millions is not receiving the attention from its manager which it should. I am fairly certain that Powell would be wise to resign forthwith."[14]

Congdon planned a rather indirect way to force the issue. In company organization, Powell held the post of Third Vice President. At a forthcoming Board of Directors meeting, Congdon planned to introduce a motion to the by-laws eliminating the office. The move backfired when the Directors unanimously moved to sustain the original by-law. Congdon was disgusted, both with the Directors, most of whom had expressed opposition to Powell, and with himself for not offering a more direct motion which would have outright fired the General Superintendent. The Board had hoped to avoid a confrontation but had only made the matter worse. To Tener, Congdon expressed his dissatisfaction of the whole messy affair, his own actions included. "If I am in the 'Day after the Fair' class," he wrote, "I better buy me a goldheaded cane, and totter among my apple trees, and not delude myself with the idea that I can do any business."[15]

But Congdon was far from tottering among his apple trees. Powell's fate was sealed in a lengthy letter which Congdon wrote to Gordon R. Campbell, Secretary to the C&A and Superior and Pittsburgh Mining Companies. In addition to all of the known charges, Congdon denounced Powell, who, the Duluthian charged, was a tool of Phelps Dodge and had been negligent in his duties to the C&A mines. Under extreme pressure from the Board, Powell tendered his resignation.[16]

Finding and hiring a new General Superintendent would prove almost as difficult as dismissing the old one; nevertheless, Congdon had a replacement in mind. On December 27 he sent a telegram to his close friend, John C. Greenway, General Manager of the Oliver Mining Company on the western Mesabi. It read: "Two of your friends here would be much gratified if you would take charge of their mining interests in Arizona. I think it would be to your advantage to do so and it would please me beyond expression." Earlier, Congdon had been emphatic about replacing Powell with "the very best man we can get for that job," and Greenway, in his opinion, was that person.[17]

Congdon's selection of Greenway was an excellent one, but it was not without its complications. Greenway's credentials both as a mining engineer and as an administrator were impeccable. Educated at Phillips Academy at

Andover, the University of Virginia, and Yale, he had joined the "Rough Riders" during the Spanish-American War where he met Theodore Roosevelt. The two became lifelong friends. Following military service, the young engineer took a job in Michigan as a junior administrator with Oliver Mining Company. His leadership caught the attention of Thomas Cole. Early in 1905, Greenway was appointed General Superintendent for the Oliver on the western Mesabi, and during the next four years he managed not only the company's mining operations but also developed the small communities where Oliver's employees lived.[18]

In November 1909, Greenway's career took a startling and unfortunate turn. Called into the office of William J. Olcott, president of the Oliver, he was summarily fired for disloyalty. Greenway was, of course, dumbfounded. Greenway's biographer concludes that Olcott's motives were "not entirely clear." Greenway appealed the decision to the highest echelon of Oliver officials. After a bitter struggle which created great dissension among Oliver's top administrators, the decision was reversed, but not until Greenway had made some permanent enemies within company ranks. Greenway retained his job, but it was a pyrrhic victory. It was clear that his employment with Oliver was over.

Greenway's last days with Oliver mining coincided with Powell's resignation. Congdon, in his involvement on the western Mesabi, had known and admired Greenway as an engineer and friend for several years. When Congdon and Hartley convinced Tom Cole that the sandy ores of the western Mesabi were worth development, it had been Greenway who built the washing plant at Trout Lake. When Congdon's son, Walter, was injured in an accident while working at Bovey, the father had lived with Greenway while his son recuperated.

To secure Greenway's appointment as general manager in Bisbee, Congdon had to sell the idea to the C&A Board of Directors, some of whom were the same steel company officials who had been responsible for Greenway's dismissal. Following Congdon's nomination of Greenway, one by one the affirmations of Greenway's appointment to the C&A came in. On December 29, the appointment hit a snag. George Tener, who had already wired Congdon his approval of Greenway, wrote Congdon saying that "the New York stockholders have requested me as a director of the Superior and Pittsburgh to delay any action towards appointing Mr. Greenway an officer of that company until they have a little time to consider the matter and lay their views before the board." The following day one of the stockholders wired that while he had a very high opinion of Greenway, he still had reservations. Something, obviously, was wrong.[19]

In a series of letters to Gordon Campbell, Secretary of the C&A Mining Company, Congdon analyzed the problem. The "New York stockholders" who oppose Greenway, he believed, meant those Oliver officials who were responsible for firing Greenway. Congdon concluded that Greenway had been caught between rival forces within the Oliver administration. But the ramifications turned out to be much broader than just Oliver. A high ranking official in the Montana copper mining business (probably John D. Ryan) was contemplating a merger of the entire copper mining industry, and some of the Oliver officials were part of this plan. The details were not entirely clear, but Greenway was a pawn in the affair. Congdon was right. The opposition to Greenway's appointment in Bisbee was only peripheral to a much larger struggle.[20]

It is unknown if Congdon used this information as leverage or if the details became widely known, but Congdon won the C&A Board of Directors approval for the new manager. On January 14, 1910, Congdon wrote Greenway of their decision, "It was thought best to make [the] change in the management as of June first."[21]

In July 1910, after settling his affairs, Greenway left the Mesabi for Arizona to take command of the C&A operations at Bisbee. The past several months had been turbulent times for the mining engineer, but the change, both in job and location, suited him perfectly. He wrote to a friend that he was "delighted with the place, the climate, and the people," and to another acquaintance he enthusiastically declared, "I am in love with this country. It even beats Itasca County, Minnesota." The friendship between Congdon and Greenway had been long-standing, and now the bond became even closer. Congdon, of course, saw his friend whenever he visited Bisbee, and Greenway was a guest at Glensheen whenever his duties would permit.[22]

The new General Manager provided the leadership that had been lacking in the C&A operations. For one thing, the relationship between management and employees took a new turn. Paycheck deductions made directly to the C&A store were eliminated, thus putting the store on a competitive basis with other retailers. Sunday work was abolished—a policy which the workers did not at first approve because it meant a decrease in pay. To increase production, Greenway asked for and received approval from the C&A Board of Directors for a new $3 million smelter. With a favorable relationship between cost of production and market prices the stock of C&A began to rise.[23] Congdon's choice of Greenway as General Manager had been a wise one, and the company began to move steadily ahead.

15
Expansion at Ajo

THE CALUMET AND ARIZONA (C&A) COMPANY HAD BEEN INTERESTED
for some time in expanding their properties, but until Greenway took over the
general manager's position the Board of Directors had been hesitant. Greenway's leadership provided that opportunity. In 1911, the general manager,
quite by chance, was asked to examine a core sample taken from Ajo, an old
and nearly abandoned mining site about one hundred ten miles west of Tucson. One can hardly imagine a location more desolate and remote than Ajo.
Situated in a dry basin surrounded by hills, the mining camp had acquired its
name from the wild garlic (in Spanish, "ajo") which springs to life and
then grows in profusion after brief rain showers.[1]

Greenway dispatched Ira Joralemon, chief geologist for C&A, to examine
the Ajo location. Upon his return, Joralemon's report was not optimistic, but
he thought there might be possibilities. In April 1911, Joralemon, this time
accompanied by Greenway, revisited the site. In Joralemon's words, "Ajo was
at its lowest point. . . ." There were only a few men in camp trying to extract
enough high grade copper to eke out a living.[2]

This handful of men was the last of a long history of miners at Ajo dating all the way back to the pre-California gold rush days. The earliest of the
"modern" efforts to work the area had come from a California company in
1854. It had been a crude operation. Ore was hauled three hundred miles by
ox cart to San Diego and from there shipped all the way to Swansea, Wales for
refining. A shorter route to the sea was implemented by loading the ore on
barges at Yuma and floating them to the mouth of the Colorado. This was
followed by the construction of a small smelter at Ajo, but it was limited in
capacity and production, and the company finally gave up. From that date
until 1911, the history of Ajo was broken into flurries of speculation by promoters of some of the wildest mining schemes ever imagined. The most
successful venture came towards the end of the century when John Boddie
formed the Cornelia Copper Company to operate a mine named for his wife.
Boddie, a dry goods salesman and totally ignorant about mining, was thoroughly taken in by a con artist who claimed to have invented a "perfect

combustion" machine out of which would flow pure copper. Though the contraption was a hoax, Boddie's faith in his Cornelia mine never faltered. As if a change in name would improve his luck, in 1909 Boddie, after several other abortive attempts at mining, reorganized his company into the New Cornelia Copper Company.[3]

Boddie's ore body at Ajo, however, was unlike copper ore found elsewhere. Here the ore was a flinty sulfide, and, some people said, could not be profitably mined. Greenway, however, had no intention of operating a "conventional" copper mine.[4]

Greenway's first job was to option the New Cornelia to the C&A. After six months of hard negotiation with Boddie, Greenway was at last successful in signing an agreement for 70 percent of the 1.2 million New Cornelia shares at $1.60 per share. Boddie retained the remaining 30 percent with which he intended to make a long overdue payment to his stockholders.

The "hit and miss—and mostly miss" techniques heretofore applied at Ajo were not Greenway's style. There is an old dictum in mining which says the first thing to do is "find out how much you have and where it is." To do just this, Greenway brought in Edmund J. Longyear from Minnesota to test-drill for the Calumet and Arizona.[5]

Greenway also acquired the services of another expert, Dr. Louis D. Ricketts, one of the best mining geologists in the southwest. A Ph.D. in chemistry and economic geology from Princeton, Ricketts hardly looked like the board room consultant. "The Doc," as he was affectionately known, cared little for his physical appearance often wearing "shapeless, clay-stained khakis (frequently held up by two nails pinned at the waistline), denim shirt, and slouch hat," but as one individual put it, he was "the best mining engineer in the world." Greenway with his drive, energy and administrative skills, Longyear with his diamond drill, and Ricketts with his technical knowledge made the perfect triumvirate. In 1911, the three men began five years of hard work.[6]

The Calumet and Arizona also began five years of expensive investment. Before mining could proceed some 12 million tons of low grade copper ore (overburden, as it is known in the mining business) must be removed from the surface at an estimated cost of $6 million. Heretofore, the low quality of this ore had caused engineers to discard it as waste. It was Ricketts who headed a research team that devised a technique for treating crushed overburden with an electrolytic process which turned a time consuming effort into a profitable enterprise. A small refining plant was built at the C&A smelter in Douglas, Arizona, but in a short time it proved inadequate, and a second plant was constructed at Ajo. Joralemon reports that "Greenway and Ricketts spent hundreds of thousands of dollars in the experiments."[7]

A major breakthrough came when they reported to the C&A directors that a process had been developed for leaching copper with sulfuric acid at a cost of eight and one-half cents a pound. Copper was selling at the time for fourteen cents a pound which meant a profit of five and half cents. With a new smelter capable of handling an increased capacity, the revolution in mining at Ajo had just begun.[8]

Greenway was determined to mine ore from an open pit. This meant steam shovels, and the general manager felt that only one man was right for the job, Mike Curley, who had worked with Greenway on the western Mesabi. As Joralemon put it, Curley "knew everything there was to know about steam shovel operations."[9]

A number of developments were occurring simultaneously with the refining process. A series of wells, at a cost of $1 million, were drilled into the subsurface water north of the mining site, and from here a pipeline was extended six miles south into Ajo. Another new corporation, the Tucson, Cornelia, and Gila Bend Railroad, constructed a spur line from Gila, a stop on the Southern Pacific, to Ajo, and in January 1916 the first train arrived at the smelter.[10]

As the site grew, a town was taking shape. From his Mesabi experience, Greenway realized that the environment in which his employees lived would be very important to the success of the operation. Congdon agreed and Greenway accepted a plan whereby Hans Lovald, the man who had directed the construction of Westhome in Yakima, would be hired to supervise the construction of the town. After spending a month in California studying Spanish architecture at the missions, Lovald was ready to begin construction. While Ajo, from the beginning, was a company town, it was quite unlike the stereotyped "company towns" of other industrial areas. Built around a plaza, it was far enough away from the mine to eliminate the noise and yet was close enough to be convenient. A company store became the major retailer but operated alongside privately owned businesses. The Ajo school buildings were the most modern of their kind. A water and sewage system, electric power, and paved streets served the community. A modern hospital, where a fee deducted from worker's wages paid for services, attended to the medical needs of Ajo's residents. The town, however, was not ethnically integrated, and a separate housing section was constructed for Mexican employees. Greenway's biographer notes, however, that "although not up to the standards of the rest of the town, the quarter, with durable homes, electricity, running water, a park, and a dance pavilion, far surpassed the squalid Mexican districts that were associated with many of the mines in the Southwest."[11]

Greenway kept Congdon fully informed of the developments at Ajo. Six months after the first drilling began, he wrote Congdon reassuringly that, "Ajo still seems to be worth while." Congdon, never one to allow over-enthusism to cloud a more cautious approach, was skeptical. Commenting to Greenway about the value of another mine, the Duluthian added a postscript derisively pointing out that "[even if the value of the mine] is only half true. . . it beats Ajo." By July 1914, Greenway could offer a definitely encouraging report. Describing the most recent research and development, the general manager concluded with, "I now believe Ajo will net us at least $60,000,000." It was, indeed, a welcome letter.[12]

World copper prices were down in the early summer of 1914, but with the assassination of the heir to the Austro-Hungarian throne in Sarajevo followed by Austria's declaration of war on Serbia on July 18, 1914, Europe rapidly prepared for war. "I shall earnestly recommend that we continue process work at Ajo," Greenway wrote, "I think our policy should be to press forward on this work with an idea of getting Ajo ready for production, if possible, by the time the European demand for copper comes. . . ." A year later the news from Ajo was again encouraging. A rail connection with the Southern Pacific was in the last stages of completion, and work on the new smelter was progressing nicely. The development of Ajo had come at a most fortuitous time. The price of copper was rising, and the future looked promising. At Ajo, as in Bisbee, the investment had been extensive, but once the mine was up and running it yielded steady returns.[13]

Congdon had already involved his two sons in the mining business, and now it was his daughters' turn. With his faith in Ajo bolstered by reports from the mine and from world events, Congdon arranged an investment in copper. "My two daughters, and Miss Currier [a friend], who visited Ajo last winter, are desirous of subscribing for some of the New Cornelia bonds," he wrote Greenway, "if you know of any stockholders who do not care to exercise all their subscription rights, I would be glad to have them assign part of what they do not want to me for the use of these young ladies." Greenway accommodated his friend. It was a wise investment. Copper prices continued to rise as the European crisis mounted.[14]

16
Pacific Panorama

CONGDON'S LEGAL BUSINESS HAD ALWAYS INVOLVED A GREAT DEAL OF travel within the United States, and after his marriage he and his family traveled abroad to Europe and the Middle East. In the winter of 1914 he decided to take a trip to Australia, New Zealand, Malaysia, Hong Kong, and Japan. The trip was a different experience for Congdon, and he kept a diary, entitled *Pacific Panorama*, in which he carefully recorded his daily activities along with his impressions.[1]

The trip combined business with pleasure. The countries of the southwestern Pacific as well as China and Japan have always attracted the interest of people in the Pacific Northwest. Australia and New Zealand relied heavily on an agricultural economy, and their horticultural production competed with American products. The Chinese and Japanese markets have long interested American businessmen. With Congdon's "second home" in Yakima and his interest in fruit production, the western Pacific frequently caught his attention.

At 11:34 A.M. on February 4, the passenger liner, *S.S. Tahiti*, sailed from San Francisco through the Golden Gate for the South Pacific with Congdon aboard. With him were two traveling companions, William A. Dyche and J. L. Alabaster, both longtime friends from Evanston, Illinois. Although whitecaps covered the ocean's surface, the sea was "light" and the northwest wind mild. Their eventual destination was New Zealand. The *Tahiti's* officers, in order to provide their passengers with a sense of time and place, regularly posted the ship's longitude and latitude as well as hour and minute of the day. Congdon began his daily entry with this information and set his watch meticulously, noting each time zone change as the ship traveled westward.[2]

By the end of the second day Congdon had struck up an acquaintance with J. B. Clarkson, a wholesale hardware dealer from Christchurch, New Zealand. In a rather lengthy conversation, Clarkson described New Zealand society for Congdon, explaining at some length the positive values of state socialism. Congdon accepted Clarkson's evaluation without comment, but later noted that the man was the only one whom he had met who made such claims for his government. When queried by Congdon about the advisability of extending a socialistic system to the United States, the New Zealander replied that it would not work in a country where the population was large and heterogenous. Congdon was unconvinced with Clarkson's arguments and ended his diary commentary with, "The only hope of success in N.Z. is education for all."[3]

To relieve the tedium of ocean travel the men played deck quoits (like horseshoes with rope rings tossed at an upright peg) during the day and bridge in the evening. When the sea was rough, Dyche took no meals and remained in his cabin, but Congdon and Alabaster felt no discomfort. As the ship pushed steadily toward the equator the heat rose to an oppressive eighty-six degrees.[4]

The first port of call was Tahiti, where they arrived on February 16. The coral-rimmed harbor, with its breaking surf at the base of 8,000-foot mountains, presented a magnificent view, a much needed change in scenery from the monotonous tedium of endless ocean. Congdon carried no camera, and Alabaster served as the group's photographer, recording on film both people and landscape. Congdon described the native population as "the plumpest people I ever saw. . . a rich brown color. . . unusually large [compared to the] white derelicts floating around here." He concluded that the "Caucasian race apparently breaks down in this environment."[5]

In Tahiti, the visitors bought their first souvenirs and trinkets—Congdon a carved canoe paddle (shipped to son Ned via Wells Fargo Express) and a piece of red and white cotton cloth commonly used by the natives for dresses and trousers. These were the first of a variety of mementos obtained by Congdon, and by journey's end his list of purchases became rather lengthy.[6]

After two days in Tahiti, the journey continued southwest to the island of Roratonga. The lack of a suitable harbor forced an offshore anchorage, but the passengers were taken ashore in a surfboat towed by an "antiquated and decadent" power launch. Anxious to view the island, the three men hired a horse-drawn surrey to transport them about. Their driver introduced himself as Prince John Pirongo, son of the last native king, and Alabaster recorded the occasion with a group picture—including "Prince John." The contrast between Tahiti and Roratonga was immediately recognizable. The latter displayed greater economic prosperity in a more orderly community. Congdon observed the contrast, noting that liquor was unavailable on the island, that there were no Chinese, and that syphilis (which Congdon estimated infected at least 75 percent of the Tahitians) was practically unknown. All of these differences the

Duluthian attributed to the government. Tahiti was ruled by France while Roratonga was governed by New Zealand.

On February 20, the ship weighed anchor for Wellington, New Zealand.[7] Upon their arrival, the view of the city's harbor reminded Congdon of Duluth with its steep hills rising behind the bay. The people of Wellington presented a sharp contrast to both Roratonga and Tahiti. New Zealand was heavily populated by the English, a disturbing presence to Congdon, and he made no effort to hide his distaste. To Congdon, the British were pretentious and considered all other nationalities inferior. The women he pronounced "beastly homely, as usual in an English country. . . . [but] men not so bad." The Americans took lodging at the Grand Hotel—"a genuinely bad English Hotel [sic]." Even the theater, which the three attended that evening, was done, in Congdon's opinion, in poor taste. A bit of risqué humor (a girl, when asked by a woman what a co-respondent was, replied that "it was the wrong man in the right place") went unappreciated by Congdon, and he pronounced the entire production as well as the audience "extremely mediocre." A contingent of about 2,000 New Zealand troops with their tropical knee length uniform trousers caught Congdon's eye, and he thereafter dubbed Wellington, "the City of the Naked Knees." But, he added, they looked "much better than English soldiers."[8]

The socialistic economy drew the Duluthian's criticism. Not only were the large industries owned and operated by the government, which to Congdon was a disturbing intervention, but he also singled out the civil service system for scorn. A reward pension at the end of thirty years service (especially for boys who began work at ages 12 and 14) resulted, he thought, in laziness. "Work is a by-product," he wrote after observing a number of golf courses, bowling greens, tennis courts, and cricket grounds. He concluded that, "this desire to play [particularly in a largely English population] probably makes the people satisfied with their paternalistic government." This condemnation was confirmed when he overheard a conversation which endorsed pending legislation to provide three pounds a week for the unemployed.[9]

Although he had his doubts about the society, the island was beautiful, and to see the countryside Congdon and his two companions took a trip by rail two hundred miles north to Rotorua in the heart of the mountains. This was Maori territory, and the Americans were entertained at dinner with songs and dances by a native group. A side trip by rented automobile the next day brought them deeper into the countryside. Dyche was particularly taken with an ancient wooden battle-ax and made every effort to buy or barter for it, at first to no avail. Only when he raised his offer to six pounds and threw in his white silk handkerchief, was the bargain consummated. Congdon refused the barter system, but purchased a number of items.[10]

At Auckland, the group observed a market where Jonathan apples were displayed. Upon inquiry, Congdon discovered that the fruit had been imported from the Wenatchee Valley in Washington state. The proprietor informed him that the sale price was greater than any fruit he had handled that year. Although Congdon made no note in his diary, the thought of marketing his own fruit in the South Seas surely must have entered his mind.[11]

Economic conditions in the agricultural area were less than placid and stable. Inequitable railroad rates created problems, the government had frightened off investment capital, and, in Congdon's view, labor was trying to run the country. During a recent dock worker's strike, 1000 farmers had taken over the operation of the port. Violence and cries of "Scab!" followed, but a greater tragedy was averted when a cache of explosives was discovered before it could be used. Congdon grudgingly admitted that labor unions were necessary, but he also believed they should not be allowed to run the government.[12]

Life was not all serene in the country. Without comment, Congdon recorded the observations of a woman who blamed much of the trouble on "womans [sic] suffrage [which] puts the power in the hands of the labor people and those seeking to destroy the government. These [labor] men whip their women and make them vote as they wish, while many other women did not vote, thus giving them [the men] the power of government, which power they use to destroy all government." Congdon noted two additional vices—an old age pension program and a state-mandated minimum wage. The first, he observed, was usually spent on liquor while the second destroyed an individual's initiative. All of these, plus endemic English lethargy, contributed to the problems. That the work day did not begin until 8 A.M. drew Congdon's reproach. He wrote, "If the Englishman and those of his blood will not work for himself, he will have to work for more energetic people like the Germans, Japanese or perhaps the Chinese."[13]

Congdon was particularly interested in New Zealand's fruit ranches, and he was able to arrange a visit to the Horticultural Society of New Zealand. Local growers, he was informed, produced a particular variety of apples (unidentified in diary), many of which were exported to South America.

Despite a rather large production, however, apples were imported from Washington state along with canned fruits from California. The Duluthian listened intently and concluded that New Zealand farmers knew little about apple production.[14]

The following day Congdon was taken on a tour of the area where he observed apples, pears, apricots, peaches, and plums. Here he was on familiar ground, and he noted with great interest all aspects of the industry—varieties of fruit, soils and subsoils, orchard spray methods, insecticides, growing season, market selection, irrigation practices, and land prices. Nothing escaped his close inspection.[15]

On March 16, the trio was off again, this time aboard the *S. S. Manuka* bound for Hobart, Tasmania. En route, Congdon had time to reflect on his impressions of New Zealand. The soil, he concluded, was not as fertile as he had expected. Much of the island was nonarable, and land was overpriced. The climate was ideal with sufficient rainfall which permitted farmers to operate marginally well on otherwise poor soil. Sheep and cattle raisers did better than horticultural producers. "Yakima growers never need fear [competition from] them because the people lack the force and ability to do the work necessary to produce an apple in competition with Yakima," he thought. The government, Congdon wrote, "is the limit," and he described as he had done previously and at great length the deficiencies of a socialistic economy. The people were the greatest disappointment. Their chief object, in his opinion, was some form of recreation, an activity which was encouraged by the government. Even the women, he wrote, were "without exception the homeliest and worst dressed" he had ever encountered—including those in England and Germany—a receding chin their most noticeable facial flaw. On the whole the inhabitants of the Southern Island were a cut above their fellow countrymen from the Northern Island but only because the former were largely Scots.[16]

At Hobart, Congdon set his watch back again and recorded in his diary, "Lat. 42° 50′ S. Long. 147° 10′ E. Temperature 8 A.M. 57." The stop in Tasmania was part of a planned itinerary. Here, as in New Zealand, were apple orchards plus a different crop for the South Seas—fields of hops. Again, Congdon took it all in with great interest. In packing the apples, he noted that corrugated cardboard was placed on the sides and ends of the wooden boxes. Upon departure for Melbourne, Congdon wrote that, "Hobart people are better looking and acting than the New Zealanders."[17]

The ship arrived at Melbourne at 7:30 A.M. on Sunday, March 22, and after a good breakfast Congdon and his traveling companions attended services at the Methodist Wesleyan church. A "good pious sermon," Congdon recorded, "but nothing remarkable," and added chauvinistically, "Congregation's appearance not up to that of the Methodist church in Duluth." Afterwards, the three men took a tram out to the ocean where they were shocked by women openly changing into their beach clothes. Indicative of the degenerate conditions, Congdon later noticed with distaste, was the hotel waiter who smoked a cigarette while on duty.[18]

As the originator of an irrigation project himself, Congdon was interested in Australian water systems, and he arranged a field trip with an official of the government's Irrigation Department. During a tour of the watered tracts of land, the official gave him a report on the cost per acre to irrigate. He explained that the major purpose of the department was not to make money but instead to encourage farmers to settle on the land. Sales were limited, however, to whites only—no others need apply.[19]

Congdon was especially interested in the agricultural laborers union. Although permitted by legislation, the same law, in some parts of the country, also made arbitration compulsory. But, the official quickly added, this provision did not prevent strikes, and the only recourse for the growers, in his opinion, was to form producers organizations.[20]

Next, to obtain a balanced view, Congdon called upon one of the prominent labor members of Parliament, whom the Duluthian described as an "honest believer in the 'cause'." Further investigation took him to two additional government officials—the Commonwealth Statistician and the Clerk of the Arbitration Court. The former was particularly outgoing and Congdon learned that, at least in the statistician's opinion, the labor legislation was "Utopian" and "violated economic laws" and therefore was "impossible and must surely fail." These views coincided with Congdon's own and were confirmed the following day when he met with one of the leading labor dispute "solicitors." The man volunteered the information that most of the social legislation had come about as a result of employers "sweating" their workers, i.e., paying low wages while pushing employees beyond their normal endurance. The answer, the solicitor speculated, lay in treating laborers fairly, whereupon the unions, he felt, would become inactive. Congdon spent a total of ten days touring the agricultural areas in the Melbourne vicinity and traveling as far north as Sydney and inland to Toowoomba. During that time he examined all aspects of the agricultural economy of the district. Little, if anything, escaped his attention, and his diary reads like a textbook on agricultural economics.

Regarding the city, he wrote, "I like Melbourne much. It is well laid out with wide streets principally at right angles. Rather flat. Reminds me much of Minneapolis, and has a climate much like that of Los Angeles. The people are altogether the best we have seen anywhere. Apparently energetic and intelligent—they look like Americans." It was a welcome change from New Zealand and Tasmania.[21]

As interesting as it had all been, he was glad to be on his way. "I am glad to leave Australia," he confided to his diary, "This terrible monotony of its mediocrity gets onto ones [sic] nerves after a time. Melbourne is an exception, at least so far as the appearance of the people goes. But as a whole, they are mentally as flat as a desert plain." To Congdon, the explanation was perfectly evident, and he added, "To begin with, they are all English," the cardinal flaw in Congdon's estimation. Based upon his observations of the last two weeks, he predicted that the fate of the British empire was apparent and close at hand, "Today with this modern gush about the brotherhood of man and social uplift, ignorance is ruling the Empire—and it approaches its end."[22]

On August 4, the party was again at sea, bound for a brief call at Port Darwin and then on to Surabaja, Java. The mercury climbed as they neared the equator, and the diary entry reads, "Hot, very hot." His hotel in Surabaja was the most modern in the city. The "private bath" was a tiled tank with a dipper with which to pour water over oneself. A large mosquito-netted bed included a "Dutch wife," a roll of fabric about three feet long to place between one's legs to keep them apart and thus cool.[23]

As had been his previous habit, Congdon toured extensively on the island. A trip to a large crater introduced him to his first volcano. A rail excursion to Djokjakarta on the southern coast and Jakarta on the western end of the island took him to a city of 80,000 where only 1,500 were European. From a Dutch proprietor he purchased several souvenirs to add to his growing collection: buckles, brooches, carved wooden boxes, and several pieces of batik. The processes involved in the production of batik (the word, he explained in his diary, meant 'drawing in wax') fascinated him, and he took great delight in describing in some detail each step—fifteen in all. Needless to say, his curiosity and interest resulted in the acquisition of a large collection from a variety of people and shops. Despite a small Dutch presence, the population was predominantly native Indonesian, and Congdon was less critical of the relationship between the two races than he had been of the New Zealand and Australian populations.[24]

The group had originally planned to travel directly from Java to Hong Kong. Reservations en route, however, could not be obtained, and a delay in Singapore became necessary. As the group moved northward through Southeast Asia, Congdon noticed that a greater proportion of the population was Chinese. Singapore, for example, contained (by Congdon's conservative estimate) 60 percent Chinese.[25]

As long as they were unavoidably detained, the party decided to see something of the nearby area, and with this in mind journeyed northwest to Kuala Lumpur where they visited a rubber plantation. Congdon was immediately interested and insisted that the owners describe the process whereby the trees were tapped and the rubber obtained for processing, all of which he dutifully recorded in his diary. While on a trip to the Batu caves, the trio passed a Hindu temple, and Congdon was moved to reflect on Oriental religion and the effectiveness of Christian missionaries in the Orient. The former, he thought, had little effect on the native population other than to care for them when they were ill. On the subject of the latter he was equally pessimistic. "Religion," he wrote, "is more or less a matter of opinion—and to ask the herds of the East to abandon their opinions and take ours is childishly ridiculous. Especially when the white man, who brings them this religion, stands ready at all times to skin them if he can."[26]

A visit to a tin mine drew as much of Congdon's interest as had the rubber plantation. It was the intensive use of hand labor that attracted his comments. From an open pit mine, native workers using a hoe ("the universal tool of the East") filled their hand baskets with ore and brought them to a concentrator where the tin was separated from the matrix. The superintendent informed Congdon that they expected to reopen a flooded mine by pumping out the water at a rate of 3,000 gallons an hour. A comparison immediately came to Congdon's mind, and he noted to himself that pumps operated on the Mesabi extracted that much each minute.[27]

The stay in Singapore was brief, and the men booked passage on the *S. S. Japan*, a liner of the British India Line, for departure to Hong Kong on May 6. But, as Congdon disdainfully noted, "Being British, she was not ready, of course." The ship, an "old derelict" as Congdon pronounced her, was packed with Chinese passengers bound for their homeland. Most of them carried their worldly goods in all sorts of packages and lived on deck throughout the voyage. The passenger accommodations were less than desirable—undoubtedly, if not deliberately, Congdon was convinced, caused by the ship's owners. When he questioned the ship's captain about the absence of life preservers, the officer registered surprise that anyone should be concerned. Congdon was furious and exclaimed in his diary—and probably to the ship's officers—that the vessel "was a joke as a passenger carrier and its agents liars. . . ." And, he added, "No man should ever take a British ship if he can get a Dutch, German, Japanese, or Austrian or if he can swim to his destination."[28]

Two travelers unofficially joined Congdon and his friends; the first was a Russian (Kossakovsky—no first name recorded) and the second, Bishop Hamilton, a "holiness semi-missionary" (denomination unidentified, but probably Methodist) who was returning home to California. The first of these was a "perfect gentleman;" the second, Congdon barely tolerated.[29]

Clara had asked her husband, should the occasion arise, to inquire about the Methodist schools in Penang (on the northwestern coast of the Malay peninsula). The church operated both a boys and girls school there, as well as several schools in Singapore. Congdon took the opportunity of the bishop's presence to find out more about them. The clergyman reported that all were doing very well, and that the students "eagerly go to these schools." In fact, the bishop elaborated, conditions were so favorable that a Chinese company recently had offered to buy the land, build a schoolhouse, and furnish additional pupils. Congdon could not restrain himself from a diary entry which reads: "As one goes through the East and sees the industry, efficiency and ability of these Chinese, as well as their wealth, it seems ludicrous to bestow charity on them. It would be wiser for Americans to send missionaries to New York City."[30] Their arrival at Hong Kong at noon on May 12 probably avoided any future tension. Here the bishop departed for the Philippines.

Before their departure from the British colony, the three took the ferry to Kowloon and from there a train up the estuary to Canton. Upon arrival, they were met by a launch which conveyed them upriver to their hotel, a magnificent structure built on an island. The journey impressed Congdon as the "most wonderful ride I ever had. It cannot be described." His impression was gained in part from literally thousands of houseboats on the river, some anchored, others moving about propelled by women and girls at the oars.

The hotel, although English, was better than Congdon expected, but a Chinese birthday party which lasted into the early hours of the morning prevented the travelers from getting a good night's sleep.[31]

The next morning they hired three "chairs" and a tour guide. Through the narrow crowded streets they went, past stores and shops of all sorts until they arrived at the Temple of the 500 Genii where they observed life-size wooden figures each representing a different idea or thought (only 499 remained since the figure of the Emperor had been destroyed after the revolution). From here they toured a lacquer shop, where Congdon bought two boxes, and then on to the ancestral temple of the Chan dynasty. Its religious significance reminded Congdon that he had yet to meet anyone (including the bishop) who would argue that the religious teachings by missionaries in the Orient had done any good. Yet, he observed, the Christian missionary is anxious to destroy the Oriental religion in order to substitute his own. As the chairs passed a Roman Catholic church, Congdon qualified his opinions on the Christian religion in the Far East. "I must say that I admire that organization [Roman Catholic]. I believe it is the best organized body of men in the world, and I believe that it is due to the fact that they select their best men as their rulers, not mediocrities."[32]

American foreign affairs became the subject of an editorial in the *Hong Kong Herald* and drew Congdon's approbation. It read,

> [President] Wilson's didactic statement that the United States is not making war against the people of Mexico . . . is the veriest piffle. Not only has the dignity of the President, but the prestige of the United States has received a severe shock when the rebels said that they would not interfere with the Americans so long as the Americans do not interfere with them.

It was embarrassing to read such disparaging remarks in the foreign press about one's own country—however much one might agree. Nevertheless, the editorial, Congdon agreed, summed up the faults of the man who, in his opinion, was incapable of governing the United States.[33]

In the early morning rain and fog of May 19th, the party sailed from Hong Kong and arrived at Nagasaki the following afternoon. Japanese culture, in contrast to other places Congdon had visited, was strikingly different. Their stay here was brief but allowed enough time for souvenir shopping. Late that evening they boarded the train for Moji, the entry point to the island of

Honshu. They encountered few Americans, and those they did meet were either tourists like themselves or employees with the American legation.[34]

From Moji, the party boarded a train for Kobe. The passenger cars were crowded with high ranking Japanese army and navy officers on their way to the funeral of the Dowager Empress in Tokyo. From Kobe, Congdon and his friends motored north through Osaka to Kyoto. Congdon was especially anxious to go to the shop of Y. Namikawa, the "great cloisonné maker"—as one of the travel books described him. Upon arrival, the Japanese craftsman graciously received his guests, and following a tour of his facilities Congdon purchased several pieces. Then it was on to a second and equally well-known cloisonné craftsman, where again Congdon made several purchases.[35]

Congdon had read about two other Japanese art forms, brocades and embroideries, and found two dealers from whom he acquired samples of their work. One of the guide books recommended that tourists view the art form of damascening, or metal inlay. Art critics declared that the Japanese had carried this technique to perfection in recent years. A visit to two shops confirmed this judgment for Congdon and resulted in more purchases.[36]

The following morning Congdon and Alabaster went to the shop of a cut-velvet specialist who had taken first place at a recent world exhibition. Again, Congdon availed himself of the opportunity and acquired several pieces. He expressed surprise that none of the shops were closed despite a national day of mourning for the Dowager Empress, whose body was being transported from Tokyo to Kyoto for burial. The only ceremony which marked the solemn occasion was the tolling of a bell which could be heard throughout the night.[37]

By this time Congdon had become thoroughly attracted to Japan. He admired their precision and efficiency which resulted in a high quality of workmanship. For his wife and daughters he made several purchases: for Clara embroidered crepe silk for a dress, the same material in different colors for Helen and Marjorie, a yellow embroidered silk blouse for Elisabeth, and a piece of embroidered white silk with a stork pattern for himself—simply because he liked it. He could hardly contain his admiration for exquisitely made Japanese products, and he bought other items of fabric and ivory.[38]

Congdon's time in Japan was running out, and it seemed that he could not absorb an appreciation of their culture fast enough. The trains were still crowded, this time with army and navy officers returning from the funeral.

Congdon traveled first class and found himself in the company of some of Japan's highest ranking military personnel, ranging from generals to vice admirals. An officer provided their names and titles to Alabaster who relayed them to Congdon, who listed them in his diary and included drawings of the insignia braid on their uniform sleeve cuffs. It was a unique experience.[39]

On May 28, Congdon received a cable indicating that a legal case in which he was involved was scheduled for trial June 24. He immediately booked passage on the *Empress of India* for June 6 (scheduled to arrive at Vancouver June 18) and cabled home his itinerary.

Congdon had not visited Tokyo, and he was determined to remain long enough at least for a short stay there. Although Alabaster and Dyche would have liked to remain with Congdon, they chose to sail for home on the *S.S. Minnesota*. The next day Congdon left for Tokyo.[40]

The brief stay in Japan's capital was most enjoyable. His room at the Imperial Hotel contained a private bathroom — the first he had seen in a long while. Congdon shopped, went to the theater (he could not understand the language, but the Japanese style of acting fascinated him), and lunched with an American newspaper editor. He wanted to see the house (a national shrine) of Maresuke Nogi, the military officer who had led his country to victory in the Russo-Japanese War. It was one of the few disappointing experiences in Japan. The house was small (Congdon described it as a weather-beaten frame house of the North Dakota type) constructed from "plain lumber and plaster." A faint blood stain on a mat marked the spot where the warrior hero had committed suicide in order to "follow the Great Emperor."[41]

The most spectacular site in Tokyo was the tombs of the "Forty-seven Ronin," men who had committed hara-kiri as an act of devotion to their leader. Congdon approached the shrine with due respect. That evening he paid them homage in his diary, "To my mind the admiration and respect which the Japanese pay to this famous act of personal loyalty and devotion throws much light on their character, and shows them to be large-souled."[42]

Japanese dedication to their culture impressed the American, and while he did not completely understand their customs he felt that here was a society which was first among the Oriental people. At a luncheon with Carl Crow, the manager of the *Tokyo Advertiser*, the newspaperman described various Japanese objects and customs as a "moral anchorage." But, alas, Crow quickly added, the present generation has lost its religion and has nothing to replace it.[43]

But Crow's estimation did not deter Congdon's admiration. Prophetically, he wrote,

> See what the Jap. [*sic*] has done. First, and above all he is absolutely his own master. No white nation ventures to tell him what to do. No other yellow or black country can say this. Second [,] he has in operation in his county every modern invention known to the world, and he is running it himself, not hiring white men to do it, as is the case of those yellow peoples who have any of these things. Third [,] he has all the charitable organizations, such as hospitals, asylums, etc. which any civilized nation has, and can justly claim to be a civilized people, as they are. . . . They do not have the hypocrisy that the Anglo Saxon has . . . therefore they do not pretend to such virtue as we do, and perhaps they do not have it. But using virtue in its larger sense, I believe they do. With their centralized authority and their submission thereto, their intelligence, their physical endurance, I believe Japan will be a great power for a long time.

Although Congdon had seen very little of the Japanese military, he speculated on their quality based on what he had observed in other parts of the Japanese culture. "I believe," he wrote with conviction, "that the Japanese are invincible as soldiers, other things being equal, against the same number of soldiers from any other nation, and that they will remain so until the doctrine of the New Democracy and the Uplifters permeates them and convinces them that they are all the equal of the Mikado and as fit to rule as he—which doctrines will promptly dispose of them, and put them in the same class as the Englishman and the American viz: good promisers and talkers but poor doers." A little later during his stay he returned to the same theme: "If we dont [*sic*] have a war with Japan for 25 years, and if we keep on our course of the last 5 years for those 25 years, and Japan is amply financed, I have no doubt that she will defeat us."[44]

On June 6, Congdon sailed for home on the *Empress of India*, a British passenger liner. He did not confide a sense of nostalgia to his diary, but there could be no doubt that Japan left a profoundly deep and lasting impression.

The trip home was uneventful. As on the voyage west across the Pacific, Congdon dutifully reversed his watch according to the ship's position. Upon arrival at Victoria, British Columbia, the ship was put into quarantine, but the delay was short. A change of vessel was required, and the following morning the *S. S. Iroquois* with Congdon aboard sailed for Seattle. From there he caught the eastbound Northern Pacific for North Yakima.[45]

En route, a perusal of the newspapers revealed that little had changed in national politics and economic conditions during his absence. Disturbed (and not without some political prejudice—and perhaps with an unconscious anticipation of how the Japanese might have handled a similar situation) he wrote, "Everybody [in the United States] seems to be trying to destroy everybody else, not only financially but in every way." President Woodrow Wilson, he judged, continued to lead the country down ruinous paths. It was a rude re-entry into America.[46] The brief stopover at North Yakima set his mind a little more at peace. Walter and the new ranch supervisor met him at the train. "The ranch looks fine," he noted with pleasure. Heermans came over from Olympia, and the two of them took a tour of the orchards and alfalfa fields. Congdon approved. "Looks good," he wrote with satisfaction.[47]

With Walter accompanying him, they left for St. Paul where Congdon conferred with the other attorneys who were involved in the case for which he had returned. Then he took the train north to Duluth where Clara, Marjorie, Helen, and Ned met him. "Mighty glad to get home," he penned with genuine sincerity.[48]

17

National Affairs

THE FIRST DECADE AND A HALF FOLLOWING THE TURN OF THE CENTURY marked a particularly turbulent period in American life as the nation searched for stability and order. Nowhere was the unrest more evident than in economics and politics.[1]

The agrarian reform movements of the late nineteenth century had pointed the way toward a new relationship between private enterprise and government. It remained for the progressive movement to forge the tie between the two. It was time, the progressives argued, to actively involve the agencies of government in restoring equality and opportunity to industrial America. If the invisible forces of economic determinism had created a divided society, the instruments of government could be used to set matters right.

The reform impulse was not lost on the industrialists and businessmen. Efficiency became the credo of business, and now they hoped to apply it to government. Chambers of commerce, now organized more effectively than ever, stressed the need for cleaner, safer, and more economically operated cities. Reform-minded businessmen began to visualize the ideal municipality as an extension of commercial values: a clean, attractive community with an atmosphere of growth and progress which served to raise the level of the economy.

Reform knew few political, social, or economic boundaries, but it was the Republican party that spearheaded the movement, if for no other reason than its control of Congress and the presidency. The business community, at first wary and even alarmed at the ascendancy of Theodore Roosevelt to the presidency following the assassination of McKinley, came to understand and to be reassured by his staunch advocacy of regulated American capitalism. By 1904, after his election to the office in his own right, it was clear that the president meant to exercise the powers of the federal government to police business and require a manner of operation which was consistent with the public interest. To many industrialists and businessmen, this meant a restoration of capitalistic competition. Even the goliaths were "safe" so long as they behaved themselves.

Chester Congdon believed strongly in the principles of the Republican party. It was this political body, after all, which had saved the Union, which had efficiently utilized the natural resources of the United States, and which had developed the forces of industrialism that had rapidly turned America into one of the foremost nations of the world.

But, there still remained, Congdon noted, large corporations which sought to place themselves above the harmonious scheme envisioned by the progressives. The panic and depression of 1907 gave evidence that disruptive forces could still attack, if not destroy, the new economic order. Writing to his former law partner, William Billson, who had retired to Pasadena, Congdon was convinced that the financial distress was the work of financiers who were anxious to "do two things: first, to show the American people what would happen . . . if they were so foolish as to elect a President [Roosevelt] who would not listen to their orders [and] second, they propose to fight it out with labor, and compel labor to be more tractable and to be content with lower wages." With these two goals in mind, the Duluthian concluded that, "it is my own judgment that they precipitated the panic in this country." The particular culprits in this case, Congdon was certain, were Morgan and Rockefeller who had, over a period of time, hoarded currency only to loan it out at exorbitant interest rates at a later date.

In addition, although Congdon did not believe the move was entirely engineered, the larger corporations would absorb smaller ones which succumbed to financial distress. The evidence of this could be seen in the two metal industries, steel and copper, with which Congdon was most intimately acquainted. "I do not think," he confided to Billson, "that any of these people are anxious to see the market improve at present, at least not until they have acquired all the loot which they are able to carry." Clearly, as Congdon saw it, the giants of industry and finance were taking an unfair advantage. The countervailing force must be government action.[2] Teddy Roosevelt could not have said it more succinctly.

If governmental action were called for, then it remained for responsible citizens to become involved. By January 1908, Congdon was already working with prominent Republicans in Minnesota to select delegates to the national convention. Frank B. Kellogg, a St. Paul lawyer, wrote to Congdon asking the Duluthian to sound out political sentiment regarding his status within the Republican party in northeastern Minnesota. Congdon's reply was reassuring.

There was, he wrote Kellogg, considerable popularity for the St. Paul lawyer in the north which "will favor your selection as a delegate. . . and your re-election to the National Committee."[3]

William Howard Taft, Roosevelt's Secretary of War and the president's hand-picked successor, would go into the convention with a distinct, but not unchallenged, advantage, and Congdon was anxious to have Kellogg, a Taft supporter, represent Minnesota to assure Taft's nomination. Delegates to the national convention were selected by a series of caucuses beginning with each county, and these meetings were followed by caucuses at the district level where delegates were selected to attend the national convention. Writing to Greenway, Congdon reviewed the delegates who might be chosen, and again expressed his preference for Taft. Current political opinion had it that "Taft men" would be elected delegates, but Congdon took nothing for granted.

Despite Roosevelt's influential endorsement, Taft was not entirely confident of his nomination, and he wrote Congdon explaining that Kellogg had recommended the Duluthian as one who had a "good opportunity for observation [and a] fine political judgment, and can give me the situation as it is." Congdon's reply was positive and he predicted that, "Unless conditions materially change in Minnesota, it will send to the National Republican Convention a delegation which will support you through thick and thin." But, he added, "your supporters should keep busy." He concluded with a statement of his own unqualified stand, "I am profoundly impressed with the importance to the country of the election of the right man this Fall [sic] for President."[4]

Congdon and the others were not to be disappointed. William Howard Taft was nominated at the summer Republican convention, in large part due to pressure applied by Roosevelt. In the fall elections, Taft won easily over the old Democratic war horse, William Jennings Bryan, but his plurality was less than Roosevelt had received in 1904. The Republicans retained control of the Congress although several state governorships fell to the Democrats. On the brighter side, in each state lost to the Democrats, Taft ran far ahead of other Republicans on the ticket. With the presidency safely in the hands of a man who Roosevelt thought would continue his example as a forceful executive, Teddy went off to Africa to hunt big game. J.P. Morgan quipped, "I hope the lions win."

It is not fair to assign to Taft all of the blame for what happened in the next few months. The Republican party which he inherited was already divided.

Roosevelt had been the bonding agent which held the party together by sheer weight of his forceful personality; that cohesive element was now gone.

Smoldering troubles within the GOP developed into flame almost immediately with the departure of Roosevelt. A liberal wing of the Republicans (the "insurgents") in the Congress had long hoped to curb the power of Joe Cannon, Speaker of the House. During the first month of Taft's presidency, Cannon threw down the gauntlet with a speech in which he advocated a revised higher tariff schedule. The insurgents, particularly those from the agrarian Middle West accepted the challenge, and the battle was on, with Taft forced to choose sides. The president wavered between the conflicting factions of his party, finally sided with Cannon, and suffered humiliation with him when the insurgents won.

Next, Taft's handling of the Payne-Aldrich tariff legislation was disastrous for the president. The insurgents favored a lower tariff schedule than the one proposed. In a somewhat ambiguous final version, however, the bill failed to provide for any downward revision. The agrarian wing of the Republican party was up in arms. Taft only poured fuel on the fire when he announced in a speech at Winona, Minnesota that the bill was "the best tariff ever passed by the Republican party."

But the real affront to the Republican reformers, and especially to Roosevelt, came during the battle over conservation. Taft had appointed Richard Achilles Ballinger, a conservative Seattle lawyer, as his Secretary of the Interior. The new Secretary and his backers took opposing sides from Gifford Pinchot, Roosevelt's appointee to head the newly created Department of Forestry. Ballinger had previously served as Commissioner of the General Land Office, and, following his appointment as Secretary of the Interior, it was charged that while serving in his former job he had turned over to private interests some federal coal lands in Alaska. The accusation turned into a nasty entanglement, especially after Gifford Pinchot became involved by bringing the matter before the Congress. Open warfare erupted, with Taft caught in the middle, between Ballinger and Pinchot. Taft, much to the dismay of the insurgents, aligned himself with Ballinger. As if this were not enough, the president fired Pinchot.

These three episodes were not the only trouble areas between the Old Guard and the insurgents, but they accentuated the greatest differences between Taft and Roosevelt. By early 1909, the conservatives in the Midwest, where the disagreements between the two groups were most pronounced, began to form "Taft Republican Clubs" and the insurgents organized into "Progressive Republican" groups.

When Roosevelt returned from Africa in June 1910 it was inevitable, given his personality and the divided party, that he re-enter politics. Roosevelt, however, refused to undercut his successor, and announced that he fully expected Taft to be the Republican nominee in 1912. Indeed, the former president vehemently lashed out at both the Old Guard and the Progressives. A speech which he delivered in Kansas, however, seemed to indicate that while he supported party unity, his sentiments lay with the reformers. Congdon, as well as the rest of the nation, grew increasingly confused over Roosevelt's actions.

The off-year congressional elections of 1910 illustrated just how deeply the party split was. The Democrats, for the first time since 1892, won control of the House. The Republicans retained a bare majority in the Senate. In the Midwest, solid victories for the agrarian progressives indicated that there would be a new challenger in the party: Robert M. LaFollette, insurgent from Wisconsin.

In 1911, Roosevelt gradually moved toward his decision to run for the presidency in 1912. The differences between him and Taft were steadily widening. In late January 1912, Roosevelt, acting out a carefully orchestrated draft, threw his hat into the ring. LaFollette had taken himself out of the race by delivering a long and rambling speech which cast doubt upon his capabilities. The Republican candidacy was reduced to two. The decision would rest with the delegates to the national convention.

The Republican convention in Chicago in the summer of 1912 was one of the most bitter political battles ever fought. The contest for delegates was vicious, but the nomination was never in doubt. During the months leading up to the convention, the Republican National Committee reviewed the credentials of both the Taft and Roosevelt delegates. Time after time the contested seats were awarded to Taft. The first demonstration of power came when the Taft forces elected Elihu Root convention chairman. The climax came when Taft won the nomination on the first ballot, whereupon Roosevelt and his followers walked out to form their own Progressive Party. A reporter wrote that Roosevelt looked like an "amiable orangutan," but the candidate announced that he "felt as strong as a bull moose." The latter name stuck, and the bull moose became the nickname as well as the symbol of the new party.

The Democrats, jubilant over the split in the opposition party, could taste victory long before November. There were really only two major contenders for the nomination: Speaker of the House Champ Clark and New Jersey Governor Woodrow Wilson. After a long series of political maneuvers, Wilson won the nomination.[5]

Roosevelt's political mutiny left the Minnesota Republicans angry and sick at heart. In the opinion of many people he had betrayed the party and sullied his political reputation beyond repair. Congdon believed that a far better strategy would have been for Roosevelt to "retire to a dignified life at Oyster Bay [the Roosevelt home on Long Island]." Had he done this, Congdon believed, "nothing in the world could prevent his nomination for the Presidency in 1916."[6]

Everything had been thrown into turmoil, including the way Minnesota Republicans should respond to recent events. How much loyalty was owed the Bull Moosers by the state Republican party, many of them former Roosevelt supporters? In the confusion there was some speculation over the responsibilities of the Republican electors in the state and their sworn duty to cast a ballot for their party's nominee. The confusion spread to the role of Minnesota's Republican National Committee. Was this body to set the policy for Minnesota Republicans?

Irving A. Caswell, Republican Party National Committeeman for Minnesota, sought Congdon's advice and received a long letter in reply. First of all, the Duluthian wrote, we must identify what a faction of the Republican party is trying to accomplish. They (Roosevelt's supporters) are, Congdon stated, attempting to create and organize both a national and a state "Roosevelt party." Second, since one of the state's gubernatorial candidates had declared in favor of the Bull Moose, the same people were trying to nominate and elect this candidate governor. And third, they were trying to control the organization of the Republican party in Minnesota.

On the first of these objectives, the creation of a Roosevelt party, Congdon declared in his letter, the attempt was doomed to failure largely because the rebel cause was not built on issues or principles but rested solely on the personality of its candidate. Congdon denounced Roosevelt's talk of principles as "tommy rot." In the Duluthian's opinion, Roosevelt had sold his political soul to corporate interests who made large contributions to his campaign expenditures. That Roosevelt could distinguish between "good" and "bad" corporations (as he claimed), Congdon seriously doubted, and the "new party is to be founded to make president a man who is devoid of truth, patriotism, honor or shame."

Roosevelt had stated that judicial opinions unfavorable to Progressive programs might be reviewed by popular ballot, and this was particularly repugnant, Congdon wrote. In his view, the stability and order of the nation was based upon principles stated in the Constitution and laws. These principles, Congdon argued, were not subject to the interpretation of any one man or electoral whim, as Roosevelt proposed to make them, but must be interpreted by the courts.

Congdon continued to condemn Roosevelt. He believed that the Republican party must, without question, remain with those persons who had been chosen to head it long before the Bull Moose split. Congdon was emphatic that the electors were morally and legally bound to cast their vote for the Republican candidate. The party organization must prevail.

In Congdon's view there were several choices which party dissidents might take: first, leave the party if there was a disagreement on principles; second, stay in the party and fight for progressive principles, or third, stay in the party and betray it by delivering it wholly or in part to its enemies [i.e., continue to call yourself a Republican but deliver the electoral machinery to the insurgent Progressives.] Only the first two, in Congdon's view, were honorable choices, and he concluded that, "the majority will agree that the wise progressive will adopt the second alternative."[7]

In the presidential election of 1912, Roosevelt won a plurality of Minnesota votes beating the Democratic candidate, Wilson, by a margin of 19,568 ballots. Taft ran a poor third.[8] At the national level, Wilson won the presidency. The only consolation for Congdon was that his state had not gone Democratic.

The election of 1916 four years later was also a troublesome time for Congdon. Woodrow Wilson, whom Congdon regarded as quite unfit to occupy the White House, had come to the presidency espousing the principles of his New Freedom. Where Roosevelt had been willing to accept corporate growth and even monopoly of business enterprise provided the large industrial giants practiced self-discipline, Wilson saw an industrial society composed of smaller competitive units. Competition was the key to industrialism, and the government, if it must intervene, ought to use its powers to regulate monopoly and thus strengthen competition. In Wilson's words, "America should restrict the wrong use of competition [so] that the right use of competition will destroy monopoly." Congdon agreed in principle with Wilson, but it was

Wilson's reluctance to take strong government action against the malefactors of wealth that offended Congdon.

A second issue disturbed Congdon. By mid-1915, and the opening days of the campaign of 1916, the issue of America's reaction to the conflict in Europe was uppermost in the public mind. Despite repeated German acts of aggression against the United States, Wilson chose merely to lecture them on their international responsibilities. The nation was divided. On the one hand, Wilson had kept the United States out of war; on the other, Congdon believed, he had done so at the cost of America's honor. Wilson's statement that a "nation could be too proud to fight," had only encouraged the Germans to grow bolder in their submarine attacks.

To his friend, John C. Greenway, Congdon wrote, " The greatest disaster that could occur to the country would be to continue the Democratic party in power, because they have demonstrated not only their ignorance of the need for self-protection but they have shown that they have no knowledge whatever of the motives which move nations." Anticipating that Greenway might favor the election of Theodore Roosevelt (who had been trying to goad Wilson into taking stronger measures by denouncing the president for his "spineless" treatment of "professional pacifists, flubdubs and mollycoddles"), Congdon tried to persuade his Arizona friend that Roosevelt was not the best man. The Bull Moose had aroused too many animosities, in Congdon's opinion, in the campaign of 1912. Rather, in the next election Congdon preferred "to nominate a Republican with progressive ideas and principles [and] one who had staid [sic] with the party." William E. Borah, Republican Senator from Idaho, would have been Congdon's choice.[9]

The only point upon which Greenway agreed with Congdon was that the Democrats ought to be turned out of power. "The whole result [preparedness] will depend largely upon the attitude of the occupant of the White House," the mining engineer emphasized, "With this thought in mind, the name of one man immediately suggests itself, Roosevelt." But, as much as Roosevelt would have liked to have taken the national helm, he knew it was impossible, and he had informed Greenway that Hiram Johnson, his running mate in 1912, would be a good choice. If Johnson were not first on the ballot, Roosevelt would support Charles Evans Hughes with Johnson as vice president.[10]

After the political circus of 1912, Congdon hoped that the Republican convention of 1916 would be more placid, that the delegates would arrive "largely uninstructed," and that the selection of the nominee would be made "after due conference."[11] If his expectations were not entirely realized, at least the proceedings came off with unusual smoothness, and the nomination went to Charles Evans Hughes. The only mildly disruptive element (if anything Roosevelt did could be described as "mildly") at the convention was the former president's attempts to convince the party to adopt a more vigorous defense stance against Germany. Roosevelt was to have his chance, however, when he received the nomination from the Progressives. The former Bull Mooser, however, realized it was all in vain and declined with a recommendation that the convention disband and support Hughes (some of the delegates did as Roosevelt suggested while others went over to the Democrats).

Woodrow Wilson won the Democratic nomination and campaigned on keeping the peace. His more vocal supporters adopted the slogan, "He kept us out of war!" Congdon's views were more accurately prophetic. "If Mr. Wilson is re-elected," he wrote Greenway, "I forsee before the expiration of his second term a war in which hundreds of thousands of American youth will needlessly die. I fear this will happen even if he is not re-elected. Never, since Lincoln's time, was it so important to have a real man as President as it is now."[12]

Wilson went on to win the election of 1916 and was inaugurated for a second term. When the Germans announced the continuation of unrestricted submarine warfare, Wilson, on April 2, 1917 asked a joint session of the Congress for a declaration of war. The Senate approved on April 4, 1917, and the House concurred two days later.

When the Republican party national convention met in Chicago in 1916, the office of Minnesota's National Republican Committeeman was held by E. B. Hawkins of Duluth. His predecessor, Irving A. Caswell, had been removed from office by the national committee in the spring of 1912 on charges of disloyalty (Caswell had been a Roosevelt supporter). Hawkins, therefore, held the position temporarily until a formal election could be held at the convention.[13]

Rumor had it that Caswell wanted the job again and would be a candidate, but instead he announced that the demands of time and financial resources were beyond his limits. The news came as somewhat of a surprise since it was estimated by those present that thirty-seven out of a total forty-eight votes were Caswell's. Upon news of his withdrawal, his supporters nominated Chester Congdon as their candidate.

Congdon's name was not the only one put forth. In what seemed like a spur-of-the-moment decision, the person who was supposed to have nominated Caswell changed his mind and instead nominated U.S. Senator Knute Nelson. The switch was interpreted by some of the delegates as the work of former governor Adolph O. Eberhart to stop Congdon. One of the delegates was later quoted saying, "It [the nomination of Nelson] was clearly a misuse of the senator's name in a brazen attempt to embarrass the delegates and mix up the situation. There was not a man present who was not a friend of the senator and who would not have voted for him were he a candidate, but we knew that he was not and would not be." The delegate, who preferred to remain anonymous, further declared that "Mr. Eberhart will find that he has created more trouble for himself in his campaign for United States Senator than he will care to dwell much upon."

Despite protests, a roll call vote was taken on the two candidates. Many of the delegates who voted for Congdon made it clear that in doing so they did not intend to cast dispersions on Senator Nelson. In the balloting Congdon received thirty-four votes and Nelson five. In view of such a lopsided decision, the Eberhart ploy (if that is what it was) had failed, and following a motion to cast a unanimous ballot for the majority candidate, Congdon was elected. From the rejected minority came an explanation of the Nelson nomination. It was not, they explained, an attempt by Eberhart to gain strength and votes by nominating Nelson. Rather, they did not like to see "an important office passed about in this manner," and they had chosen this method to register a protest. Whatever had happened, Minnesota had a new Republican Party National Committeeman. Moreover, the choice of Chester Congdon was regarded very favorably throughout the state of Minnesota.[14]

Nineteen sixteen was a busy year for the Congdon family. There was a heavy snowfall in January, and it looked like spring would be a long time coming. In early February, Chester went to the Pacific Northwest on business. Upon his return, he reported that he had never seen as much snow between Puget Sound and Duluth. Later the same month, he was invited to give an address to the Methodist Episcopal Church Men's League. Congdon chose the subject of patriotism, and the speech consisted of more substance than the usual rhetoric on the subject. Two days later, Chester and Clara left for the East, she to visit relatives and friends, he to take care of business affairs. The couple arrived home in time for David Ericson, a Duluth artist, to paint Clara's portrait.

In April, Chester, Clara, Elisabeth, and Marjorie accompanied by Walter and his family, journeyed to Westhome in Yakima. The Heermans family from Olympia came over for a short visit. It was a delightful occasion. Clara recorded in her journal, "Many visitors and much activity during the two months we spent there." Chester was forced to depart earlier than the family in order to attend the Republican convention in Chicago. Traveling by automobile, the rest of the family went through Yellowstone and arrived in Duluth on July 10.

Between August 16 and 19, Chester was ill "with pain like indigestion." Two doctors saw him, but could find nothing seriously wrong. A week later he felt well enough to visit some friends at their home on the Brule River. Late September saw him off again to Yakima, this time alone; afterwards, he and Clara traveled to New York in early October. Chester had business in St. Paul in early November, but he went home to Duluth to cast his ballot for Hughes. The early election returns were encouraging, and on November 7, election day, the family held a celebration dinner in honor of what they mistakenly thought would be a Hughes victory. That same evening Chester left for St. Paul, fully expecting to wait there for the official announcement of Hughes election. Congdon was disappointed when Wilson's victory was announced.

On November 10, he called Clara from his apartment in the St. Paul Hotel saying that he did not feel well. Doctors were called, and they informed Clara that she should summon the children. Walter, Ned, Elisabeth, and Helen came as quickly as possible. Marjorie was visiting in the East, Robert was in school, and both were delayed in their arrival.[15]

The next few days were critical. Dr. Hubert Davis at first thought it was an attack of pleurisy but quickly realized it was much more serious. Several days passed before the doctors identified the problem as a blood clot on one lung. Both doctors advised against trying to move him to a hospital. November 20 was a particularly bad day and his suffering increased. At 7:00 A.M. on November 21, 1916, after suffering an acute dilation of the heart, which produced a pulmonary embolism, Chester Adgate Congdon passed away. He was sixty-three years, five months, and nine days old.[16] His body was placed in the private railroad car of John H. McLean, General Superintendent of the Oliver Mining Company, and brought to Duluth.

The *Duluth Evening Herald* published an editorial summarizing public sentiment regarding Congdon's death. It read (in part):

> He was always a good citizen, eager to have his part in every forward move-ment in directions that he judged to be wise, and his share in the develop-ment of better things in public life in this state had been far greater than many people know. Not because he was a rich man, but because he was a good man with sound instincts and large capacities for service and with an ever increasing will to give his energy and means to public enterprises . . . will his death be a blow to the community, the state, and the nation.[17]

The funeral was held on November 24. Clara's journal entry for that day reads, "It was cold but lovely and quiet in the afternoon."

A full and distinguished life had come to an end.

Notes

CONGDON ANCESTRY

1. Guilford G. H. Congdon files, unpublished mss., information compiled by Marjorie Congdon, hereafter cited as G.G.H.C., files; Bertie [Albert Congdon] to Clara [Bannister Congdon], January 6, 1935, Chester Adgate Congdon Papers in possession of Mary and William P. Van Evera, Duluth, Minnesota, hereafter cited as CAC Papers, VEC (Van Evera Collection); there may have been an earlier ancestor, John Congdon, Benjamin's father, who emigrated from Wales to Virginia, see Guilford Congdon's marginal note in entry on "Chester A. Congdon," *The National Cyclopaedia*, Vol. 17, p. 342, photocopy in CAC Papers, VEC.

2. G.G.H.C., files; *Minutes of the Annual Conferences of the Methodist Episcopal Church for the Year 1868* (New York: Carlton and Lanahan, 1868), "East Genesee Conference," 154, General Commission on Archives and History, The United Methodist Episcopal Church, Madison, New Jersey, hereafter cited as *Minutes, ME Church* (1868).

3. *Minutes, ME Church* (1868), 154.

4. Whitney R. Cross, *The Burned-Over District: The Social and Intellectual History of Enthusiastic Religion in Western New York, 1800–1850* (Ithaca: Cornell University Press, 1950), 3–13.

5. Clara Bannister Congdon, "Journal," 10, Glensheen files, hereafter cited as CBC, "Journal," notes that "in those days appointments were made for one or two years so they [the Methodist Episcopal clergy] moved often"; Clara's "Journal" consists of a summary of yearly events, highlights, and activities of the family beginning with 1853; some specific dates by month and day are recorded; the pages are unnumbered; the entries are in chronological order with the exception of the first few entries which are repeated (with new wording and a typewritten chronology of events inserted); some of the events recorded in the "Journal" were entered on a different date from that upon which the event occurred, e.g., occurrences in her husband's life before they met; in view of the foregoing, when using material from Clara's "Journal" in the narrative and citing a reference thereto, it seemed expedient to number the pages and refer to those page numbers in the "Notes;" the original "Journal" is in the Glensheen files without numbered pages; a photocopy in author's possession contains the numbered pages; *Minutes, ME Church* (1868), 154–155.

6. G.G.H.C., files.

7. CBC, "Journal," 10; *Minutes, ME Church* (1868), 155, gives the daughter's name as "Nellie," but this is an error; CBC, "Journal," 11, the ME Church governing board hoped to strengthen its churches on the Pacific Coast, and there was some discussion about moving Congdon to California; nothing, however, developed regarding the move.

8. *Minutes, ME Church* (1868), 154–155; Bertie [Albert] to Clara, January 6, 1935, CAC Papers, VEC; G.G.H.C., files.

9. *Corning Democrat,* May 28, 1868; *Minutes, ME Church* (1868), 155; Minutes of the ME Church list the cause of death as "typhoid pneumonia" while the *Corning Democrat* cites "angina and heart attack." Since there is no record of typhoid which turned into pneumonia, death probably resulted from a heart attack.

10. *Minutes, ME Church* (1868); N. B. Harmon and H. E. Hiller, "Penisons, Board of," in Nolan B. Harmon, ed., *The Encyclopedia of World Methodism* (New York: The United Methodist Publishing House, 1974), 1880; Carolyn Ocheltree to author, May 9, 1988; in the years listed below, the ME Church provided compensation to the surviving members of the Congdon family in the following amounts:

1868 – NONE	1873 – NONE
1869 – $50.00	1874 – $66.43
1870 – $40.00	1875 – $29.77
1871 – NONE	1876 – NONE
1872 – $35.14	(NONE THEREAFTER)

11. Bertie and Mother to Chester [Adgate Congdon], June 20, 1869; Bertie and Mother to CAC, July 25, 1869; Bertie and Mother to CAC, May 1, 1870; Bertie and Mother to CAC, May 15, 1869, all CAC Papers, VEC.

12. Wayne E. Morrison (compiled by), "Town and Village of Ovid, Seneca County, New York," Copyright 1980; oral interview by author with Wayne E. Morrison, Ovid, New York, May 28, 1988; oral interview by author with Wisner Kinne, Ovid, New York, May 28, 1988; CBC, "Journal," 5.

SYRACUSE UNIVERSITY

1. *The University Herald* [student newspaper], October 31, 1873; in 1874, the newspaper ran an editorial protesting the reduced tuition for sons and daughters of Methodist clergymen; the tuition advantage in 1871, however, presented an opportunity which could not be turned down; *The University Herald,* October 26, 1874, Syracuse University Archives, Syracuse University, hereafter cited as Syracuse University Archives; CBC, "Journal," 7.

2. *The University Herald,* October 31, 1873; the history position was taken by Rev. Charles W. Bennett, who in later years became a personal friend and correspondent of Congdon's.

3. W. Freeman Galpin, *Syracuse University: The Growing Years* (Syracuse: Syracuse University Press, 1960) 2:1–20.

4. J.P. Durbin to Issac Owen, May 31, 1850, quoted in Rockwell D. Hunt, *History of the College of the Pacific, 1851–1951* (Stockton: College of the Pacific, 1951), 1–10; CBC, "Journal," 5.

5. Hunt, *College of the Pacific,* 4, 6–37, 210–213. The institution's name, however, was short-lived. The inclusion in the title of the word "Wesleyan" was a duplication of several other Methodist schools, and the California founders preferred a name more

appropriate with the setting. At the first meeting of the Board of Trustees, the name was changed to "University of the Pacific." Under this title, the school continued until 1911 when the name was changed to "The College of the Pacific."

6. Hunt, *College of the Pacific*, 34–37; CBC, "Journal," 16, 19.

7. Clara B. Congdon, June 1945, typewritten page, CAC Papers, VEC.

8. CBC, "Journal," 16–17; Clara B. Congdon to Executive Secretary [Syracuse Alumni Association], June 23, 1945; Elisabeth Congdon, untitled typewritten page, May 1950, CAC Papers, VEC; Alumni Files, Syracuse University Archives.

9. *Syracuse University Catalog* (1871), 4–6, Syracuse University Archives.

10. Galpin, *Syracuse University*, (1871), 1:40; *Syracuse University Catalog*, College of Liberal Arts, 30–40, Syracuse University Archives; CBC, "Journal," 23.

11. Syracuse University, *Annals*, 1871–1875; *Syracuse University Catalog*, 1871, 1872, 1875; "First Junior Exhibition of the Syracuse University Class of '75;" "Syracuse University General Program, Anniversary Exercises, June 1875;" "Syracuse University Class Day Progamme of '75;" Syracuse University, "Commencement [Miscellany]," n.d., *The University Herald*, September 28, 1872, October 30, 1872, October 11, 1873, October 31, 1873, October 6, 1874, October 26, 1874, June 22, 1875, July 1, 1875, March 7, 1876, June 13, 1876, all Syracuse University Archives.

12. Elisabeth Congdon, untitled typewritten page, May 1950, CAC Papers, VEC.

13. CBC, "Journal," 3.

14. "Syracuse University, Class of 1875, June 23rd, Commencement Exercises"; "[Petition] To the Faculty of the College of Liberal Arts of Syracuse University," [1875]; Syracuse University, *Annals*, 28 (1875), Syracuse University Archives. Unfortunately, none of the senior theses have been retained.

15. "Syracuse University, Class of 1875, June 23rd, Commencement Exercises," Syracuse University Archives; in 1896 Syracuse University established a Phi Beta Kappa Chapter; both Chester and Clara were accorded alumni status, Chester in 1904 and Clara in 1908, Douglas W. Foard, National Secretary, Phi Beta Kappa, to author, December 12, 1991, author's files.

AFTER GRADUATION: AN UNCERTAIN TIME

1. CBC, "Journal," 5; G.G.H.C. files.

2. Clara Bannister Congdon to Executive Secretary, June 23, 1945; CBC, "Journal," 4, 5, 25, 28; Elizabeth Mitchell to author, May 5, 1988; following a fire in 1926, Alexandra College was closed, and women students were not readmitted until 1935 and only then as students in Albert College. Although the historical references do not identify either Albert or Alexandra College as Methodist schools, Clara, in her "Journal" records a visit to the school by a Methodist church official, Diane Rebar to author, May 13, 1988; Wyoming Seminary, founded in 1844, is one of the few schools in the United States to continuously enroll both boys and girls and to offer boarding as well as day students since it opened.

3. G.G.H.C. files; CBC, "Journal," 25.

4. C.H. Green to CAC, December 15, 1877, CAC Papers, VEC.

5. *Chippewa Herald,* September 6, September 27, and October 4, 1878; CBC, "Journal," 6.

6. CAC to Mother, December 11, 1878, CAC Papers, VEC.

7. CAC to Mother, February 14, 1878, CAC Papers, VEC.

ST. PAUL

1. CAC to Harry C. Heermans, [undated, 1881(?)], Harry C. Heermans Papers, Manuscripts and University Archives, University of Washington Libraries, University of Washington, Seattle, Washington, hereafter cited as Heermans Papers.

2. G.G.H.C., files.

3. Mother to CAC, February 11, 1880, CAC Papers, VEC; CBC, "Journal," 1–2, the entry reads, "There was not much farming done, but it was home."

4. Mother to CAC, [undated, 1880(?)], CAC Papers, VEC.

5. Charles W. Bennett to CAC, February 5, 1880, CAC Papers, VEC.

6. Bennett to CAC, January 3, 1880, CAC Papers, VEC.

7. Mother to CAC, [undated, 1880(?)]; Bennett to CAC, January 3, 1880, both CAC Papers, VEC.

8. *Duluth Evening Herald,* September 3, 1923, hereafter cited as *DEH.*

9. CAC to Heermans, [undated, 1881(?)], Heermans Papers.

10. Heermans to CAC, September 1, 1881, Heermans Papers.

11. CBC, "Journal," 29, 32, 36–37, 39.

12. CBC, "Journal," 36–38.

13. CBC, "Journal," 42, 45, 48, 53; the cause of John's death is not recorded in Clara's "Journal."

14. CBC, "Journal," 40, 43, 48.

15. William W. Billson to [U.S.] Attorney General, March 31, 1881; CAC to [U.S.] Attorney General, April 13, 1881; Billson to [U.S.] Attorney General, December 6, 1881; D.B. Searle to [U.S.] Attorney General, June 22, 1883; CAC to [U.S.] Attorney General, July 3, 1883; Searle to [U.S.] Attorney General, December 26, 1883, all Chronological File, Minnesota, National Archives Trust Fund Board, National Archives, Washington, D.C.

16. CAC to [U.S.] Attorney General, April 13, 1886; G. Baxter to [U.S.] Attorney General, May 27, 1886, both Appointment File, Minnesota, National Archives Trust Fund Board, National Archives, Washington D. C.

17. CBC, "Journal," 40, 43.

18. CBC, "Journal," 38, 41, 47.

19. CBC, "Journal," 36, 38.

THE VENTURE ON GRAYS HARBOR

1. Here and two paragraphs below, [n.a.], *Southwestern Washington, Topography, Climate, Resources, Productions, Manufacturing Advantages, Wealth and Growth,*

with *Illustrated Reviews of the Principal Cities and Towns, and Pen Sketches of Their Representative Business Men* (Olympia: Pacific Publishing Company, 1890), 10, 167–168, 187–193, 203; Louis Tuck Renz, *The History of the Northern Pacific Railroad* (Fairfield, Washington: Ye Galleon Press, 1980), 143–146; Edwin Van Sycle, *The River Pioneers: Early Days on Grays Harbor* (Aberdeen: Friends of Aberdeen Public Library, 1982), 206.

2. Incorporators of the Ontario Land Company were Harry C. Heermans, Corning, New York; Quincy W. Wellington, Corning, New York; Frank A. Garrett, Syracuse, New York; William C. Bennett, St. Paul, Minnesota; and Chester A. Congdon, "Ontario Land Company, Articles of Incorporation," April 1, 1886, Book N, 478–482, Minnesota Historical Society, St. Paul, Minnesota, hereafter cited as MHS. Although not included as an original incorporator, Matthias H. Arnot, banker from Elmira, New York, was an investor in the company; W. W. Clayton, *History of Steuben County, New York, with Illustrations and Biographical Sketches of Some of Its Prominent Men and Pioneers* (Philadelphia: Lewis, Peck & Co., 1879), 261; George A. Mellor, "The Arnots of Elmira," *The Chemung Historical Society Journal*, Vol. 9, No. 2, June 1964, 1261–1267; Thomas E. Byrne, *Chemung County, 1890–1975* (Elmira: Chemung County Historical Society, 1976), 476–478; "History of the Arnot Family," newspaper clipping file, Arnot Art Gallery, Elmira, New York, [n.p.]; Irvin W. Near, *A History of Steuben County, New York and Its People* (Chicago: The Lewis Publishing Co., 1911), 518–521.

3. *Southwestern Washington*, 199–203.

4. *Daily Washingtonian Industrial Edition*, January 25, 1913, Hoquiam Timberland Library, Hoquiam, Washington, 27; CAC to Heermans, March 17, 1890, Heermans Papers.

5. *Southwestern Washington*, 201–203.

6. CAC to Albert [S. Congdon], July 23, 1890, Heermans Papers.

7. CAC to Heermans, March 17, 1890, Heermans Papers.

8. Here and below, Heermans to M. H. Arnot, October 28, 1903; "List of Stockholders in Harbor Land Company," August 21, 1908, Heermans Papers.

9. Heermans to Albert [S. Congdon], November 21, 1890; Heermans to A.S. Congdon, November 19, 1890; Quincy W. Wellington to Heermans, March 29, 1890; Wellington to Heermans, March 30, 1890, all Heermans papers; the latter two letters are illustrative of Wellington's financial involvement in Hoquiam.

10. Heermans to A.S. Congdon, December 2, 1890; Heermans to A.S. Congdon, January 14, 1891, both Heermans Papers.

11. CAC to A.S. Congdon, November 4, 1891; CAC to A.S. Congdon, November 7, 1891; Heermans to A.S. Congdon, February 3, 1891; Heermans to A.S. Congdon, December 27, 1890; Heermans to A.S. Congdon, October 6, 1891; CAC to H.P. Barbour, April 27, 1891, all Heermans Papers.

12. Heermans to A.S. Congdon, [n.d., but filed with the 1892 correspondence in Heermans Papers]; Heermans to A.S. Congdon, January 4, 1892; CAC to A.S. Congdon, March 28, 1892; CAC to A.S. Congdon, January 18, 1892, all Heermans Papers.

13. For a discussion of the effects of the panic of 1893 on the Olympic Peninsula, see Robert E. Ficken, *The Forested Land: A History of Lumbering in Western Washington*

(Seattle and Durham: Forest History Society and University of Washington Press, 1987), 78–82.

14. Here and two paragraphs below, CAC to Heermans, January 16, 1895, Heermans Papers; Congdon included in his correspondence a detailed description of construction costs.

15. CAC to Heermans, March 15, 1895, Heermans Papers; there was another advantage to be gained in moving quickly: a large supply of unused rails left over from the Northern Pacific construction into Aberdeen was available, and the partners planned to buy and use these for their own railroad, CAC to Heermans, March 15, 1895, Heermans Papers.

16. CAC to Heermans, March 25, 1895; CAC to Heermans, April 6, 1895, both Heermans Papers.

17. Heermans to Arnot, October 28, 1903; the extension of the railroad was to cost the citizens of Hoquiam and the land companies a total of $66,000; Heermans to Editor, *Washingtonion* [*sic*], November 20, 1908, both Heermans Papers; in 1908, the Northern Pacific refused to use Grays Harbor for anything except outbound lumber shipments, Renz, *Northern Pacific Railroad*, 197–198; Northern Pacific Railway Company Records, Branch Line Data, Western District, Tacoma Division, Grays Harbor Branch, p. 2, MHS.

18. Heermans to Frank A. Garrett, September 16, 1903, Garrett, a resident of Syracuse, was one of the original incorporators of the Ontario Land Company, Heermans Papers.

19. *Corning Daily Olympian*, September 13, 1943, 1; *Corning Leader*, September 21, 1943, 10; W. W. Clayton, "Corning Water Works," *History of Steuben County, New York* (Philadelphia: Lewis, Peck, and Co., 1879), 264; Loring Brooks, "A Prospectus of the City of Hoquiam and Facts Concerning the Grays Harbor Country" (Hoquiam Timberland Library Files, [n.p.], April 1901), [unnumbered pages plus photographs]; "Annual Edition of the Grays Harbor Washingtonian," January 25, 1913, [n.p.]; CAC to Heermans, December 24, 1909, Heermans Papers.

20. *Census Data Book*, 1890–1970, Washington/Northwest Room, Washington State Library, Olympia, Washington; Shirley Dallas to author, undated, author's files.

21. *STATE ex rel. SHROPSHIRE v. SUPERIOR COURT OF PACIFIC COUNTY et al.* (Supreme Court of Washington, January 6, 1909).

22. Heermans to John T. Welch, February 3, 1909; CAC to Heermans, February 25, 1913, both Heermans Papers.

23. Heermans to Charles W. Whitcomb, June 11, 1906; Heermans to CAC, August 28, 1908, both Heermans Papers.

24. Heermans to Jennie B. Crawford, May 15, 1912; Heermans to George L. Abbott, August 1, 1908, both Heermans Papers; *Daily Washingtonian* [Hoquiam], July 22, 1910, July 27, 1910; John Hughes, "Hoquiam's Grand Hotel, circa 1890," *The Daily World* [Aberdeen], December 8, 1974; oral interview by author with Jerome T. Heermans (son), June 12, 1984, Olympia, Washington.

25. CAC to Heermans, September 1, 1908, Heermans Papers; the sale was postponed, but the profits were not spectacular.

26. CAC to Heermans, February 25, 1913, Heermans Papers.

27. Heermans to CAC, August 27, 1914, Heermans Papers.

28. CAC to Heermans, August 9, 1907, Heermans Papers; see also as example of a loan, an agreement dated September 3, 1914 in which Congdon loaned $50,000 to the Ontario Land Company for which he received 1,700 shares in the Hedley Gold Mining Company, both Heermans Papers.

RAYMOND

1. Here and two paragraphs below, Harry C. Heermans to CAC September 5, 1905, Heermans Papers.

2. Here and below, CAC to Heermans, September 11, 1905, Heermans Papers.

3. CAC to Heermans, November 3, 1905, Heermans Papers.

4. A.C. Little to Heermans, September 17, 1906; Little to CAC, September 17, 1906, both Heermans Papers.

5. Little to CAC, September 17, 1906; Heermans to CAC, May 29, 1907, both Heermans Papers.

6. Heermans to CAC, June 28, 1907, Heermans Papers.

7. CAC to Heermans, September 16, 1907; Heermans to CAC, August 5, 1907; CAC to Heermans, August 9, 1907; CAC to Heermans, September 11, 1907, all Heermans Papers.

8. CAC to Heermans, December 9, 1907; Heermans to CAC, December 12, 1907; Heermans to CAC, December 13, 1907, all Heermans Papers.

9. Heermans to CAC, March 13, 1913; in lieu of payment on his loans, Congdon accepted additional shares in the Raymond Land and Improvement Company as well as mortgages on land acquired by the company. Heermans to CAC, September 11, 1913; Heermans to CAC, November 24, 1908; CAC to Heermans, February 12, 1909; CAC to Heermans, April 3, 1909, all Heermans Papers.

10. CAC to Heermans, September 16, 1913; Heermans to CAC, October 16, 1914, both Heermans Papers.

11. Heermans to CAC, July 1, 1915, Heermans Papers.

12. Heermans to Walter B. Congdon, August 7, 1915; Heermans to CAC, February 26, 1916, both Heermans Papers.

THE MESABI: RIVALRY FOR ORE

1. Walter Van Brunt, ed. *Duluth and St. Louis County, Minnesota*, I (Chicago and New York: The American Historical Society, 1921), 392–416; David A. Walker, *Iron Frontier: The Discovery and Early Development of Minnesota's Three Iron Ranges* (St. Paul: Minnesota Historical Society Press, 1979), 83–84. The history of the discovery and development of the Mesabi Iron Range has been told many times; Walker's book offers the most complete account.

2. CBC, "Journal," 50.

3. Walker, *Iron Frontier*, 76, 85, 108, 99–100.

4. Henry Oliver Evans, *Iron Pioneer: Henry W. Oliver, 1840–1904* (New York: E. P. Dutton & Co., 1942) 192; Walker, *Iron Frontier*, 100, 76–201, Walker offers the most complete account of the Merritt family, their discovery of ore on the Mesabi, their relationship to Henry W. Oliver, their development of a railroad from the Mesabi to Lake Superior, their involvement with Rockefeller, and their withdrawal from the Mesabi.

5. Evans, *Iron Pioneer*, 197.

6. Evans, *Iron Pioneer*, 197; June D. Holmquist, "Convention City: The Republicans in Minneapolis, 1892," *Minnesota History*, 35:64–76 (June, 1956).

7. Evans, *Iron Pioneer*, 198–200; Walker, *Iron Frontier*, 104–105.

8. Tom Congdon, "Congdon Reunion, August 9, 1975," 7, CAC Papers, VEC; Evans, *Iron Pioneer*, 216.

9. Walker, *Iron Frontier*, 206–207; Evans *Iron Pioneer*, 209.

10. George Harvey, *Henry Clay Frick, The Man* (New York: Charles Scribner's Sons, 1928); Joseph Frazier Wall, *Andrew Carnegie* (New York: Oxford University Press, 1970), 586–587.

11. Evans, *Iron Pioneer*, 209; Walker, *Iron Frontier*, 207–208.

12. Evans, *Iron Pioneer*, 209; Walker, *Iron Frontier*, 208.

13. Wall, *Carnegie*, 596.

14. Evans, *Iron Pioneer*, 211.

15. Walker, *Iron Frontier*, 144–201.

16. Wall, *Carnegie*, 600–601.

17. CAC to John S. Pardee, May 29, 1913, CAC Papers, Congdon Office Corporation, Duluth, Minnesota, hereafter cited as CAC Papers, COC.

18. Evans, *Iron Pioneer*, 220–221; MEMORANDUM OF AGREEMENT, Oliver Iron and Steel Company Records, Records 1863–1930, 1959, 64:6, Folder 1, Box 1, Archives of Industrial Society, Hillman Library, University of Pittsburgh, Pittsburgh, Pennsylvania.

FAMILY

1. Walter Van Brunt, ed., *Duluth and St. Louis County* (Chicago and New York: The American Historical Society, 1921), 1:266–333.

2. CBC, "Journal" 48–49, 67–72, 75–77; interview with Richard O. Sielaff who verified that expenses for the Congdon household were meticulously recorded using a system of double entry bookkeeping, see "Ledgers," Glensheen files.

3. CBC, "Journal" 52–53, 58–59, 78–80, 83–84, 95–99, 106–107, 111–112, 114–116.

4. CBC, "Journal," 58–59.

5. CBC, "Journal," 83–84, 91–93, 94–99, 108–109.

6. CBC, "Journal," 73–74; Glensheen files.

7. CBC, "Journal," 78–80.

8. "Glensheen," Glensheen files.

9. Here and below, Michael Lane, *Glensheen: The Construction Years*, [Duluth: University of Minnesota, Duluth, n.d.], 4–7.

10. Here and two paragraphs below, Lane, *Glensheen*, 10–26.

11. CBC, "Journal" 106–107, the Congdons acquired a yacht, the *Hesperia*, and enjoyed sailing on Lake Superior; on July 1, 1916 the boat was destroyed by fire.

12. Glensheen files.

13. Lane, *Glensheen*, 5, 10, 14, 20.

14. Lane, *Glensheen*, 14.

15. Charles W. Leavitt, Jr. to Hooper Bros. and Thomas, April 11, 1907, Glensheen files; horticultural challenges always interested Chester and Clara Congdon. Raising apples in the winter climate of northeastern Minnesota was particularly risky, but the weather hazard only made Congdon more determined. John Norton to CAC, June 25, 1910, Glensheen files; Congdon wrote to the St. Louis County Attorney, who was himself somewhat of a horticulturalist, inquiring about the varieties of apples which could survive the harsh winters. In reply, the attorney wrote, "There is no doubt but what St. Louis County could be a fruit producing region if the same care and attention was given it that is given to growing fruit in the West." The letter went on to list eleven varieties that might thrive in the Duluth area, Glensheen files.

16. Glensheen files; several full-time gardeners served the Congdons over the years beginning with John Kenney. George Wyness, who had previously worked at Henry C. Frick's Massachusetts estate, came in 1921, and upon his retirement was followed by his son, Robert, who retired in 1979, Ada Fourie, *Their Roots Run Deep* (University of Minnesota, Duluth, n.d.), 1–22.

17. Glensheen files.

18. CBC, "Journal," 91–93; Lane, *Glensheen*, 22.

19. CBC, "Journal," 110–112; following her husband's death in 1916, Clara remained at Glensheen until her death in 1950 at the age of 97. Elisabeth Congdon willed the estate to the University of Minnesota with the proviso that the University not take possession until her death. She continued to reside at Glensheen until 1979. Today, the house and grounds serve as a tour home. By 1994, the site had attracted 1.6 million visitors.

20. Here and below, CAC to Frank Crassweller, April, 14, 1915, Glensheen files.

21. *Journal of the House of the Thirty-Sixth Session of the Legislature of the State of Minnesota*, H.F. No.917, 922, March 17, 1909 [introduced]; April 21, 1909 [passed unanimously]; *Journal of the Senate of the Thirty-Sixth Session of the Legislature of the State of Minnesota*, H.F. No. 917, received from the House, March 23, 1909, 60; April 20, 1909, [passed unanimously]; Thomas J. Schindler to Michael J. Lane, November 1, 1983; *Proceedings of the Common Council*, Duluth, Minnesota, "Ordinance, by Mayor W. I. Prince," June 2, 1913; *Proceedings of the City Council*, Duluth, Minnesota, Ordinance No. 606, June 2, 1915, Lane letter and Duluth city ordinances are in Glensheen files.

AGRICULTURAL DEVELOPMENT IN YAKIMA

1. Rose Boening, "History of Irrigation in the State of Washington," *Washington Historical Quarterly*, IX (1918), 9–10, 21–45, X (1919), 259–276; [n.a.], *An Illustrated History of Klickitat, Yakima, and Kittitas Counties with an Outline of the Early History of the State of Washington* ([n.p.], Interstate Publishing Company, 1904), 318; C. Brewster Coulter, "New Settlers on the Yakima Project, 1880–1910," *Pacific Northwest Quarterly*, 61 (January 1970), 10–21.

2. *Illustrated History*, 212.

3. Susan Boone, "Chester A. Congdon: Pioneer Irrigationist," p. 3 unpublished manuscript, author's files.

4. Bruce Mitchell, "Flowing Wealth: the Story of Water Resource Development in North Central Washington, 1870–1950," *Wenatchee Daily World*, March 6, 1957; Bruce Mitchell to author, February 2, 1985, author's files; *Laws of Washington Territory Enacted by the Legislative Assembly*, Tenth Biennial Session, 1885–6 (Olympia: Thomas H. Cavanaugh, Public Printer, 1886), 508–511.

5. Untitled, "Notice of 150 feet per second appropriation," from Yakima Valley Canal Company files, Yakima, Washington, hereafter cited as YVCC files.

6. Yakima County Auditor, *Water Rights Index Book*, [1894], Vol. A, 210, 223; untitled notice of 50 feet per second appropriation, YVCC files.

7. "Articles of Incorporation of the North Yakima Canal Company," May 23, 1894, YVCC files. The Tieton River flows into the Natches a few miles above the point where Congdon planned his intake; water from the Tieton, as such, was never used.

8. CAC to Alfred Bannister, June 6, 1893, YVCC files, photocopy in Boone.

9. CAC to Bannister, July 6, 1893, YVCC files, photocopy in Boone.

10. CAC to Bannister, May 18, 1894, YVCC files, photocopy in Boone.

11. CAC to Bannister, June 13, 1894, YVCC files, photocopy in Boone.

12. CAC to Bannister, December 1, 1894, YVCC files, photocopy in Boone.

13. The pipe across Cowiche Canyon was designed and patented by Bannister, *Annual Report of the Commissioner of Patents for the year 1903*, 58th Congress, 2nd Session, Document No. 177, Patent No. 738, 394, "Wooden Stave Pipe."

14. Regretfully, no patent was taken out on this unique water wheel; following its installation in the canal, the design was copied by other canal builders, oral interview with John Shannon, May 28, 1984; *Yakima Herald*, September 20, 1894; Click Relander Collection, Yakima Valley Regional Library, Yakima, Washington, hereafter cited as Relander Collection.

15. *Yakima Herald*, August 16, 1894, transcript, Relander Collection.

16. *Yakima Herald*, August 16, 1894, transcript, Relander Collection.

17. Kenneth E. Maine to author, June 10, 1988, author's files;

18. CAC to Bannister, telegram [no date], YVCC files, photocopy in Boone.

19. Ed Whitson to CAC, June 4, 1895, YVCC files, photocopy in Boone.

20. Bannister to CAC, June 24, 1895 (telegram); CAC to Bannister, June 25, 1895 (telegram), both YVCC files, photocopy in Boone.

21. Heermans to CAC, June 28, 1895; CAC to Bannister, July 3, 1895, YVCC files, photocopy in Boone; Maine to author, June 30, 1988, author's files.

22. CAC to Albert S. Congdon, undated, YVCC files; Maine to author, June 30, 1988.

23. The Yakima Valley Canal Company provides water for 4,000 acres, Maine to author, June 10, 1988, author's files.

24. Maine to author, June 10, 1988, author's files.

25. Correspondence in the files at Westhome (name of the residence on the Yakima ranch) contain literally dozens of letters to and from Congdon on the operation of the ranch; all correspondence regarding the operation of the ranch is located in these files, Congdon Papers located at Westhome, Yakima, Washington, hereafter cited as CAC Papers, Westhome files. The examples included in the narrative are only illustrations of the close and careful attention which Congdon gave to the details of running the ranch; "List of Books at Glensheen," provided by Michael Lane, Director of Glensheen; CAC to Walter Baragar, August 20, 1908; CAC to A. W. Speyers, August 8, 1910; CAC to Speyers, November 30, 1910; CAC to Speyers, September 29, 1910; CAC to Speyers, September 14, 1910; CAC to Speyers, September 24, 1910, all CAC Papers, Westhome files.

26. CAC to Stark Bros. Nurseries Co., November 27, 1909; Speyers to CAC, June 15, 1909, both CAC Papers, Westhome files.

27. CAC to Speyers, July 7, 1909, CAC Papers, Westhome files.

28. CAC to Speyers, July 1, 1909, CAC Papers, Westhome files.

29. The incident regarding the removal of the hops is included in H.C. Dudley, *Glorified Fishing*, Reed Whittemore, ed. (printed privately, 1978), 119, copy in author's possession.

30. CAC to Speyers, August 30, 1910, CAC Papers, Westhome files.

31. The original warehouse for processing fruit is still in use. In recent years when the method of moving fruit within the building was changed from handtrucks to fork-lifts, i.e., from moving five to six stacked boxes of fruit with a handtruck to moving larger amounts with a forklift, the only alteration required to accommodate the addi-tional concentrated weight was to place steel plates on the floor to protect the surface from wear by the forklift wheels, oral interview with Eugene Thomas by author, May 28, 1984, Yakima, Washington.

32. T.C. [Thomas Cooper] to J.M. Hannaford [President of the Northern Pacific], January 15, 1915; Cooper to Hannaford, January 8, 1915; Cooper to Hannaford, January 6, 1915; George T. Reed to Hannaford, December 7, 1914; George Dunwald to Hannaford, November 19, 1914; [N.P.] Agent to Hannaford, November 14, 1914; [N.P.] Agent to Hannaford, W.T. Tyler, and H.E. Still, November 13, 1914, Northern Pacific Railway Company Records, President's Subject File, 1444–2 through 1444–6, all MHS.

33. Oral interview by author with Susan Lovald, July 15, 1988, Duluth, Minnesota. There was speculation by workers and townspeople in Yakima that Congdon planned to retire in Yakima, but there is no supporting evidence.

34. [n.a.], *An Illustrated History of Klickitat, Yakima and Kittitas Counties with an Outline of the Early History of the State of Washington* (n.p., Interstate Publishing

Company, 1904), 212; Maurie Helland, "Congdon's Hobby," *Yakima Herald–Republic*, January 4, 1976, clipping file, Yakima Valley Regional Library, Yakima, Washington; the location of Congdon's "capitol land" is today in the vicinity of A.C. Davis High School, Yakima, Washington.

THE WESTERN MESABI

1. Walker, *Iron Frontier*, 214–238.
2. Walker, *Iron Frontier*, 224–230.
3. Evans, *Iron Pioneer*, 267–275; Walker, *Iron Frontier*, 224–230.
4. Evans, *Iron Pioneer*, 276–281.
5. Evans, *Iron Pioneer*, 282.
6. Evans, *Iron Pioneer*, 282.
7. Walker, *Iron Frontier*, 232–233; Donald L. Boese, *John C. Greenway and the Opening of the Western Mesabi* (Grand Rapids: Itasca Community College Foundation, 1975), 4–9; Edmund J. Longyear, *Mesabi Pioneer: Reminiscences of Edmund J. Longyear*, Grace Lee Nute, ed. (St. Paul: Minnesota Historical Society Press, 1951), 83; Articles of Incorporation, Book G-3, p. 492, MHS.
8. Boese, *Greenway*, 4–8.
9. Boese, *Greenway*, 4–9.
10. Boese, *Greenway*, 12–17; Walker, *Iron Frontier*, 233–235.
11. Dudley, *Glorified Fishing*, 1–19.
12. Dudley, *Glorified Fishing*, 20.
13. Dudley, *Glorified Fishing*, 23–24.
14. Dudley, *Glorified Fishing*, 27–31.
15. Dudley, *Glorified Fishing*, 32–33.

THE LEGISLATURE OF 1909: THE TONNAGE TAX

1. *General Laws of the State of Minnesota*, 1881, General Session, 55–56; William Watts Folwell, *A History of Minnesota*, 4:11, 53 (St. Paul: Minnesota Historical Society Press, 1930); Hal Bridges, *Iron Millionaire: Life of Charlemagne Tower* (Philadelphia: University of Pennsylvania Press, 1952), 166–167; Bridges states that George C. Stone, the man who originally interested Charlemagne Tower in the Vermilion range, guided this legislation through the Minnesota legislature since Tower was reluctant to invest large sums of money in mining property until his mines were in operation and he could pay taxes out of profits; Gladys C. Blakey, *A History of Taxation in Minnesota*, (Minneapolis, University of Minnesota Studies in Economics and Business 4, 1934), 49; Blakey maintains that "the law was the result of clever work on the part of certain citizens of Duluth who were raising capital for the new enterprise and who wanted to assure investors that it would not be overtaxed." She also indicates that in 1891 the Farmer Alliance made an attempt to adjust the new tax upward, and in 1895 a "powerful lobby in a disgraceful session prevented any

change;" "Brief Against the Tonnage Tax Bill, Submitted to the Committee on Taxes and Tax Laws of the House of Representatives of the Minnesota Legislature, Session of 1909, by the Delegation from St. Louis County in the House of Representatives," Hallock's Edgewater Press, Duluth, Minnesota, copy in Congdon Papers, COC; *Executive Documents of the State of Minnesota*, 1895, IV, 1058–1059, "Attorney General Report," H.W. Childs to R. C. Dunn, March 19, 1896; Folwell, *History of Minnesota*, 4:53.

2. Blakey, *History of Taxation*, 38.

3. Opinion of the Attorney General, quoted from Blakey, *History of Taxation*, 38.

4. Here and two paragraphs below, *Minnesota Reports*, (St. Paul, 1909), 106:392; *First Biennial Report of the Minnesota Tax Commission to the Governor and Legislature of the State of Minnesota*, (St. Paul, 1908), 212–218.

5. *Journal of the House of the Thirty-Sixth Session of the Legislature of the State of Minnesota*, April 6, 1907, 1206, hereafter cited as *House Journal; Journal of the Senate of the Thirty-fifth Session of the Legislature of the State of Minnesota*, April 17, 1907, 1339, hereafter cited as *Senate Journal.*

6. Winifred G. Helmes, *John A. Johnson, the People's Governor: A Political Biography* (Minneapolis, University of Minnesota Press, 1949), 31–88.

7. "Democratic State Platform, Adopted at Minneapolis Convention, August 19, 1908," printed copy in CAC Papers, COC.

8. Helmes, *Johnson*, 190–193; *DEH*, October 30, 1908.

9. CAC to Frank Billings Kellogg, August 20, 1908, CAC Papers, COC.

10. *DEH*, September 23, 1908.

11. *DEH*, October 10, 1908.

12. *Duluth News Tribune*, October 14, 1908, hereafter cited as *DNT.*

13. CAC to Kellogg, August 20, 1908, CAC Papers, COC.

14. CAC to Thomas F. Cole, October 22, 1908, CAC Papers, COC.

15. *DNT*, October 25, 1908.

16. *DNT*, October 28, 1908.

17. *DEH*, October 28, 1908; *DNT*, October 29, 1908.

18. *DNT*, October 30, 1908; *DEH*, October 29, 1908.

19. Bruce White, et al., *Minnesota Votes: Election Returns by County for Presidents, Senators, Congressmen, and Governors, 1857–1977*, (St. Paul, Minnesota Historical Society, 1977), 177–178; *Legislative Manual for the State of Minnesota* (1909), 530–531, 553.

20. *Minnesota Reports*, Vol. 106, 392–430.

21. *House Journal*, Thirty-sixth Session, January 25, 1909, 153; printed copy of H.F. No. 227, dated January 25, 1909 in CAC Papers, COC.

22. Lynn Haines, *The Minnesota Legislature of 1909* (Minneapolis: [printed privately], 1910), 37; *House Journal*, Thirty-sixth Session, March 17, 1909, 935–936.

23. *DNT*, March 26, 1909.

24. *DNT*, March 31, 1909.

25. "Report of the Tax Committee on the Construction of a Steel Plant in Minnesota by the United States Steel Corporation," Pamphlet Number 565, Northeast

Minnesota Historical Center, University of Minnesota, Duluth, Duluth, Minnesota. Congdon served on this committee.

26. George D. Swift to CAC, February 15, 1909, CAC Papers, COC.

27. Here and two paragraphs below, *DNT,* March 31, 1909; *DNT,* April 1, 1909; *DNT,* April 2, 1909; *DNT,* April 3, 1909; *DNT,* April 4, 1909. Before leaving, Representative Bjorge delivered a lengthy defense of his bill to the Senate, typescript copy of this speech entitled, "Speech of the Honorable H.O. Bjorge before the Senate Committee of the Legislature of the State of Minnesota at the Senate Chamber, St. Paul, Minnesota on Wednesday Evening, March, 31st, A.D. 1909, on the subject of the tonnage tax on iron ore," CAC Papers, COC.

28. Here and below, *DNT,* April 7, 1909; *DNT,* April 8, 1909.

29. Here and below, *DNT,* April 9, 1909.

30. *DNT,* April 13, 1909; *DNT,* April 14, 1909.

31. *Senate Journal,* Thirty-sixth Session, April 14, 1909 through April 16, 1909. A copy of an amendment to the bill is in the CAC Papers, COC, but there is no indication that it belonged to Congdon or that he intended to offer it.

32. *DNT,* April 16, 1909.

33. Here and below, *DNT,* April 18, 1909; *DNT,* April 19, 1909.

34. Johnson's veto message is contained in his letter to Hon. A. J. Rockne, Speaker of the House of Representatives, April 20, 1909, Outgoing Correspondence, John A. Johnson Papers, MHS.

35. *DNT,* April 21, 1909; *DNT,* April 22, 1909.

THE LEGISLATURE OF 1911: REDISTRICTING THE STATE

1. *The Legislative Manual of the State of Minnesota Compiled for the Legislature of 1911,* by Julius A. Schmahl, Secretary of State (Minneapolis: Harrison & Smith, 1911), 503, hereafter cited as *Legislative Manual,* 1911; the *Duluth News Tribune* praised Congdon's leadership declaring that "Congdon . . . is already recognized as one of the leaders in the house. To his counsel the members will listen attentively," *DNT,* January 8, 1911.

2. *DNT,* January 5, 1911.

3. John Avery Bond, "Legislative Reapportionment in Minnesota," unpublished Ph.D. dissertation, University of Minnesota, 1956, 190–191.

4. Bond, "Legislative Reapportionment," 192–194.

5. *Legislative Manual, 1911,* 146–147; the Senate Committee of Reapportionment was chaired by James Hackney (R-Ramsey County) and consisted of one member from each congressional district; *DNT,* January 25, 1911.

6. *DNT,* January 19, 1911.

7. *DNT,* January 23, 1911.

8. *DNT,* February 2, 1911; *DNT,* February 11, 1911.

9. Lynn Haines, *The Legislature of 1911* (Minneapolis: privately published by Lynn Haines, New York Life Building, 1911), 70–79; both Haines and Bond speculate

that the reapportioned senators went to areas that opposed the tonnage tax; *DNT*, February 15, 16, 1911.

10. Bond, "Legislative Reapportionment," 197.

11. *DNT*, February 22, 1911.

12. Bond, "Legislative Reapportionment," 198.

13. Bond, "Legislative Reapportionment," 199–200, speculates that the latter part of the amendment was inspired by the liquor interests who saw an opportunity to eliminate two county optionist legislators; Bond, "Legislative Reapportionment," 201; *Journal of the House of the Thirty-seventh Session of the Legislature of the State of Minnesota* (St. Paul: McGill-Warner Co., 1911), February 21, 1911, 427–429, hereafter cited as *Journal of the House.*

14. *DNT*, February 23, 1911; true to his platform commitment, Eberhart continued to demand a reapportionment bill and to threaten an extra session if results were not forthcoming.

15. *Journal of the Senate of the Thirty-seventh Session of the Legislature of the State of Minnesota* (St. Paul: McGill-Warner Co., 1911), March 16, 1911, 685–688, hereafter cited as *Journal of the Senate*; Bond, "Legislative Reapportionment," 245, maintains that it was Senator Haycraft, a "proposed victim of the [Congdon] amendment who aroused his supporters in the Senate to secure the defeat of the bill."

16. Bond, "Legislative Reapportionment," 202–204, also shows that while H.F. 477 would have improved equality of representation, wide discrepancies between districts would still have existed in several senatorial districts, e.g., District 49 (Ottertail) with a population of 46,036 elected one senator as did District 7 (Faribault) with a population of 19,949.

17. Bond, "Legislative Reapportionment," 206.

18. *Journal of the Senate*, (date missing), 272.

19. *Journal of the Senate*, April 6, 1911, 1050–1052.

20. *Journal of the House*, April 7, 1911, p. 1367; *Journal of the House*, April 17, 1911, 1658.

21. *Journal of the House*, April 17, 1911, 1658–1659.

22. *Journal of the House*, April 18, 1911, 664, 1668.

23. *Charles R. Fowler and W. D. Washburn, Jr. v. Julius A. Schmahl as Secretary of State*, Hennepin County District Court, Finds and Order, including Memorandum, September 15, 1911, Archives, Hennepin County Court, Minneapolis, Minnesota; brief in CAC Papers, COC.

24. *Fowler v. Schmahl*, CAC Papers, COC.

25. *Fowler v. Schmahl, Memorandum*, September 15, 1911.

26. Draft copy in CAC Papers, COC; *DNT*, November 1, 2, 3, 4, and 5, 1912; *DEH*, November 1, 2, 4, 1911.

27. *Minnesota Constitution*, Article XIV, Section 1.

28. *Legislative Manual*, 1913, 508–509; Bond, "Legislative Reapportionment," 207–208; in 1913 the Minnesota legislature passed the "Seven Senators" amendment and submitted

it to the voters in the general election of 1914. Once again, the amendment received a majority of those voting on that particular issue, but failed to receive a majority of the total votes cast in the election. Thus, for the last time the "Seven Senators" amendment was defeated.

29. *Journal of the House*, Extra Session, June 4, 1912, 1;

30. *Journal of the House*, Extra Session, June 11, 1912, 41–45.

BISBEE

1. The above from Evans, *Iron Pioneer*, 292–293; Ira Joralemon, *Romantic Copper: Its Lure and Lore* (London and New York: D Appleton-Century Company, 1934), 127–129; Dwight E. Woodbridge, "Arizona and Sonora—II: Bisbee Camp," *The Engineering and Mining Journal*, Vol. 81, No. 21, (May 26, 1906), 991, hereafter cited as *E&MJ*; Evans and Woodbridge relate quite a different narrative from Joralemon. According to the latter, early in 1898, the two Hoatson brothers were visited in Calumet, Michigan by John Graham, a friend who had worked with them earlier in their careers at Butte, Montana. Graham carried with him specimens of malachite and azurite, both copper bearing rocks. There were more like these, Graham claimed, in the vicinity of Bisbee, and "they were just as good as the [Copper] Queen." Immediately, both Hoatsons left for Bisbee. There they found several old friends, many of them "Cousin Jacks" or Cornishmen who had worked for the two captains in Michigan. It was from these men that the Hoatsons learned more about the extent of the copper deposits, both known and anticipated. One piece of information was especially interesting. Some of the currently operating drifts, i.e., tunnels running at horizontal angles off the main shaft, headed toward the Irish Mag and showed an ever increasing amount of high-grade ore. And, they learned, the Irish Mag was for sale for $550,000. For several days the two captains climbed over the rugged surface of the site. There was little to encourage them—lots of seams of iron oxide with only an occasional copper stain cutting across the limestone beds. Legend has it that during his exploration, Jim Hoatson became tired and lay down to doze. As he slept he dreamed that he saw a vast ore body nine hundred feet beneath his feet—a deposit greater than anything he could imagine. Moreover, the outcroppings, although worthless in themselves, provided a surface map of the underlying ore bodies. On the strength of this "vision" the Hoatsons made arrangements with Costello to purchase the mine. Upon their return to Calumet, the two captains began to raise money to begin operation on the "Irish Mag." With the Hoatsons reputation, which extended over a quarter century of mining, upon which to rely, investors began to buy shares at sixty cents each in the new Lake Superior and Western Copper Company, headquartered "in a dingy little office above a drug store in Red Jacket, Michigan." Woodbridge states that the Calumet and Hecla Company of Calumet at first decided to carry the enterprise, but later changed their mind. It was probably the Hoatsons reputation that attracted investors.

2. Robert Glass Cleland, *A History of Phelps Dodge, 1834–1950* (New York: Alfred A. Knopf, 1952), 121.

3. The narrative of how Cole became interested varies. The role of Hoatson's sister, Cole's wife, is described by Woodbridge. Evans states that Hoatson and Briggs called Cole into the office in Red Jacket where they showed him maps of the "Copper Queen" and the "Irish Mag." Joralemon omits details of the initial encounter between Hoatson and Cole; Evans, *Iron Pioneer*, 293–294, states that Cole began by trying to interest Boston investors.

4. Evans, *Iron Pioneer*, 292–295; Joralemon, *Romantic Copper*, 130; Cleland, *Phelps Dodge*, 122; Evans states that in order to facilitate a wider distribution of stock, Henry W. Oliver reduced his holdings to half the original amount.

5. Cleland, *Phelps Dodge*, 122; Evans, *Iron Pioneer*, 294–295.

6. Cleland, *Phelps Dodge*, 228; Evans, *Iron Pioneer*, 295; Dwight E. Woodbridge, "Arizona and Sonora—IV: The Calumet and Arizona Group," *E&MJ*, Vol. 81, June 23, 1906, 1180.

7. Joralemon, *Romantic Copper*, 132.

8. Woodbridge, *E&MJ*, June 23, 1906, 1180.

9. Woodbridge, *E&MJ*, June 23, 1906, 1180.

10. Dwight E. Woodbridge, "Arizona and Sonora—I," *E&MJ*, Vol. 81, May 12, 1906, 896, this, figure, of course, would have included all copper producers; L.W. Powell to CAC, December 2, 1907; L.W. Powell to CAC, December 12, 1907; Thorald F. Field to CAC, November 27, 1907; A.J. Huneke to CAC, November 27, 1907, all CAC Papers, COC.

11. Charles Briggs to CAC, February 12, 1908; Briggs to CAC, February 13, 1908; Briggs to CAC, February 25, 1908; CAC to Briggs, February 28, 1908, all CAC Papers, COC. Briggs repeatedly wrote Congdon expressing his concern about the cost of production in relation to the price of copper, see Briggs to CAC, May 24, 1908; Briggs to CAC, May 30, 1908; Powell to CAC, May 30, 1908; Field to CAC, June 28, 1908; CAC to Field, July 6th, 1908; CAC to Field, July 7, 1908; Field to CAC, July 12, 1908; Powell to Briggs, July 20, 1908, all CAC Papers, COC.

12. CAC to Powell, July 1, 1909, CAC Papers, COC.

13. CAC to Powell, July 19, 1909, CAC Papers, COC.

14. CAC to Briggs, December 6, 1909; CAC to Cole, December 14, 1909, both CAC Papers, COC.

15. CAC to Briggs, December 6, 1909; CAC to George E. Tener, December 24, 1909, both CAC Papers, COC.

16. CAC to Gordon R. Campbell, December 27, 1909; also see Briggs to Campbell, December 27, 1909, both CAC Papers, COC; despite criticism and pressure, Powell continued as General Superintendent until his resignation in mid-1910.

17. CAC to Campbell, December 27, 1909; CAC to John C. Greenway (telegram), December 27, 1909, both CAC Papers, COC.

18. Here and below, for the career of Greenway prior to his coming to Arizona, see Donald E. Boese, *Greenway.*

19. CAC to Tener, December 27, 1909; CAC to Henry R. Rea, December 28, 1909; CAC to Tener, December 28, 1909; Tener to CAC, December 29, 1909; Rea to CAC, December 30, 1909 (all telegrams), all CAC Papers, COC.

20. CAC to Campbell, December 31, 1909 (two letters, same date); CAC to Tener, December 29, 1909 (telegram); three unsigned telegrams to CAC, December 30, 1909, January 2, 1910, January 4, 1910; CAC to Campbell, January 3, 1910; CAC to Campbell, January 4, 1910 (two letters, same date); Tener to CAC, January 5, 1910, all CAC Papers, COC; for a description of John D. Ryan's involvement with Amalgamated Copper, see Michael P. Malone, *The Battle for Butte: Mining Politics on the Northern Frontier, 1864–1906* (Seattle and London: University of Washington Press, 1981).

21. CAC to John C. Greenway, January 14, 1910, CAC Papers, COC; one is left to wonder why Greenway accepted the Arizona position in view of the composition of the Board of Directors of the C&A.

22. Quoted in Boese, *John C. Greenway*, 187.

23. Boese, *John C. Greenway*, 188; on firm footing at last, the company was on its way as a successful enterprise.

EXPANSION AT AJO

1. Boese, *John C. Greenway*, 188–189.

2. Boese, *John C. Greenway*, 188.

3. Both Boese and Joralemon have written excellent histories of mining at Ajo between the mid-1850s and 1911, see Boese, *John C. Greenway*, 189–191 and Joralemon, *Romantic Copper*, 166–189; also see Cleland, *Phelps Dodge*, 229–230; [John C. Greenway], "Success After Failures: The Story of the New Cornelia Copper Company as Related Informally by Col. John C. Greenway," *Arizona Mining Journal*, January 1920, 17.

4. Here and below, Boese, *John C. Greenway*, 191–193; Joralemon, *Romantic Copper*, 188–197.

5. Boese, *John C. Greenway*,, 191.

6. Joralemon, *Romantic Copper*, 133; Walter R. Bimson, *Louis D. Ricketts (1859–1940), Mining Engineer, Geologist, Banker, Industrialist, and Builder of Arizona* (New York: The Newcomen Society of England, 1949), 7–26.

7. Cleland, *Phelps Dodge*, 231–232.

8. Boese, *John C. Greenway*, 193, credits Greenway with perfecting the leaching method, a process which he later patented in his own name; Joralemon, *Romantic Copper*, 195.

9. Boese, *John C. Greenway*, 193.

10. Boese, *John C. Greenway*, 192–193; Joralemon, *Romantic Copper*, 194–195; Cleland, *Phelps Dodge*, 232; [John C. Greenway,] "Success After Failures," 17, Greenway states that the well supplied 1200 gallons of water at 102 degrees F. per minute.

11. For a full description of the town of Ajo see Boese, *John C. Greenway,*, 194–195; there are several photographs of Ajo in Cleland, *Phelps Dodge,* between pages 232 and 233; oral interview with Susan Lovald by author, July 15, 1988, Duluth, Minnesota, notes in author's files.

12. Greenway to Walter [Congdon], July 20, 1914; Greenway to CAC, June 7, 1912; CAC to Greenway, August 6, 1912, all CAC Papers, COC.

13. Greenway to Briggs, August 8, 1914; Greenway to Walter [Congdon], June 1, 1915, both John C. and Isabella Greenway Papers, MS 311, Arizona Historical Society, Tucson, Arizona, hereafter cited as Greenway Papers.

14. CAC to Greenway, August 16, 1916; William J. Nash to CAC, August 23, 1915, Greenway to CAC, August 23, 1915; CAC to Greenway, August 27, 1915, all Greenway Papers.

PACIFIC PANORAMA

1. CBC, "Journal," 113; it was the only time in Congdon's life that he kept a record of his daily thoughts and activities; his diary for the Pacific trip was published for the family by his son, Robert, under the title of *Pacific Panorama;* the diary is in the Van Evera collection.

2. Judy Copland to author, February 25, 1988; *Northwestern University Alumni News,* March 1936; *The Evanston Review,* August 23, 1934, 22–23. *Evanston Index,* March 23, 1895; clipping files, Evanston Historical Society, Evanston, Illinois; Dyche, a graduate pharmacist, went on to become the business manager of Northwestern University; he married the daughter of Congdon's Syracuse University mentor, Charles W. Bennett; J.L. Alabaster lived in Evanston and commuted to Chicago where he was employed by Caxton Publishing Company.

3. CAC, *Pacific Panorama,* 6–7, hereafter cited as CAC, *Pacific.*

4. CAC, *Pacific,* 8.

5. CAC, *Pacific,* 12–13.

6. CAC, *Pacific,* 13–14.

7. CAC, *Pacific,* 14–16.

8. CAC, *Pacific,* 19–20.

9. CAC, *Pacific,* 21.

10. CAC, *Pacific,* 22–26.

11. CAC, *Pacific,* 27–28.

12. CAC, *Pacific,* 28–34.

13. CAC, *Pacific,* 30–31, 36.

14. CAC, *Pacific,* 36–38.

15. CAC, *Pacific,* 38–40.

16. CAC, *Pacific,* 45–49.

17. CAC, *Pacific,* 49–53; the use of a pulp fiber tray and box was later developed by Paul Friday (called the "Friday Pack") and used by fruit growers in the state of Washington, Dick Larsen to author, September 6, 1991, author's files.

18. CAC, *Pacific*, 53–55.
19. CAC, *Pacific*, 55–57.
20. CAC, *Pacific*, 55–56.
21. CAC, *Pacific*, 56–64.
22. CAC, *Pacific*, 70–72.
23. CAC, *Pacific*, 73–80.
24. CAC, *Pacific*, 81–96.
25. CAC, *Pacific*, 98–99.
26. CAC, *Pacific*, 100–102.
27. CAC, *Pacific*, 102–104.
28. CAC, *Pacific*, 105–107.
29. CAC, *Pacific*, 106–107.
30. CAC, *Pacific*, 108–109.
31. CAC, *Pacific*, 112–115.
32. CAC, *Pacific*, 117–121.
33. CAC, *Pacific*, 123.
34. CAC, *Pacific*, 125–127.
35. CAC, *Pacific*, 127–129.
36. CAC, *Pacific*, 129–130.
37. CAC, *Pacific*, 130–134.
38. CAC, *Pacific*, 135–137.
39. CAC, *Pacific*, 139–140.
40. CAC, *Pacific*, 140–141.
41. CAC, *Pacific*, 141–145; Richard Storry, *A History of Modern Japan* (New York: Pelican, 1960), 139–140.
42. CAC, *Pacific*, 145–146; Storry, *A History of Modern Japan*, 79–80.
43. CAC, *Pacific*, 146–152.
44. CAC, *Pacific*, 164–165.
45. CAC, *Pacific*, 157–173.
46. CAC, *Pacific*, 173–175.
47. CAC, *Pacific*, 175.
48. CAC, *Pacific*, 175–176.

NATIONAL AFFAIRS
1. Historical literature on American politics and economic life at the turn of the century is voluminous. Two excellent works on economic and political affairs and the involvement of the American business community for this period are Robert Wiebe, *Businessmen and Reform* (Chicago: Elephant Paperbacks, Ivan Dee, Inc., 1989), and George E. Mowry, *Theodore Roosevelt and the Progressive Movement* (New York: Hill and Wang, 1946).
2. Here and below, CAC to W. W. Billson, December 10, 1907, CAC Papers, COC.

3. Frank B. Kellogg to CAC, January 5, 1908; CAC to Kellogg, January 11, 1908; CAC to Kellogg, January 12, 1908; CAC to Kellogg, January 17, 1908, all CAC Papers, COC.

4. William Howard Taft to CAC, January 17, 1908; CAC to Taft, January 30, 1908; Taft to CAC, February 4, 1908; CAC to L.M. Willcuts, February 17, 1908, all CAC Papers, COC; Congdon volunteered to serve as a delegate to the Republican national convention. "My only thought," he wrote Willcuts, "about going is that I might do some good which otherwise would not be done."

5. For a survey of these affairs, see Mowry, *Theodore Roosevelt*, 40–203.

6. CAC to Greenway, July 10, 1915, Greenway Papers.

7. CAC to Irving Caswell, July 9, 1912, CAC Papers, COC.

8. White, et al., 18.

9. CAC to Greenway, July 10, 1916, Greenway Papers.

10. Greenway to CAC, July 31, 1915, Greenway Papers.

11. CAC to Greenway, July 10, 1915, Greenway Papers.

12. CAC to Greenway, July 10, 1915, Greenway Papers.

13. *DNT*, June 9, 1916.

14. Here and two paragraphs below, *DEH*, June 12, 1916.

15. CBC, "Journal," 117–122.

16. "Certificate of Death," City of St. Paul, Department of Public Safety—Bureau of Health, Division of Vital Statistics, No. 2655, St. Paul, Minnesota.

17. *DNT*, November 22, 1916.

Bibliography

PRIMARY SOURCES

Interviews

Adams, Jean and Salisbury, Yakima, Washington, June 12, 1984.
Bonson, Ann, Yakima, Washington, June 12, 1984.
Boone, Charles, Yakima, Washington, June 12, 1984.
Copeland, Thomas B., St. Paul, Minnesota, August 12, 1992.
Heermans, Jerome T., Olympia, Washington, June 16, 1984.
Larsen, Dick, Wenatchee, Washington, August 2, 1984.
Lovald, Susan, Duluth, Minnesota, July 15, 1988.
Maine, Kenneth, Duluth, Minnesota, 1982–1994.
Morrison, Wayne, Ovid, New York, July 15, 1986.
Sielaff, Richard O., Duluth, Minnesota, April 7, 1989.
Shannon, John, Yakima, Washington, June 13, 1984.
Thomas, Eugene, Yakima, Washington, June 13, 1984.

Government Documents

Annual Report of the Commissioner of Patents for the Year 1903, Document 177, 58th Congress, 2nd Session (Washington: Government Printing Office, 1904).
Census Data Book, 1970, State of Washington, Office of Program Planning and Fiscal Management, Vol. 1, 1972, Washington State Library, Olympia, Washington.
Department of Public Safety—Bureau of Health, Division of Vital Statistics, Certificate of Death, November 21, 1916, City of St. Paul, Minnesota.
Executive Documents of the State of Minnesota, 1895–1896, IV, Attorney General, Biennial Report, Minnesota Historical Society, St. Paul, Minnesota.
Executive Documents of the State of Minnesota, 1907. Governor John A. Johnson's Annual Message to the Legislature, Minnesota Historical Society, St. Paul, Minnesota.
General Laws of the State of Minnesota, 1881, Minnesota Historical Society, St. Paul, Minnesota.
Journal of the Minnesota House of Representatives, 1909, 1911, Minnesota Historical Society, St. Paul, Minnesota.
Journal of the Minnesota Senate, 1909, 1911, Minnesota Historical Society, St. Paul, Minnesota.
McVey, Lord, and Hall, *First Biennial Report of the Minnesota Tax Commission*, 1908, Minnesota Historical Society, St. Paul, Minnesota.

Minnesota Reports, 1909, Minnesota Historical Society, St. Paul, Minnesota.

Minnesota Secretary of State, "Articles of Incorporation of the Ontario Land Company and the Chemung Iron Company, 1887," Minnesota Historical Society, St. Paul, Minnesota.

National Archives Trust Fund Board, Atlanta, Georgia, National Archives, Washington, D.C.

STATE ex rel. SHROPSHIRE v. SUPERIOR COURT OF PACIFIC COUNTY et al. (Supreme Court of Washington, January, 6, 1909.)

Water Rights Index Book, Yakima County Auditor, Yakima, Washington.

Manuscript Collections

Chester A. Congdon Papers, Van Evera Collection, Duluth, Minnesota.

Chester A. Congdon Papers, Congdon Office Corporation, Duluth, Minnesota.

Chester A. Congdon Papers, Glensheen, Duluth, Minnesota.

Chester A. Congdon Papers, Westhome, Yakima, Washington.

Clara B. Congdon, "Journal," Glensheen, Duluth, Minnesota.

Davis, Kellogg, and Severance Records, Minnesota Historical Society, St. Paul, Minnesota.

John C. and Isabella Greenway Papers, MS 311, Arizona Historical Society, Tucson, Arizona.

Guilford G. Hartley and Family Papers, Minnesota Historical Society, St. Paul, Minnesota.

John H. Hearding File, Northeast Minnesota Historical Center, University of Minnesota, Duluth, Duluth, Minnesota.

Harry Clay Heermans Papers, Manuscripts and University Archives, University of Washington, Seattle, Washington.

John A. Johnson Papers, Minnesota Historical Society, St. Paul, Minnesota.

Frank B. Kellogg Papers, Minnesota Historical Society, St. Paul, Minnesota.

Edmund J. Longyear and Family Papers, Minnesota Historical Society, St. Paul, Minnesota.

Materials Relating to the Oliver Iron Mining Company, James S. Steel compiler, Minnesota Historical Society, St. Paul, Minnesota.

Northern Pacific Railway Company Records, Minnesota Historical Society, St. Paul, Minnesota; President's Subject File: Vol. 9 [front cover, Vol. 1 on spine], File 1.B.7.1B, page 64; Vol. 12 [front cover, Vol. 4 on spine], File 1.B.7.2F, page 809; Vol. 14 [front cover, Vol. 6 on spine], File 1.B.7.2F, pages 115, 133; Vol.21 [front cover, Vol. 13 on spine], File 1.B.7.3B, page 409; Vol. 22 [front cover, Vol. 14 on spine], File 1.B.7.2B, page 656; Vol. 50 [front cover, Vol. 26 on spine], File 3.A.10.1B, pages 446, 447, 476; Branch Line Data, Western District, 1922, Tacoma Division,Grays Harbor Branch, 1922.

Oliver Iron Mining Company Papers, Minnesota Historical Society, St. Paul, Minnesota.

Oliver Iron and Steel Company Records, Archives of Industrial Society, Hillman
Library, University of Pittsburgh, Pittsburgh, Pennsylvania.
Ontario Land Company File, Spokane Public Library, Spokane, Washington.
Click Relander Collection, Yakima Valley Regional Library, Yakima, Washington.
Yakima Valley Canal Company Papers, Yakima, Washington.

Newspapers

Alameda Daily Argus, Alameda California, 1895.
Chippewa Herald, Chippewa Falls, Wisconsin, 1878.
Corning Journal, Corning, New York, 1868, 1886, 1878, 1879.
Daily Olympian, Olympia, Washington, 1943.
Daily Washingtonian, Hoquiam, Washington, 1903, 1910.
Daily World, Aberdeen, Washington, 1974.
Duluth News Tribune, Duluth, Minnesota, 1908–1911.
Duluth Evening Herald, Duluth, Minnesota, 1908–1911, 1916.
Evanston Review, Evanston, Illinois, 1934.
University Herald, Syracuse University, Syracuse, New York 1871–75.

SECONDARY SOURCES

Books

Ahlstrom, Sydney, *A Religious History of the American People* (New Haven, 1972).
Blakey, Gladys, *A History of Taxation in Minnesota* (Minneapolis, 1934).
Boese, Donald L., *John C. Greenway and the Opening of the Western Mesabi* (Itasca
Community College Foundation, 1975).
Bridges, Hal, *Iron Millionaire: The Life of Charlemagne Tower* (Philadelphia, 1952).
Brooks, Loring, *A Prospectus of the City of Hoquiam and Facts Concerning the Grays
Harbor Country* (1901).
Chrislock, Carl M., *The Progressive Era in Minnesota* (St. Paul, 1971).
Clayton, W. W., *History of Steuben County, New York* (Philadelphia, 1879).
Cleland, Robert Glass, *A History of Phelps Dodge, 1834–1950* (New York, 1952).
Congdon, Chester A., *Pacific Panorama—1914,* Robert Congdon, ed. (privately pub-
lished, 1938).
Cross, Whitney, *The Burned-Over District: The Social and Intellectual History of Enthu-
siastic Religion in Western New York, 1800–1850* (New York, 1950).
Day, Frank A. and Theodore M. Knappen, *Life of John Albert Johnson: Three Times Gov-
ernor of Minnesota* (Chicago, 1910).
Dudley, Harry C., *Glorified Fishing: Memoirs of a Mining Engineer,* Reed Whittemore,
ed., privately published, 1978.
Evans, Henry Oliver, *Iron Pioneer: Henry W. Oliver, 1840–1904* (New York, 1942).

Ficken, Robert F., *The Forested Land; A History of Lumbering in Western Washington* (Seattle, 1987).

Folwell, William Watts, *A History of Minnesota*, I, (St. Paul, 1921).

Fourie, Ada, *Their Roots Run Deep* (published privately, no date).

Galpin, Freeman W., *Syracuse University* (Syracuse, 1960).

Gray, James, *Business without Boundaries: THE STORY OF GENERAL MILLS* (Minneapolis, 1954).

Haines, Lynn, *The Minnesota Legislature of 1909* (Minneapolis, 1909).

_____, *The Minnesota Legislature of 1911* (Minneapolis, 1911).

Harvey, George, *Henry Clay Frick, The Man* (New York, 1928).

Hazeltine, Jean, *The Historical and Regional Geography of the Willapa Bay Area*, Washington (n.p., 1956).

Helmes, Winnifred G., *John A. Johnson, The People's Governor* (Minneapolis, 1949).

Hunt, Rockwell D., *History of the College of the Pacific* (Stockton, 1951).

Hunt, Herbert, *Washington, West of the Cascades* (n.p., 1932).

Jackson, Gary L., *Remembering Yakima* (Yakima, 1975).

Joralemon, Ira, *Romantic Copper* (New York, 1934).

Lane, Michael, *Glensheen: The Construction Years* (published by the University of Minnesota, Duluth, no date).

Longyear, Edmund J., (Grace L. Nute, ed.), *Mesabi Pioneer* (St. Paul, 1951).

Lyman, W. D., *History of the Yakima Valley* (Chicago, 1919).

Near, Irvin W., *A History of Steuben County, New York and Its People* (Chicago, 1911).

Pletcher, David M., *Rails, Mines and Progress: Seven American Promoters in Mexico, 1867–1911* (Ithaca, 1958).

Renz, Louis, *The History of the Northern Pacific Railroad* (Fairfield, Washington, 1980).

Sandvik, Glenn N., *Duluth, An Illustrated History of the Zenith City* (Duluth, 1983).

Storry, Richard, *A History of Modern Japan* (New York, 1960).

Van Brunt, Walter, ed., *Duluth and St. Louis County* (Chicago and New York, 1921).

Van Sycle, Edwin, *The River Pioneers: Early Days on Grays Harbor* (Aberdeen, 1982).

Walker, David A., *Iron Frontier: The Discovery and Early Development of Minnesota's Three Ranges* (St. Paul, 1979).

Wall, Joseph Frazier, *Andrew Carnegie* (New York, 1970).

Waller, O.L., *Right of State to Regulate Distribution of Water Rights* (n.p., 1914).

White, Bruce, et al., *Minnesota Votes: Election Returns by County for Presidents, Senators, Congressmen, and Governors, 1857–1977* (St. Paul, 1977).

Writers Group, *Chemung County . . . Its History* (Elmira, 1975).

Articles and Unpublished Materials

Alumni Files, Syracuse University, Syracuse, New York. n.a., "History of the Arnot Family," n.d., Arnot File, Arnot Art Gallery, Elmira, New York.

Bimson, Walter R., "Louis D. Ricketts (1859–1940): Mining Engineer, Geologist,

Banker, Industrialist, and Builder of Arizona," The Newcomen Society of England, 1949.

Boening, Rose, "History of Irrigation in the State of Washington," *Washington Historical Quarterly* renamed *The Pacific Northwest Quarterly*, 259–276, 21–45, 1910.

Bond, John Avery, "Legislative Reapportionment in Minnesota," (unpublished Ph.D. dissertation, University of Minnesota, 1956).

Boone, Susan, "Chester Adgate Congdon, Pioneer Irrigationist," n.d., unpublished manuscript, copy in author's possession.

Cornell, Gerald D., "Henry W. Oliver, Jr., and the Development of the Oliver Mining Company," 1984, unpublished manuscript in possession of the author.

Coulter, Calvin B., "The New Settlers on the Yakima Project, 1880–1910," *Pacific Northwest Quarterly*, 10–21 (January, 1970).

_____, "Building the Tieton Irrigation Canal," *Pacific Northwest Quarterly*, 11–18 (January, 1958).

_____, "The Victory of the National Irrigation in the Yakima Valley, 1902–1906," *Pacific Northwest Quarterly*, 99–122 (April, 1951).

Holmquist, June D., "Convention City: The Republicans in Minnesota, 1892," *Minnesota History* 35:64–76 (June, 1956).

Hughes, John, "Hoquiam's grand hotel, circa 1890," *The Daily World*, Aberdeen, Washington, Sunday, December 8, 1974.

Mathewson, E. P., "History of the Ajo District," (paper read before the Tucson Literary Club, November 1933), Tucson, 1933.

Mitchell, Bruce, "Flowing Wealth: the Story of Water Resource Development in North Central Washington, 1870–1950," (*Wenatchee Daily World*, March 6, 1967).

Pardee, John S. "An Appanage of Steel," unpublished manuscript, Northeast Minnesota History Center, University of Minnesota, Duluth.

White, Thomas W., "Main Street on the Irrigation Frontier: Sub-Urban Community Building in the Yakima Valley, 1900–1910," *Pacific Northwest Quarterly*, 94–103 (July 1986).

Index

Adgate, Chester, 9
Adgate, Hannah, 9
Agriculture, crops, 71–74. *See also* Horti-
culture
Ajo, Ariz., copper mines, 113–117; com-
pany town, 115–116
Alabaster, J. L., Pacific travels, 118–131
Alexandra College, Belleville, Ont., 19
Apples, raised, 71, 153n15; exported,
121–122
Arcturus Mine, 81–82
Arnot, Matthias, banker, 30, 32,38
Australia, described, 123–124

Ballinger, Richard Achilles, secretary of
the interior, 135
Bannister, Alfred, oversees irrigation
project, 65–70
Bannister, Edward, oversees canal pro-
ject, 70–71
Bannister, Rev. Edward, 13–14
Bannister, Elizabeth, 14, 15
Bannister, Mary, 29
Barrager, Walter, ranch foreman, 72–73
Baseball, college team, 16
Baxter, George B., U.S. district attorney,
28
Bennett, Rev. Charles W., 24–25, 27, 29,
55, 146n2
Bennett, William C., 29, 49; mining in-
terests, 149n2
Billson, William W., U.S. attorney,
25–26, 28; law practice, 48, 49, 51, 133
Bisbee, Ariz., copper mines, 104–112
Boddie, John, mine owner, 113–114
Borah, William E., senator, 139

Brazil, mining ventures, 83–84
Briggs, Charles, mining interests, 105,
106, 107–108
Briggs Mine, copper mine, 107
Bryan, William Jennings, candidate, 134
Bush, John C., construction supervisor,
60

Caldwell, Edward F., and Co., New York,
60
Calumet and Arizona Copper Co., Bis-
bee operations, 106–112; Ajo opera-
tions, 113–117
Calumet and Hecla Co., 160n1
Calumet and Pittsburgh Co., 107
Campbell, Gordon R., mining interests,
109, 111
Canals, for irrigation, 65–71
Canisteo Mining Co., Mesabi proper-
ties, 81; leases, 83
Cannon, Joe, speaker of the house, 135
Carnegie, Andrew, steel manufacturer, 5,
51; interests in Mesabi, 49, 52–53, 54,
76–77
Carnegie–Oliver Steel Co., activities,
xix; vertical organization, 52; sold, 77
Caswell, Irving A., politics, 137, 140
Chemung Iron Co., organized, 80;
leases, 80–81, 83
China, described, 126–127
Chisholm, taxes, 92
Clark, Champ, politics, 137
Clarkson, J. B., hardware dealer, 118
Cole, Thomas F., 88, 89, 110; Mesabi
interests, 82–83; interests in copper,
105–106, 107

Cole Mine, copper mine, 108
Coleraine, built, 83
Congdon, Albert Sylvester (brother), 9,
10, 11, 28, 29; student, 23; investments,
31; company manager, 33, 34; oversees
irrigation project, 69
Congdon, Benjamin, 8
Congdon, Chester A., company attorney, xix, xx, 76, 78; legislator, 7, 91–92;
birth, 9; childhood, 10, 11; education,
12, 13–18; becomes a lawyer, 19–22; St.
Paul law practice, 23, 24, 28, 48; personality, 25; assistant U.S. district attorney, 25–26, 28; marriage, 26–27;
land investments, 30–42; invests in
Raymond, 43–47; moves to Duluth,
49; joins Oliver, 51, 53, 54; Duluth law
practice, 55; builds house, 56–60; en-
vironmental interests, 60–61; Yakima
Valley interests, 62–75; irrigation project, 64–70; agricultural projects,
71–74; style of management, 72–73;
gift of capitol site,74–75; interests in
Mesabi, 78–83; interests in Brazil,
83–84; characterized, 83, 84; legislative candidate, 87, 91, 95, 97; opposes
tonnage tax, 88–91, 94; work on redistricting, 98–103; Arizona mining
interests, 104, 106– 112, 115–117; Pacific
travels, 118–131; politics, 133–134, 136,
137–140; national committeeman,
140–141; illness, 142; death, 142–143
Congdon, Clara Hesperia Bannister, 131,
143; education, 13, 15–18; birth, 14;
teacher 19–20; personality, 25; marriage, 26–27; journal, 27; travels, 29,
142; moves to Duluth, 49; activities,
55; builds house, 56–60; temperance
supporter, 73; interest in missions,
126; death, 153n19
Congdon, Edward Chester ("Ned")
(son), 27, 29, 60, 131, 142

Congdon, Edward Herbert (brother), 10
Congdon, Elisabeth Mannering (daugh-
ter), 55, 142; education, 56; will, 153n19
Congdon, Hannibal (grandfather), 8
Congdon, Helen Augusta (sister), 10
Congdon, Helen Clara (daughter), 27,
29, 131, 142; childhood, 55; education,
56
Congdon, John (son), 27
Congdon, John (ancestor), 145n1
Congdon, Laura Jane Adgate (mother),
9–11, 28, 29; sells farm, 23–24
Congdon, Laura Sophia (sister), 9, 10, 11
Congdon, Marjorie (daughter), 27, 29,
131, 142; childhood, 55; education, 56
Congdon, Mary (grandmother), 8
Congdon, Robert (son), 55, 142; educa-
tion, 56
Congdon, Sylvester Laurentus (father),
8–10
Congdon, Walter Bannister (son), 27,
131, 142; childhood, 55; education 56;
accident, 110
Congdon, Walter Hibard (brother), 10
Congdon Mine, copper mine, 107
Conservation, as political issue, 135
Copper, mines, 104–117; types of ore, 114;
mining process, 115
Copper Queen, mine, 104, 107
Cornelia Copper Co., mine, 113
Costello, Martin, mine owner, 105, 106
Crow, Carl, newspaper manager, 129–130
Curley, Mike, steam shovel operator, 115

D'Autremont, Charles, mining interests,
106
Daley, Jim, prospector, 104
Davis, Dr. Hubert, 142
De la Barre, Walter, miller, 4–5
Del Norte Mine, copper mine, 107
Democratic Party, platform, 86; cam-
paign, 136–137

Diamond Mine, 81, 82
Douglas, Dr. James, minerologist, 104
Drills, diamond faced, 5
Dudley, Harry C., mining engineer, 83–84
Dudley, William B., developer, 65
Duluth, growth, 48; land preservation, 60–61
Duluth Commercial Club, opposes tax, 93
Dyche, William A., 55; Pacific travels, 118–131

East Hoquiam Co., organized, 31, 32; finances, 38, 46
Eberhart, Adolph O., governor, 97, 99, 103; politics, 141
Economic conditions, assessed, 3–7, 133
Elections, 1906, amendment approved, 86
Elections, 1908, campaign, 86–91
Emerson, George H., 38; lumberman, 31, 33
Ericson, David, artist, 142
Evans, Henry Oliver, biographer, 77

Farmer Alliance, 156n1
Field, Thorald, geologist, 107, 108
Finney, Charles Grandison, evangelist, 8
Florada, Edward, mining supervisor, 50
Flour milling, growth, 4–5
Fowler v. Schmahl, representation case, 102
Fraser, C. D., mining interests, 106
French, William A., Co., St. Paul, interior decorators, 59
Frick, Henry C., 153n16; steel company manager, 51, 52, 53, 77, 84

Garrett, Frank A., mining interests, 149n2
Gary, Elbert, steel company official, 82–83

Gates, Frederick T., steel company official, xix
Gayley, James, steel company official, 80
Gilbert, James M., developer, 65, 68
Gilchrist, Percy C., 5
Glensheen, built, 56–60
Gogebic Range, leases, 76
Gold, mined, 106
Gold Flint Mine, copper mine, 28
Graham, John, mining adviser, 105
Grays Harbor, Wash., development, 30–42; improvements, 39–40
Grays Harbor City, Wash., site, 31–32
Grays Harbor Co., organized, 31; activities, 32; stock, 34; finances, 38; failure, 44
Grays Harbor Terminal Co., railroad, 35
Greenway, John C., mining superintendent, 83, 109–113, 114, 115, 116; politics, 139

Hamilton, Bishop ———, missionary, 126
Harbor Land Co., organized, 31, 32; stock, 34; finances, 38
Hartley, Guilford G., Mesabi interests, 81–82
Haven, R. D., mayor, 93
Hawkins, E. B., politics, 140
Haycraft, Julius E., senator, 159n15
Hedley Gold Mining Co., 151n28
Heermans, Harry Clay, 12, 29, 131; aids Congdon, 26; investments, 30, 31, 32, 33, 34, 35, 37, 38, 40, 41; builds water works, 38; develops utilities, 39, 40; investments, 40, 41; invests in Raymond, 43–47; reports on canal, 69
Heermans, John, investments, 39
Heermans family, 142; befriends Congdon, 12; moves to Washington, 40
Hesperia, yacht, 153n11
Highways, on north shore, 61

Hiller and Burbank, construction engineers, 69
Hiscock, Gifford, and Doheny, Syracuse, 19, 20
Hoatson, Capt. James, mining foreman, 105, 106
Hoatson, Thomas, mining interests, 106
Hoatson Mine, copper mine, 107, 108
Hops, as crop, 73
Hoquiam, Wash., businesses, 30; land, 32, 34, 35; railroad, 34–38; water works, 38–39; growth, 39
Hoquiam Water Co., organized, 38
Horticulture, experimental, 72–73. *See also* Agriculture, Apples
Horticultural Union, ranchers' association, 73
Hughes, Charles Evans, candidate, 139, 140, 142
Hugo, Trevanion W., opposes tax, 92
Hull, Judge William E., 102

Illinois Steel Co., Chicago, 81
Immigrants, in work force, 4; political power, 100
Irish Mag, copper mine, 104–106, 107
Iron ore, companies, xix–xx; changes, 76; in Brazil, 83–84; taxes, 85–96. *See also* individual ranges
Irrigation, projects, 62, 63, 64–70; in Australia, 123

Jacobson, Jacob F., candidate, 86–87, 88, 90, 91
Japan, described, 127–130
Java, described, 124–125
Johnson, Hiram, politics, 139
Johnson, John Albert, governor, 86, 91, 94–95; candidate, 87–88; death, 97
Johnston, Clarence H., Sr., architect, 57–58

Joralemon, Ira, geologist, 113, 115
Junction Mine, copper mine, 107, 108

Kellogg, Frank Billings, lawyer, 88, 133–134
Kendrick, John W., railroad official, 36, 37
Kenney, John, gardener, 153n16
Kenyon and Maine, Chicago, architects, 74
King, Thomas M., steel company owner, 77

La Follette, Robert M., elected, 136
Lake Superior, north shore preserved, 60–61
Lake Superior and Pittsburgh Co., 107
Lake Superior and Western Copper Co., mining properties, 105, 106
Lake Superior Consolidated Mines, 53, 54
"Lake Superior Group," interests in copper, 104
Land, grants, 3; speculation, 31, 40
Law and lawyers, training, 19, 20
Leavitt, Charles Wellford, Jr., landscape architect, 58, 59
Liquor, as political issue, 99
Little, A. C., town promoter, 43–47
Lone Jack Mine, opened, 53
Longyear, Edmund J., mining engineer, 81, 114
Lovald, Hans O., construction supervisor, 74, 115
Lowell Mine, copper mine, 107
Lumber industry, growth, 39

Mainzer, Jacob, lawyer, 24
Mallman, John, mining superintendent, 81
Marengo Co., mining venture, 84
McGolrick, Bishop James, 92

McLean, John H., mining official, 142
Melbourne, Aust., described, 124
Merritt, Leonidas, sells mining rights,
  51
Merritt brothers, Mesabi interests, 49,
  50, 53
Mesabi Iron Range, xx; developed, 5, 6,
  48, 52; ore described, 5, 49, 78, 81, 82;
  leases, 76, 78–79; mining ventures,
  78–83
Methodist Episcopal church, clergy, 8–9;
  schools, 13, 14
Mexicans, mine workers, 116
Minnesota, boundaries, 6–7
Minnesota constitution, amendments
  proposed, 85–86, 91, 100–103
Minnesota legislature, ore taxation
  issue, 85, 91–96; issue of redistricting,
  97–103
Minnesota Supreme Court, cases, 86,
  91
Morgan, J. Pierpont, banker, xix, 76–77,
  133, 134
Morrison, Bishop James D., 92

Natches River, used for irrigation, 63, 64,
  65–68
National Steel Co., merger, xx
Nelson, Knute, senator, 141
New Cornelia Copper Co., mines, 114
New Zealand, described, 120–122
North Yakima, Wash., described, 62–63
North Yakima Canal Co., organized, 65;
  irrigation project, 65–69
North Western Lumber Co., 30, 31
Northern Pacific Railroad, spur lines,
  30, 34–35, 36, 37–38, 44, 73–74; bank-
  ruptcy, 37

Olcott, William J., mining company
  official, 110
Oliver, Henry W., steel company official,

xix, xx; interests in Mesabi, 49–51,
  52–54, 76, 77–80; interests in copper,
  106
Oliver Iron Mining Co., 82; organized,
  51; growth, 55; stock, 77–78; leases, 78;
  opposes tax, 92; officers, 110
Oliver Mine, copper mine, 107
Olympia, Wash., utilities, 40
Ontario Land Co., 33; organized, 30;
  subsidiaries, 32; finances, 42, 43–44,
  45, 46

Painted Rocks, Washington, 67, 70
Panic of 1893, impact, 34, 51, 53
Panic of 1907, impact, 133
Payne–Aldrich tariff, 135
Phelps Dodge Corp., interests in copper,
  104, 105, 107, 109
Pierce, Stephenson, and Mainzer,
  St. Paul, 23
Pinchot, Gifford, head of forestry
  department, 135
Pirongo, Prince John, 119
Pittsburgh and Duluth Co., 107
Pittsburgh Junction Co., 107
Population, state growth, 97
Powell, L. W., mining superintendent,
  107, 108–109
Progressive Party, issues, 132; beginnings,
  136, 138, 140

Railroads, growth, 3; costs, 36
Raymond, Wash., town developed,
  43–47
Raymond Land and Improvement Co.,
  43–47; shares, 151n9
Reapportionment, of legislative seats,
  97–103
Republican Party, protectionist policy,
  50; platform, 87; reform issues, 132,
  133; conventions, 134, 136, 140; split,
  135–136, 137–139, 141

Ricketts, Dr. Louis D., geologist, 114, 115
Roberts, W. D., railroad official, 36
Robertson, S. C., banker, 27
Rockefeller, John D., 133; steel interests, xix; iron ore interests, 53–54; business interests, 76, 77
Roosevelt, Theodore, 110; president, 132; politics, 134, 135, 136, 139, 140; candidate, 136, 137–138
Root, Elihu, politics, 136
Roratonga Island, described, 119–120

St. Louis County, representation in legislature, 97, 98, 99, 100, 101, 102, 103
Schmahl, Julius, secretary of state, 101
Schwab, Charles, company negotiator, 77
Searle, D. B., U.S. district attorney, 28
"Seven Senators" amendment, 159n28
Silver, mined, 106
"Six Senators" amemndment, 100–101
Soule, John F., investments, 31, 39, 40
Southern Pacific Railroad, spur line, 115, 116
Spencer, Herbert, social theories, 5–6
Speyers, Albert, ranch manager, 71, 72, 73
Stearns, J. O., investments, 39
Steel industry, companies, xix, 76–77; smelting process, 5; vertical organization, 5, 52
Stone, George C., mining interests, 156n1
Sumner, William Graham, sociologist, 6
Swift, George D., mining company official, 92
Syracuse University, founded, 13; course of study, 15–18

Taft, William Howard, campaign, 134, 136, 138; president, 135
Tahiti, described, 119–120

Tariff, as political issue, 135
Tasmania, described, 122
Taxes, on iron ore, 51, 85–96
Tener, George, mining adviser, 50, 106, 110
Thomas, Sidney Gilchrist, 5
Tin, mined, 125
Tischer's Creek, flowage, 56, 57, 58
Tower, Charlemagne, mining interests, 156n1
Traphagen, Oliver, architect, 56
Tucson, Cornelia, and Gila Bend Railroad, spur line, 115

United States Congress, grants to railroads, 3
United States Steel Corp., organized, xix–xx, 77–78; leases, 80–81; mines low–grade ores, 82–83; plans for steel mill, 92; opposes tax, 92
United States Supreme Court, decisions, 105
University of Minnesota, receives Glensheen, 153n19
University of the Pacific, founded, 14

Vermilion Iron Range, opened, 6; leases, 76
Virginia and Ely Railroad, incorporated, 76

Washburn, Cadwallader, milling interests, 4
Washington, water rights issue, 64; capitol controversy, 74–75
Washington State Supreme Court, decisions, 39
Water, rights and usage, 64; sold, 67
Water works, systems built, 38
Weed, Alfred B., developer, 65
Wellington, Quincy C., banker, 30, 32, 33, 38

Wellington, N.Z., described, 120
Whitson, Edward, developer, 65, 68
Wilson, Woodrow, candidate, 137, 138;
    president, 127, 131, 138–139, 140, 142
Winchester, Dr. C. W., school adminis-
    trator, 12
Woman's Christian Temperance Union,
    issues, 73
World War I, impact, 116, 139; U.S. entry,
    140

Wyness, George, gardener, 153n16
Wyness, Robert, gardener, 153n16

Yakima, Wash., investments, 41; as capi-
    tol site, 74–75
Yakima Valley, Wash., described, 62; irri-
    gation, 63–70; horticulture, 72–73
Yakima Valley Canal Co., name, 65; irri-
    gation project, 70

About the Author

Roy O. Hoover is Professor Emeritus of history at the University of Minnesota, Duluth. He did his graduate work at Washington State University where he received his Ph.D. Before moving to Minnesota he taught at Northland College in Ashland, Wisconsin, and in the Pacific Northwest at Yakima Valley Community College.

A Lake Superior Lawyer was designed and produced under the direction of Emily Strayer of The Kutenai Press, St. Paul, Minnesota with assistance from Luther Strayer and Tracy E. Smith. The text is Minion and the titles are Weiss Bold, set by Mary Buscher of Stanton Publication Services in St. Paul. This edition is a lithographic reproduction of the limited edition hand printed at The Kutenai Press.